RATTLE OF THE KEYS

RATTLE OF THE KEYS

True story of
a wrongful conviction
in Ada, Oklahoma

by
Matt Thompson

Ongoing Remembrance

≈

In memory of the families and loved ones of the falsely accused; and lest not forget Calvin Lee Scott, a black man also innocent of a Pontotoc County rape charge, for which he spent 20 years in prison, until his release in 2003.

The mouth of a loose woman is a deep pit.
Proverbs 22:14

Time alone will bring the just man to light; the criminal you can spot in one short day.
Sophocles, OEDIPUS REX

≈

Contents

Introduction

This is a true story. The facts of the case are from pre-trial interviews, conversations and phone calls, trial transcripts, investigator's reports and sworn affidavits. All of the new evidence is documented and was formally presented at some point in the appeal for a new trial. Some names have been changed.

I started keeping a journal from the first day in jail. I didn't know how I would ever prove my innocence, but I did know that I was an innocent man starting a prison sentence. The journal entries in the second part of the book carry you through the ups and downs of prison days and my appeals.

Experience as I did...the arrest, conviction at trial (acquittal on one charge) and sentencing for a crime I didn't commit. After nineteen months in prison, discover with me as new evidence comes to light: investigator's reports and sworn affidavits, about Rita and her accusations against men of rapes, beatings, abductions, knifings, shootings, devil-ritual participation, animal killing, break-ins, molestation of her children, and setting fire to her home.

Waiting for my legal appeal and new evidence to save the day, I was on a rollercoaster of hope...for justice.

MATT THOMPSON

Chapter 1   Meeting Rita

I was arrested on a Friday. Good Friday, in fact…of 1991. The Ada detective cuffed me in the Administration building hallway, of East Central University in Ada, Oklahoma, at the very stroke of noon. I was waiting, with half-a-hundred other college students, for class to begin. We were prepared to take a business law test. Oh, how dramatic it was.

That was a moment that forever changed my life. It was a turning point that divides my life as "before" and "since". I was falsely accused of a rape, of which I would eventually be convicted at trial and sent to prison. It all began almost two weeks before, on the eve of St. Patrick's Day, Saturday, March 16, 1991.

My girlfriend Krissy and I, and our ten-month old son lived in a small two-bedroom apartment on the south side of Ada, at Sander's Apts. I went to ECU and worked part time as an accounting clerk at the Chickasaw Nation. Krissy worked full time there. She had a red Pontiac Firebird that we both drove, as I didn't have my own car. I rode a bicycle a lot.

The week leading up to this particular Saturday was my spring break from school, and I worked full time all week. During the week, I would take a few valiums in the evening and drink beer. I would take about five of the little yellow pills and drink beer along with them. I took the last pills on Thursday, March 14.

On the evening of Friday, March 15th, I walked to the Village Club bar, which was only a few blocks from my apartment. For the last few days, Krissy and I had been mad at each other and were talking of breaking up, which we did from time to time, so we were going our own separate ways this night. She was driving her car to the Tiger's Den bar and I was walking to the Village Club. Krissy and I communicated fairly well and allowed each other breathing room. Our son Josh was staying at my parents, pretty close by as the crow flies, at 907 S. Constant.

At the Village Club I played pool, hung out, drank beers and left the bar when it closed at 2:00 a.m. I had seen an old friend of mine at the bar, Chuck Main. He was staying in a room at the Village Inn, the adjoining motel. He said he had a joint, and we walked to my apartment after the bar closed. We smoked a joint and talked some. He was drinking whiskey and was very drunk, nothing unusual for Chuck. He was a bundle of energy, a former wrestling champion. Chuck left the next day before noon. I think his girlfriend picked him up. I went for a jog soon after waking up and stayed around the house the rest of the day.

I again went to the Village Club on Saturday evening. At midnight it would be St. Patrick's Day, and green beer would be flowing. Krissy went to the Tiger's Den bar again. Chuck was at the bar as was my girlfriend's boss, Karla. I hung out, played pool and drank beer, then walked back alone to my apartment when the bar closed at 2:00 a.m. I was hungry and there was nothing to eat in the apartment, so I was waiting for Krissy to get home so I could take her car to Hardee's to get something.

I remember Krissy getting home about 2:40 a.m. I had been waiting anxiously on her, wondering if maybe she had gone to a party or something and wasn't coming home. She went straight to bed in our bedroom. I took her bright red 1986 Firebird, and drove to Hardee's restaurant at 12th and Mississippi.

This night, I parked on the north side of Hardee's, but went in the south door. The reason I went around to the other door was that an Ada detective, Jeff Crosby, was coming out the north door and I didn't want to be seen by him. This irony, I never really thought about until after my trial. It is possible that this detective could have remembered seeing Rita sitting in the second booth on the north side.

That night I had on a pair of Guess jeans, some Dexter-type shoes and a denim shirt that was unbuttoned and untucked. As I entered and looked around, this attractive blonde woman was really giving me the eye. Right there sitting in the second booth on the north side, facing the front. We made eye contact, and she just kept on looking.

I ordered a ham & cheese sandwich and water. When I got my food, I went to sit down. She was still looking at me seductively so I decided to approach her. I asked her if I could sit down, and she said yes. I sat facing her and dug into my sandwich. She had food, fries, I remember. We began to talk and I learned she was from Boston and worked here at Hardee's. She had a distinct New England accent. We also discussed the fact that we both had green eyes because it was now March 17th, St. Patrick's Day.

I asked her if she had a boyfriend. Much to my surprise, she was very frank and said that she had a "girlfriend". But then, she sort of like peered up and down my body and proclaimed that she "likes men too"! Within this first five minutes of meeting, she was very suggestive (sexually) in her behavior, words, and the way she looked at me. I was only human, and no saint. I then asked her if she wanted to leave and go drink a beer. She said yes. We just walked out the north door and to my girlfriend's car.

We drove north, slowly, from Hardee's to the 24-hour Texaco on 10th & Mississippi. She elected to stay in the car as I went in and bought two six-packs of Bud Light and got some cigarettes. I remember the beer was on sale for $2.49 a six-pack or something like that.

Not wanting to risk getting pulled over, I suggested that I had a friend who lived nearby and we could go to his apartment and drink. She agreed and we carefully drove that way.

My friend's name was Danny Cole, and he lived just a few blocks away at 907 E. 12th, apt #7, which was right across the street from East Central University. I was very familiar with these apartments, as we had lived in apt #6 for the period of February-September 1990. My son Josh was born while we lived there. Apartment six is the attic of this three-story house. Danny's apartment was a small one-bedroom dwelling behind the main house.

I parked right next to his apartment, behind the main house. Danny didn't have a car. We each got out of our own side, and I knocked on the door. No one was home but the door was unlocked. There was nothing in the apartment except a refrigerator and a pile of carpet that had been pulled up close to the front door. Danny had told me a week or so before that he needed help pulling up the carpet. He and his landlord had made some kind of deal about his rent if he helped replace the carpet. Danny has a prosthesis below the left knee and his right arm is paralyzed, so he must have found someone to help him pull it up.

We walked in and I put one six-pack in the fridge as we drank from the other one. I told her I would drag the carpet into the small bedroom so we could sit down, which I did. I took my shirt off before I dragged the heavy carpet into the bedroom. We sat on the carpet and continued to drink, smoke and talk.

During this time, I told her about myself; where I worked, about my girlfriend and I possibly breaking up and that I was a student at ECU. We talked about her also but I don't remember what about other than what we had talked about in Hardee's. I felt very comfortable around her, which is saying a lot for me.

It all started with a kiss. We started kissing. We kissed for a few minutes and then we removed her shirt. We continued with kissing and caressing and then took her pants off. As soon as her pants were off, she came to me on her knees as I stood to take mine off. She started kissing my stomach and removed my pants before performing oral sex on me. I was comfortable and excited with her. She really became vocal and enthusiastic when we began to have sex. I was actually a little startled with her carrying on, but it felt good.

We had sex for quite a while, probably half an hour. At one point during this time, she wanted me to stimulate her anally. Perhaps she had something other in mind, but I gently stimulated her there with my finger. This pleased her with great fervor. The remnants of the valium, in action with the alcohol, would keep me from ejaculating. Finally, we got tired and stopped. Again, I did not ejaculate.

It was a little chilly in the apartment by this time of the morning, so I turned on the small combination heater/air conditioner for a little while. She told me how she had enjoyed it. She was aggressive, uninhibited and knew what she wanted to do.

After we finished getting dressed, I got the beer out of the fridge and we got in the car. I asked her if I could see her again and she said yes. She said she didn't have a phone but that she lived at 805 E. 12th, which was one block down the street. Her apartment was one block from Hardee's and one block from where we had sex.

She said that she was worried about going home to her "girlfriend" and getting caught, and asked me to drop her off a couple of blocks down from her house. I drove past her apartment, continuing west past Hardee's across Mississippi a few blocks to where the railroad tracks (bike trail now) used to be. In front of Ben's TV. We said goodbye and I said I would stop by her apartment, later in the week. She got out and I went home to bed. I estimate it was around 4:15 am when I let her out.

At 5:56 am the call to 911 reporting a rape is placed. She was seen downtown by two women out for a morning walk. She appeared hysterical and claimed to have been raped. They then called 911 and the police arrived. She was taken to the hospital to be examined. Once finished there, she returned to the police station to give her side of the story.

I will always wonder what happened, what she thought, and did, during the ninety minutes or so after I let her out and when she called the police. Did someone else, the man in the yellow car maybe, rape or harass her? Or did she get caught by her boyfriend? She only knows. This was the report she gave the police interviewer later that morning:

Rita's Statement to Police

(I –interviewer, R-Rita [formatting of the "I", "R" here; and subsequent transcriptions; was Archaic; UGH!])

I   I am going to ask you some questions. And your full name is?

R   Rita Gasteau.

I.   Do you have a middle name, Rita?

R   Tamara.

I.   And how old are you?

R.   27

I   Okay. Rita, you realize that this is a terrible thing that has happened, and I realize also that every ounce of information we can get from you is going to make this much easier for us to work. There are a lot of things that you may not want to tell us about what happened, but I don't want you to hold back, Okay? Like I told you earlier, this is kinda like the doctor that saw you out there while ago. He has done this a bunch and so have we. So don't be embarrassed about anything. Just tell us everything that happened. If you would feel better about telling Terry here about it, I will be glad to leave, and you can tell her about it. But I want you to be comfortable. What would be the most comfortable setting for you? Okay. Well, I'll tell you, why don't we go ahead and start and let me ask you some questions and you kinda tell me what happened and then at any time you feel uncomfortable, we can stop and I will leave. How's that? And then you can tell Terry the rest of the story. Will that be alright? Okay. We are going to do the interview at 11:32 in the morning or March 17, 1991, St. Patrick's Day. Okay. Why don't you just kinda…I know we have touched on this a little bit coming from the hospital here…Why don't you go ahead and just start from the beginning and tell us…Let's start at home, Okay? What you were doing at home up until now.

R   I was at home and got tired. And I went to bed, and I had forgotten that I was supposed to call about a job at about 2:45 or 3:00 am. I had woken up and it was about 2:45, so I had…I started getting dressed and Michael asked me where I was going this late. And I said, "Well, I forgot to call, so I thought I would go ahead and call." So, I went to go call and when I got done with the phone, I had started walking, like I said, and he was right there in the parking lot, and a car was parked there. And I didn't even see it. I mean I just started walking this way. You know, I don't notice anything around me. I just go. I just…face to face right on.

I.   Can you describe him for me?

R.   He was tall and had no shirt on, kinda tanned, darker than me. Sandy blonde hair. Looked like he hadn't shaved. Wearing cowboy boots and jeans.

I.   Did you notice any…

R.   He had like a something like a tattoo or something written right across…right there (on the wrists).

I.   It was very noticeable though?

R.   It was real noticeable. It looked like someone had tried to…it looked like something was written, but something was put over it. Like the tattoo was like this.

I.   Okay. Was it definitely a tattoo or a scar?

R.   It was a tattoo.

I.   Okay. What was the building there that you said you went to call? Where did you call from?

R.   From a convenience store.

I.   There at 14th and Mississippi?

R.   Uh huh.

I.   Okay. And you said you were walking back and you crossed the alley, you told me earlier.

R.   Right. Went across…straight down… and was…

I.   The car was parked on the south side of the building, which was Taco Tico, is that correct?

R.   Right.

I.   Okay. When he confronted you, did he say anything?

R.   Yeah. He said, "You thought you could get away from me before didn't you bitch." Because earlier that day I had gone to the grocery store to buy some things for a taco salad I was going to make for me and Mike, and he wasn't driving…he was one of the ones in the car but there was another guy, kinda shaggy hair, that was driving the car, so there was three of them in the car at that point. The guy that got me later on was one of the ones with this other guy that got out of the car.

  I.   Okay. There was definitely…same car?

  R.   Right.

  I.   Okay.

  R.   And they grabbed me by the arms and when I got away from them, I went and ran toward a house and stayed right there…like they were, you know, going to come near me…I was going to knock on the door because I noticed a car. I went straight to the one with a car there.

  I.   Where was this at?

  R.   This was going towards Highland or something grocery store…Homeland. Homeland grocery store on 12th Street. Straight down 12th Street.

  I.   And you had walked to Homeland from your house. About how far is that? Do you remember, in blocks?

  R.   It took me about 10 minutes to get there.

  I.   You don't have a car, right? That is the reason you walked?

  R.   No.

  I.   Okay. Do you remember who the guy was at Taco Hut, I'm sorry, Pizza Hut, that you were supposed to call?

  R.   No. I just went in there and asked for an application.

  I.   Did you get in touch with him?

  R.   And they said, "We'll call." No, I didn't.

  I.   Because they had already closed.

  R.   Right. That was…

  I.   Okay. Let's take up from where he has grabbed…or he has confronted you now and said, "You thought you could get away from me bitch." What happened then?

  R.   Well, it didn't even dawn on me who he was. At first, I thought it was Mike just following me to make sure I was Okay. So, when I turned around, I just put my arms like this…because I thought it was Mike. And when I turned around and I got…it took me a minute because I can't see that good…and when I looked at him then I noticed that it was the same guy and I looked down and all I saw was the yellow of the car and I knew it was the same car and the same guy.

I.	And about what time was this?

R.	I would say…I left the house about…it was about 2:45 because I looked at the clock right before I left and it only took me…I went in and got some cigarettes and did that…so I know it took me about six minutes. I was close to about 3:00.

I.	Okay. Does that store stay open all night? Twenty-four hours?

R.	And before that I had gone in to Hardee's where I worked and got a soda. So…

I.	Alright now. You turned around and you put your hands up…now what happened?

R.	Right. I guess it kinda shocked him, because he thought I was going to hit him or something. He just grabbed my arm and when he did, he scratched my arm and bruised it and he just grabbed my arm and then grabbed me and took the top of my hair and pushed me in the car. He never went around and opened the door for me. He just pushed me straight in.

I.	Straight through the driver's side.

R.	Right.

I.	Okay. Now take us from there. What has happened or…where were you going?

R.	Okay. He just told me to sit down and shut up and I just had my head down because I was afraid if I looked up, he was going to hurt me or something. So, I just had my head down and when I finally looked up, all I saw was when he took me out of the car, I looked and it was like a brown building and then when we got closer there was kinda like I guess lights close because I saw the cursive writing on the side of the white like a big white house and then there was two doors and he just banged into one of them, the first one.

I.	He kicked the door in?

R.	He just kicked the door in.

I.	Was it already open or was it locked?

R.	I don't know. It couldn't have been locked…he didn't kick it that hard.

I.	Okay. Kinda knee-ed it?

R.	There was just…yeah.

I.	Okay. Now what has happened? What happens now?

R.	At that point there was some carpet that was pulled out because he threw me and I fell face down on it. And I guess it was some kind of a hard rug or something that had been scrunched up and I looked up and there was nothing in the apartment. No furniture. There was nothing.

I.	Okay.

R.	There was a lot of beer and stuff sitting around.

I.	Beer bottles and beer cans and stuff?

R.	Uh-huh.

I.	Okay. Now, this is the part where we really need the details. Okay? And I know this is going to be kinda hard so go slow and take your time and we need to know what happens now.

R.	Well, first he layed down. I remember him grabbing something and drinking it and lit up a cigarette and he just pushed my hands back and he took out a knife. It was…I didn't even see the whole thing, just part of it. And I…the first thing he did was rip my shirt and he just slipped the knife down and just told me not to move.

I.	Okay. You feel kinda uncomfortable about telling me the details of what happened. Would you like for me to get up at this point and you tell Terry what he did? Okay? Why don't I do that. And I want you to keep in mind that she needs all the details. Okay? Anything that he said or made you do to you or to him or whatever. Okay? And I will leave the room.

I.	Go ahead and tell me what happened.

R.	He took his hands and shoved it on my chest and was trying to get his hands off and I kept trying to push his hands away and then he started just scratching me.

I.	On the chest?

R.	Yes. It was just like a (inaudible) scratch. He just kept scratching me and I kept trying to pull his hands away, and then after

that he hit me right here and then at that point, I decided to completely
stop fighting him because I had jaw surgery done and I had been going
through a lot of pain with that as it is, so I had to protect my face from
getting hit. And at that point, I guess I had my jacket off. He ripped my
shirt. He took my pants down. He took everything off.

    I.   He took your clothes completely off?

    R.   Yes. At that point he put it in and was going and going and
going and kept hitting me down there between the legs.

    I.   He was hitting you with his hands?

    R.   Yes. And then he turned me over and put it somewhere else
and then after that he took it out, put it back somewhere else and just
kept going and going and he just…he kept pushing me down. I
remember that. I was almost suffocating because he had me by the back
of the head and was pushing me down. And he just made some sounds
and that was it. He got off me and he put my clothes back on and then
he told me to get into the car and that is the point when I got in the car.
He pushed me some, but he didn't make me get in his side. I got in on
the other side because I knew he still had the knife on him, and I was
really scared.

    I.   What did he do with the knife during all of this? Did he put it
away or did he have it out?

    R.   Yeah. It clicked back and he put it right in his pants and
when he pulled his pants down, he set it on the side. And then when he
was done, he just put the knife back in his pants.

    I.   Was it a pocketknife? A type that folds up?

    R.   Yeah. It was pretty big. Large.

    I.   But it did fold up.

    R.   Uh-huh.

    I.   Did he make you do anything?

    R.   He put my hand on my chest and down there and that was it.

    I.   He put your hand there? What did he tell you to do?

    R.   He didn't tell me to do anything. He just put my hand there.

    I.   He just put your hand there?

    R.   And took it off. Everything was going so fast.

    I.   Is there anything else he made you do?

R.   No. He just told me when I was in the car when we were…he told me to get out and I was trying to open the car door. It was like an old car… and I was trying to open the car door. I couldn't get it opened, and he kept getting frustrated and I was afraid he was going to really hurt me at this point if I didn't get out of the car. And I kept trying to open the door, and he was still going down the road, and at this point he slowed down. He didn't completely stop. He slowed down, opened the door and threw me out. And then he stopped the car I guess about when I rolled out, the car door banged into my head and I crawled on the sidewalk right there and he stopped the car and he just stuck…he rolled down the car window on the passenger's side and said that I was his and that he would get back with me later. And that was that. I didn't even look at him. I didn't even look at the car. I just sat still. And I remember the car made a noise. It was like a muffler type.

I.   Loud?

R.   It wasn't real loud, but it was…

I.   Okay. Now back to when he had you at the house. Did you notice…did he take his clothes completely off?

R.   Well, he didn't take his pants totally off. He just pushed them down.

I.   Did he take his boots off? Kept his boots on?

R.   He left them on.

I.   Did you notice any kind of marks on his body anywhere?

R.   That was the only thing I noticed. Right there. He had green eyes. I remember that because he looked down at me and said, "You got green eyes just like me." And that was the only thing I remember.

(Discussion between detectives) PAUSE

I.   Feeling better?

R.   I hurt.

I.   You hurt? Where do you hurt at?

R.   Down there.

I.   Was he real rough with you?

R.   Yeah.

I.   I need to go back to that. And I need you to say…tell me exactly what he did. Tell me where he put it. I mean like while ago you were referring to it as somewhere. You didn't tell me. And whatever you call it, I am…

R.   (inaudible)

I.   He lifted one of your legs up?

R.   Yes.

I.   Okay.

R.   And he just shoved it in.

I.   Okay. I need you to tell me. He shoved what? Your plain everyday language for it.

R.   I don't say it.

I.   Well, you need to. You need to say it here. Okay? What did he shove?

R.   His dick.

I.   Okay. Where did he shove it?

R.   In the cervix. Whatever you call it.

I.   Okay. I need for you to say where he shoved it. Can you tell me where he shoved it?

R.   Vagina.

I.   Okay. He put it in your vagina?

R.   Yes.

I.   Okay. Then what did he do after that?

R.   He just…he pounded real hard for quite a while and then he flipped me.

I.   He turned you over on your side?

R.   Yes.

I.   Okay. What did he do then?

R.   He hiked my leg up.

I.   Lifted them up or spread them apart or what?

R.   He lifted them up like this.

I.   Were you up or were you down?

R.   My butt was up and he pushed my head down and at that point he put it in my rectum.

I.   Okay. He put what in your rectum?

R.   Dick.

I.   Okay.

R.	And then he took it out and put it back into my vagina.

I.	Okay. Tell me what (inaudible) and…

R.	It hurt real bad.

I.	Was he real rough when he did it?

R.	Yes.

I.	Did you notice anything about the way he smelled? Did he smell dirty or did he smell clean? Any odd smells?

R.	No. I didn't notice.

I.	Did he look dirty or clean?

R.	He looked messed up.

I.	Like messed up how?

R.	Spacy. Messed up. Drugged messed up. Because he couldn't…I know that when he threw me down when he first knocked in the door and he threw me down and I was looking at him, he banged into the wall before he even got to me so…and I didn't smell beer or anything on him. There was a lot of empty beer cans in the apartment, but…

I.	Did you notice his hands? Were they rough or smooth or did they feel rough?

R.	I didn't even notice.

I.	Did you notice his fingernails? Were they dirty or clean?

R.	It was dark in there and there weren't any curtains at all. There was none. That was not the place…no one had really been living there, and I remember the…when I looked up…the door we went into was right there, and there was a big window, a real big window right beside it, and I remember I looked out and there was a (inaudible) building that was going like this.

I.	Did he do anything else to you?

R.	Huh-uh.

I.	You didn't do anything else to him?

R.	No.

I.	Did he put anything in your mouth?

R.	Huh-uh.

I.	Okay. Do you remember if the car was…was it an older model?

R.	Yeah, it was an old type yellow car.

I.	About how old would you think if you guessed?

R.	I don't even know because I didn't know what kind of car it was. It looked just like that car that (inaudible)…it looked just like that…but then we saw another one just like it too.

I.	Was it a bright yellow?

R.	Yeah. You could definitely tell it was yellow.

I.	Was it dirty or clean?

R.	It was kinda dirty.

(other side of tape)

R.	…because he kept yelling at me to get out, the door was squeaking so I couldn't really get the door open.

I.	The inside of it…how did it look? Inside of the car? Were the seats torn?

R.	Decent. No. The inside looked kind of decent.

I.	Did he have a radio in it? Did he have it on or anything?

R.	No. There was no radio on. He had a radio in it though.

I.	He didn't have it on?

R.	No.

I.	Did you notice anything in the car that…tapes or anything like that lying around?

R.	No. I just kept trying to stare at the floorboard because I was kinda afraid to look out.

I.	Okay. Back at the house…were there any lights in there? Did he turn any lights on?

R.	No.

I.	How dark was it in there? Was it completely dark or…?

R.	Yeah, it was dark, but those from the building…there was lights around the building so it came into the window.

I.	There were no curtains on the windows?

R.	There was none.

I.	Okay. About…was it light enough to see very well?

R.	Not really. No.

I.	Did you see well enough to be able to see his face?

R.	Oh, I remember his face. I remember that when, earlier that day, he had harassed me then and I remember his face.

I.	You said a while ago that he hadn't shaved. It looked like he hadn't shaved for a couple of days? Okay. You said a while ago he hadn't shaved. Did he try to kiss you or anything like that?

R.	No.

I.	So, you never actually felt his face?

R.	No. But when I looked up at him, you could see it. It was dark and I could see it.

I.	Okay. But you never actually could feel it to see how rough it was?

R.	No.

I.	Okay. So, he didn't kiss you or anything like that?

R.	No.

I.	Did he say anything to you while all of this was going on? Was he talking?

R.	Well, I screamed a couple of times and that was when he started really hitting me and so I shut up.

I.	He didn't say anything?

R.	No. He didn't say anything. He just kept hitting.

I.	You didn't notice anything about the way he smelled or anything?

R.	No.

I.	Was his hair long or short?

R.	No. It was…I don't know…I guess it was about like this and then there was like a tail grown in the back.

I.	Okay. One of the little tails the little narrow ones like that or one…

R.	It was a little wider. It was probably about like this. It kind of tapered down and then went down.

I.	How was it fixed on top?

R.	It was just straight down.

I.	It was hanging down?

R.	Yeah. It was hanging down.

I.	Okay. You said something about his eyes a while ago. Did you see…did you see the color of his eyes or was it the remark he made?

R.	Well, when he put my leg up and the light was shining on his face, we were right in front of the window, and when he did that and I looked up, I could see he had …they were kind of greenish.

I.	You could see that in the light?

R.	Right. They were exactly the same color as my eyes. That was the first thing I noticed. Even when I looked up at him when I was coming out from the store towards the alley, when I looked up and saw him, I could notice the eyes too, because we have got the same color eyes.

I.	How were his eyebrows? Bushy or not bushy?

R.	I don't know. Medium, I guess. I don't remember.

I.	Did he have a smooth complexion or maybe acne scars or something like that? Do you remember?

R.	Yeah. There was a couple right here that he had.

I.	Like acne scars. Okay. How did he walk?

(Officer knocked on the door and asked if he could come back in)

I.	I know that you are getting tired Rita. I just had a couple of questions I wanted to ask you right quick. When all this happened… and I know you told the officer how it happened, did you try to fight him in any way?

R.	Yes. I did.

I.	Can you describe that to me?

R.	Yeah. I scratched him.

I.	Do you remember where?

R.	Well…the first time…well…when he put his hands on me, I was trying to pull his hands off. And then at that point he started scratching me and I kept trying to get his hands off. But before that I just like pushed him a little bit right on the chest and I scratched him. He was muscular. It looked like he had been lifting weights or something.

I.	Kind of a bodybuilder type physique?

R.	Yeah. He did. I remember scratching him right down his arm.

I.	Remember which arm?

R.	Left arm.

I.	Did he say anything when you scratched him?

R.	Yeah, he hit me.

I.	That is when he hit you?

R.	Uh-huh.

I.	Okay. Is there any other little detail you can think of?

R.	Just that tattoo that is on his arm like that. That was one thing I noticed and that he made a comment that he had the same color eyes I have. And he does.

I.	Did he have bad breath?

R.	I didn't even notice.

I.	Okay. Okay. Well, we're going to go ahead and end the interview with you at eight minutes after noon, same date, March 17, 1991. Detective Cosper wants to talk to you just a second…not to ask you any questions, just to talk to you for just a second.

Chapter 2 Twelve Days

Later that Sunday morning on St. Patrick's Day 1991, I awoke not knowing what was brewing up as I greeted the new day. Wow! I thought to myself as I remembered our encounter. What a wild woman! My friend Randy came by to smoke one with me, and I told him about her.

On Monday, another friend, Mike Sparks, came by in the afternoon to see if he could borrow my ten-speed for a while. I couldn't help telling him about this woman. Never in my life had I been with a girl that was so vocal. She really was moaning and carrying on.

Earlier in the day when I drove Krissy's car to school, I stopped by Rita's house to see if she was home, interested in possibly seeing her again. No one was home. I stopped by her house once again in the next couple of days. No answer.

Also on Monday, I went over to my parent's house to read the papers and eat. While reading the Ada Evening News from that day, my mother pointed out to me the reported rape on 12th street near the college. After reading the article, the first thought that came to mind was all the fraternity guys who lived on that block. Maybe they had a party and this happened to some poor girl. It never even entered my mind at this point that it might have been the girl I was with. Not even a thought. The newspaper article read:

Police Investigate Alleged Rape
ADA-Ada police detectives are investigating a reported rape that allegedly occurred here March 17th. The 27 –year old Ada woman told authorities she was forced into a car and sexually assaulted.

Police headquarters received a 911 call at 5:56 am, March 17. Officers were told there was a woman in the 100 block of North Broadway who was claiming to have been raped. When officers came into contact with the woman, they reported "she was extremely upset, almost hysterical."

The victim would not talk to police officers, but did show signs of an assault. She was taken to the Valley View Regional Hospital emergency room and examined. While there she spoke to female staff and details of the alleged rape were relayed to officers.

She said she had gone to Hardee's between 1:30 and 3:00 am, March 17. She then left the restaurant to buy cigarettes. She said the man forced her into an older model yellow car.

The woman said she was taken to a residence near the East Central University campus and was sexually assaulted.

She described her assailant as tall with a slim, muscular build and shoulder length, sandy colored hair.

*

On Wednesday, March 20th, I again went to my parent's house to read the papers and eat. I stood at the front hall furniture, looking through mail and papers.

"Matthew, would you have some explanation for why this was slid under my front door?" Mom handed me a small, torn piece of grocery sack, about the size of half a sheet of paper. Written in pencil was something like, "Stay away from the girl or you will be sorry." Mom's eyes had not left mine. I wasn't really finding an explanation so quickly.

"Hmmm…Where did you find it?"

"I found it just inside the door when I got home for lunch, obviously slid under the door."

"I really don't know Mom." I said that like a smart aleck, because I was uncomfortable and didn't know what else to say. I quickly retreated to the kitchen. It had to be from this girl or her "girlfriend". I figured that Rita had been caught by her girlfriend and her girlfriend was mad.

On Thursday, March 21, 1991, a tornado hit northern Ada and did considerable damage. I remember looking outside (I lived on the south side) and seeing this sinister looking cloud off to the north. My apartment was in a valley so I couldn't see the tornado itself.

My dad, brother and sister were all working in a printing company that they owned at the Ada Airport. The building itself was a converted hanger, perfect lunch for a hungry tornado. The tornado took the roof off of the National Guard Armory a couple of hundred yards away instead.

After my morning classes on Friday, March 22nd, I decided to call in sick to work and drive around, looking at the damage done by the tornado. It was a pretty day. I bought some beer about noon and stopped by Hardee's to get something to eat before I started drinking.

I parked on the south side, walked in and ordered two hamburgers from Rita, who happened to be working. I was pleasantly surprised to see her again after my failed attempts to catch her at home.

"Hi."

"Can I take your order?" she said in an uneasy manner, like she was not being herself.   I thought it strange that she didn't make direct eye contact with me for more than a second and she seemed very nervous. My mind quickly thought maybe her boss (who was right behind her) was her girlfriend or something and she was being cautious. She acted scared and was shaking really bad when she handed me my change.

As I was walking out, her boss told the other workers that she and Rita were going in the back to talk and would be right back out. I just didn't feel right about how she reacted to me. Weird. Oh well.

I sat in the parking lot to eat my burgers before I started driving again. Two workers came out and one guy went to his car and did something and then went back into Hardee's. I felt more weird vibes and was somewhat paranoid of these workers going to their cars, considering a death threat (the note) had been sent to me. I quickly finished eating and left. As I was pulling out, a thought came into my head to go by Danny's to see if he was home.

Danny was not home, but I found another death threat. It was written on a small post-it note, tacked to the doorframe. It was similar to the other one, just different wording. I think it said, "Touch the girl again and you are dead." Now I knew for sure who was sending the death threats but I was a little confused and surprised as to the magnitude of this "girlfriend's" anger. I wadded up the piece of paper and threw it on the ground.

I drove north, looking at the damage at Hammond Heights (black community across from the National Guard Armory) and I saw Mike

Sparks and some other people I knew. I talked to him for a few minutes about the tornado and asked him when he would bring my bicycle back. I then drove behind the airport and looked at the damage around the area.

I decided to go see my friend Leah who lives in Francis (northeast of Ada a few miles). I talked with her for 2-3 hours and even told her about the wild escapade with the woman. Leah and I used to date and we can tell each other things that two guy/girl friends would tell each other. I told so many people about her because she was such a unique girl and I would always remember our first meeting (oh boy).

I stayed out all night with Krissy's car. I had failed to pick her up from work at five o'clock, so like a little kid in trouble, I didn't want to go home to face the wrath caused by that.

Early Saturday morning, about 7:00 am, I stopped by my friend Teri Adair's house to see if anyone was home. I brought some donuts and talked with her roommate for a while, and then decided to drive to Francis to see if Leah or her sister was home. I was buzzed from the long night out, but relatively clear headed, enjoying the beautiful day that was developing. As I was taking a left-hand curve just over the railroad tracks, a black truck was suddenly in my lane and I had to swerve to avoid hitting it. This part of the road was notorious for wrecks and I was going to add to its mystery.

I'll never forget the image of this dark colored truck headed straight for me. My best guess is that it was a dual-axle truck. My instinct took over and I swerved to the right.

The problem with this stretch of road is that there is no shoulder on the right side, so if a car going north and taking the left curve somehow gets off the road, the car will crash. The road drops off about 3-4 inches to gravel on the side of the road. As I swerved off the road, I hit the gravel and was thrown into a spin. It all happened so fast; I had no time to do anything. I crashed through a steel pole fence and wound up caught in some barbed wire.

When I regained focus, I took stock of my body and the situation. Except for the possibility of cracked ribs, I came out of the crash with only a scratch on my forehead. The car was still running so I tried to back up. It wouldn't budge. I tried to rock it out.

I got out and discovered that I was high-centered on a small hill, with the barbed wire fence wrapped around and keeping the car from moving. Man, I was mad! The driver didn't even stop to see if I was alive. He had to have seen the dust and commotion in his rearview mirror.

This was bound to be trouble for me. Here I was, driving under suspension, on probation for a felony, drinking, and crashing my girlfriend's car into someone's yard. Krissy was already so mad at me. I reached in the car, grabbed the twelve-pack and took off across the highway for Leah's, less than a half-mile away.

A hundred yards up the road and out of sight of the car, I reconsidered and turned back for the car. I just had to try again to get her car out. I couldn't just leave it there.

Nobody will believe that I was forced off the road. Can I still get a DUI if I'm not arrested with the car? Would she report it as stolen when the police question her about it and suggest that she press charges? Can they prove that I crashed it?

I crossed the road and took another look at the position of the car before trying to work it out again. I tried three or four more times before realizing that it wasn't moving without a tow.

"Step out of the car and keep your hands where I can see them."

I looked in the rearview mirror and saw a car with a woman and two little girls in it and a man standing behind my car.

"Step out of the car and keep your hands where I can see them."

I turned to see a middle-aged man postured like a soldier, brandishing a walkie-talkie as if it were his weapon. I was certainly caught.

It just so happens I crashed into an Oklahoma State Bureau of Investigation agent's front yard. What luck! His wife and two children were in the car, looking dressed for a spring morning picnic. He called the highway patrol, and soon I was hauled to the county jail.

I was mad. It just wasn't fair! The truck ran me off the road! I refused to take a breathalyzer because I knew what it would read. They would not understand my tolerance to alcohol. I was booked for DUI for my refusal and placed in the drunk-tank to sober up for four hours. I could make my phone call at that time.

I called Krissy because I was twenty dollars short in making bail. Darn, twenty more dollars and I wouldn't have to call her! She somehow agreed to bail me out and did. The news that I had possibly totaled her car did not sit well with her. I was beaten and just wanted to go home.

The rest of the day Saturday and Sunday I was really in the dumps. My felony probation would probably be revoked and I would go to prison. I felt like such a screw-up. My self-worth and confidence were at an all-time low.

I contacted my attorney Tommy on Monday. He said he would go to work on the DUI. Krissy and my parents had torn into me for two days. I was ready to gain some serenity. Monday night I went to AA. Danny was there at the meeting.

I told him that I had stopped by a couple of times but missed him. He was a little reserved, not talking much, which was unusual for him. He said that he had spent a few days in the city jail for drunk and disorderly conduct, including the early morning Rita and I had stopped by. The AA meeting ended and we parted without much more to say. I noted that he seemed a bit preoccupied.

Needless to say, the weekend events really put a hurt on my relationship with Krissy and I planned to move back in with my parents on Monday or Tuesday. I would just try to keep my job and finish the semester in good standing.

I heard from Rita again on Tuesday, March 26th, nine days after our meeting. She called me at work in the early afternoon. I was thrown into confusion from the start, but I think this phone call is very telling, being it's the first time we had spoken again. Does it sound like two friends, or the abductor and victim?

(O-Operator, K-Kim, R-Rita)
O.   Good afternoon, Chickasaw Nation.
R.   Yes, can I speak to a Matthew Thompson?
O.   Matthew Thompson?
R.   Uh-huh.
O.   Hold on, I think he works in Finance.
R.   Okay.
O.   Does he? Do you know?
R.   I have no idea.
O.   Hold on.
K.   Finance, this is Kim.
R.   Yes, can I speak to a Matthew Thompson please?
K.   Uh-huh. One moment please.
M.   This is Matthew.
R.   Matthew?
M.   Yes.
R.   This is Rita.
M.   Oh, Hi.
R.   Hi.
   M.   What's going on?
R.   Yeah, do you remember me?
M.   Yeah.
R.   Yeah.
M.   Uh…what's up?
R.   Oh, not much.
M.   Your friend's mad at me, huh?
R.   Who?
M.   Is your girlfriend mad at me?
R.   What girl?
M.   Oh, I don't know…uh…
R.   Oh, I have no earthly idea.
M.   Oh, I got a…
R.   Oh what, you talking about at Hardee's?
M.   Yeah.

R.	Oh, when you came there?

M.	Yeah. I got a death threat.

R.	You did?

M.	Yeah.

R.	Wow.

M.	And it was left at my parent's house.

R.	Oh, wow. That ain't got nothing to do with me.

M.	And then there was one left at where I took you that night.

R.	Oh, I have no idea. That has got to be somebody else.

M.	It can't be though.

R.	I don't know. I don't think so.

M.	See, I didn't know who it was and then I went by that house again to see if that guy was home.

R.	Yeah.

M.	And there was a note on his door. So, there's…that's the only thing it could be.

R.	I don't think so.

M.	Uh…

R.	I don't think so.

M.	I don't know. It's pretty weird.

R.	I don't know. I really don't think anybody at my work would, you know, have anything against…

M.	Is that not your girlfriend at work?

R.	No. They are all friends of mine at work.

M.	Uh…

R.	So, I don't…you know…maybe she's mad at something you did there before or something. I don't know.

M.	She said, "Don't touch that girl again."

R.	Oh, she…I have no idea. That can't really have anything to do with me. I don't…I have no idea.

M.	I think that is the only way it could be.

R.	I don't know.

M.	Where are you at?

R.	Huh?

M.	Where are you at?

R.	Um. I'm just at a friend's house.
M.	Oh yeah. You just thought you would give me a call, huh?
R.	Yeah.
M.	What, do you want to get together?
R.	Yeah. I would like to.
M.	Cool.
R.	Cool.
M.	Uh…
R.	Can I see you tonight?
M.	I don't see why not.
R.	Okay.
M.	You're…I hope you are not setting me up to be killed.
R.	What? I'm not setting you up.
M.	I hope not.
R.	I am not setting you up at all. God, I just…I don't know anybody around here.
M.	Well, did you…if your girlfriend might have found out though?
R.	I don't think so. I really don't.
M.	Um. Because it's kind of weird that…see, the only other person that would have done that knew where I lived so he wouldn't have left it at my parent's house and the…
R.	I don't…uh…I can tell you right now, I don't know nothing about your parents or where they live or anything else. I just started working at Hardee's.
M.	Yeah.
R.	So, like I said, unless somebody else has a beef with you. I really…I don't, you know…I don't see that whatsoever.
M.	Yeah, because…
R.	So.
M.	Because it's kind of weird that they would leave a…
R.	Yeah, I guess so, but I mean…
M.	And that place we went to, too.
R.	I…I guess so. I just…um…I don't know anything about that. I really don't.

M.   It's kind of weird. Uh. Can I get a hold of you when I get off of work?

R.   Well, I don't have a phone. Um…is there someplace I can call you?

M.   Yeah, but uh…um…

R.   Or at a pay phone. I can call you from another pay phone or something?

M.   Uh, let me think. Oh, goodness, see I am supposed to be moving home tonight.

R.   You're what?

M.   Going to move home.

R.   Oh, you are moving home?

M.   Yeah.

R.   Oh, with your parents?

M.   Yeah. I was going to do that tonight, but I don't know if I am going to. I think I was going to go over there and stay tonight anyway. So, um…let me think. Shit. Yeah, write this number down.

R.   Okay.

M.   xxx-xxxx.

R.   Okay.

M.   And just…um…let me think of a good lie you can say. Because they are going to want…

R.   Do you even remember the other night?

M.   Hell yeah I do. I come in Hardee's and saw you and…I don't know, it's a weird deal. Seems like…I mean…because I got these death threats and the only other person I could think of I knew wouldn't do it and then…I mean…not saying it was him, and that maybe if you had told someone I was with some guy named Matthew and…

R.   No. I haven't even mentioned your name to anybody…now I just…

M.   I wonder if somebody…

R.   No, I just…you know…I was just wondering if you remembered when we were at the apartment.

M.   Yeah, I remember! I came by to talk to you, but I felt bad vibes there at Hardee's or something.

R.   Oh.

M.   I don't know. But um…

R.   Okay. What time should I call you?

M.   Just call about 7:30 or 8:00 and uh…I guess just ask for me. Yeah.

R.   Matthew. Okay.

M.   Okay.

R.   All right.

M.   All right, I'll talk to you later.

R.   So, I'll look forward to seeing you tonight.

M.   Okay.

R.   All right.

M.   Well, bye.

R.   Bye bye.

She called back just a few minutes later.

M.   Hello.

R.   Matthew?

M.   Yeah.

R.   I am sorry to call you again. This is Rita.

M.   That's Okay.

R.   Oh, it's Okay? Okay. Um…I was wondering something.

M.   What?

R.   If I saw you again…

M.   Yeah.

R.   I mean…I was kind of…you know…worried about this the last time I saw…um…You're not going to be that forceful, are you?

M.   How was that?

R.   I mean…you were pretty loaded.

M.   Yeah.

R.   You know…and you were really…I mean…real forceful and…I mean…you know…I like you and everything…I just…I don't…you know…I don't get into that…you know…what I'm saying…and I was just wondering if I saw you again if you were going to be like that again.

M.   Whatever you want.

R.   I mean…I don't really know you, you know? You were real, real forceful

M.   (laugh) Whatever you want.

R.   Okay. I just know that…I mean…you know…you don't rip a girl's clothes off and shit. You know? You be more gentle and stuff.

M.   Was I that way?

R.   Yeah. You were very much that way.

M.   Uh…

R.   I mean…you ripped my shirt and everything, you know.

M.   I did?

R.   Yeah. I just wanted to make sure you wasn't going to be that way again or whatever.

M.   Oh.

R.   I just…you know.

M.   Call back down here about, well…(talking with someone in the room; Do people answer the phone after five here? They probably don't do they?) Uh…just call me later.

R.   Call you later?

M.   Yeah.

R.   At this same number?

M.   Yeah, about…what time is it right now?

R.   I don't even know what time it is.

M.   Call me about…(What time is it?) Call me back in 15 or 20 minutes.

R.   Okay.

M.   Okay.

R.   All right, talk to you then.

M.   All right. Bye.

R.   Bye bye.

"That was weird," I thought as I hung up and got back to work. She must be confused. Weird. My first reaction was that she was confused, not me. My brain went into overdrive to try to make sense of this and immediately began to factor in the valium. That alone made me start to try to visualize that night in a way that was different than the way I remembered. I began to chase this wisp of smoke a bit, but a bit was just enough.

After work I went to my new dwelling, my parent's house. I had some homework to catch up on and was doing so at the kitchen table with Krissy and Mom. I was expecting Rita to call so I was staying close to the phone.

The phone rang and I rushed to get to it. I had to wrap around the utility room and try to shield my voice from Krissy and Mom. Here we go again with this weird stuff.

M.   Hello.
R.   Is Matthew there?
M.   Yeah. What's going on?
R.   Hey, not much. I tried calling at your work that last time and all I got was an answering service, so…
M.   Yeah, they are gone after five.
R.   Yeah. It was about ten after when I tried calling, so…
M.   Yeah. That's all right.
R.   Yeah. So, what's going on?
M.   Well, I am eating.
R.   Oh.
M.   Eating dinner. Where are you at, a friend's house?
R.   Huh?
M.   Where are you at?
R.   At who's house?
M.   I said, where are you?
R.   Oh, yeah. At the friend's house. Yeah.
M.   Um. Well, I've got to do some homework tonight.
R.   Oh, you do?
M.   Uh-huh.
R.   Can't wait?
M.   No. I'm behind.
R.   Oh.
M.   I don't got…Do you got a car?

R.   No. Well, yeah. I can get a way there.

M.   Um, well I don't think I can do it tonight. To tell you the truth I don't trust you.

R.   What do you mean you don't trust me?

M.   Because I had somebody…one of your girlfriends or somebody has a death threat out on me.

R.   Matthew, I…

M.   I guarantee it was one of your girlfriends or something.

R.   I don't…

M.   Because everybody knows me in this town, see…

R.   Yeah.

M.   Whether I know them or not.

R.   Matthew, I don't know anybody. Do you know what I'm saying?

M.   Yeah, but…

R.   I just moved here a month ago. Then evidently it is somebody that likes you.

M.   Well…and they saw me with you I guess, you know. But I can't figure out who in the hell would do that.

R.   I don't know.

M.   Uh…

R.   I mean…maybe it wasn't for you.

M.   Yeah…brought it to my parent's house and whipped it under the door.

R.   Uh…well Matthew, I have no idea.

M.   And then…

R.   I have not talked to anybody about what happened that night.

M.   And then there was one at that place.

R.   I know that night upset me and I know I haven't talked to anybody about it, you know. I kind of wanted to talk to you about it because…I mean…it was like…I mean…you forced everything on me. You know what I'm saying? I mean…you were loaded.

M.   Yeah.

R.   And you got me in the car and we went there and…I mean…you…for…I mean…you dragged my clothes off and stuff. I mean…

M.   Maybe I can talk to you tomorrow? Do you got to work tomorrow?

R.   No. I just…I've really been really wanting to talk to you about it because it has been upsetting me. I mean…I like you and everything…and uh…you know…I've wanted to see you again and really talk to you and get things right between us because that night was really bad…I mean…I don't know if you remember or not. But it…you know…it was…I mean…there's nobody around me now I can talk to. You know? I didn't want to talk to you at your work.

M.   Yeah.

R.   And…I mean…

M.   Well, can you give me a phone number I can call you at?

R.   Oh man, I don't even want to risk…you know…you calling my…you know…calling my friend's house or anything. But I mean…I don't know the stuff that's going on at my work at all. A matter of fact…um…you know…I'm not going to be working there anymore because the girl there is a real bitch and I know that when she saw you when I was working there, she freaked out and when you smiled at me I know that she freaked out. So, I don't know what's going on with that.

M.   Why did she freak out?

R.   I have no earthly idea. Maybe she likes you. I mean she said she likes a lot of guys that come in there. So…I mean…maybe you are one of them. Maybe she's been keeping tabs on you and she knew what happened that night. I have no idea. I just know I've been wanting to talk to you since that happened.

M.   I'm living in my Mom and Dad's house, you know. That's just not…I'm just moving out tonight really.

R.   Yeah.

M.   It's just not cool for me to leave because I've got a lot of homework I've got to catch up on.

R.   I just um…

M.   I'd like to talk to you tomorrow or something. I'll be down at East Central (University).

R.   Yeah, I want to talk to you. I really do. I just…I'm just wondering why you hurt me like that because…I mean…

M.   I didn't mean to.

R.   I mean…I really care about you a lot and I was just wondering why you hurt me like that. I mean…

M.   I didn't mean to. I mean at the time it didn't seem like…I didn't even…I don't remember ripping your shirt.

R.   Yeah, you did. I mean you ripped my shirt and…

M.   I probably scared you.

R.   You forced it a couple of times. Two different places, you know. I just…it freaked me out, it really did and I really liked you when I first saw you and I just didn't understand why you did that and I'm just…I mean…if you want to go someplace that…I mean…is completely out of the area…I mean that's fine with me, you know. I just wanted to talk to you about it.

M.   Well, can we get together tomorrow?

R.   Sure. I'd like to get together. There's no way you can get together tonight? I mean…I just…I know I've been kind of upset about it. I really have now. I'd like to see you.

M.   Well, the only way is that…I can call you because I don't know how long she (Krissy) is going to be here or…

R.   Yeah. Well, uh…is there a certain time I can call you back?

M.   Yeah. Um…let me think…why don't you call me back at nine.

R.   At nine?

M.   Yeah.

R.   Okay.

M.   Okay. Maybe I can be somewhere where I can talk to you or something.

R.   Okay. Because I…you know…I don't know what's going on and I just…you know…I feel bad in a sense but…I mean you know…I am really hurt about it and I just…I just want to talk to you about it that's all.

M.	Okay.

R.	I mean I don't want any hard feelings. We live in the same town and in the same area. I mean I live right up the street from the college. You know that.

M.	Uh-huh. What, 805 (her address, 805 E. 12th)?

R.	Huh.

M.	805?

R.	Yeah.

M.	I came by a couple of times.

R.	Oh, did you?

M.	Yeah, like a couple of days after I saw you. Monday or something. Nobody was home.

R.	Oh.

M.	You were probably at work.

R.	Yeah. Yeah. I got weird hours. But I got another job so I probably won't be working at Hardee's anymore.

M.	Oh really.

R.	But um…

M.	Why don't you call me at nine?

R.	Okay.

M.	Okay.

R.	All right. At the same number?

M.	Yeah.

R.	Okay.

M.	Okay.

R.	All right. Talk to you then.

M.	All right.

R.	Bye bye.

M.	Bye.

M. Hello.

R.	Hi, how are you doing?

M.	Call back in about five minutes.

R.	Five minutes?

M.	Yeah.

R.	Okay.
M.	Bye.
R.	Bye bye.

M.	Hello.
R.	Hi.
M.	Hello.
R.	Is it a good time to call?
M.	Yeah, they just left to go get a coke.
R.	Oh, Okay. I didn't know.
M.	So, what are you doing?
R.	Oh, not much.
M.	I'm studying a bit.
R.	Yeah? You still going to see me?
M.	Not tonight.
R.	I thought you said you were going to?
M.	No, I said I might but I…hell, I can't. I'm here at my
parent's house.
R.	Yeah, but you could leave.
M.	Hell, I can't leave. That would cause them some trouble.
Hell, I'd…haven't …I've been through some trouble in the last few
days. I wrecked my girlfriend's car last weekend. I got a DUI.
R.	Oh. Yeah, we could go someplace where nobody knows
about though, just for a few minutes.
M.	I can't leave though. Hell, when I was talking to you a while
ago, I told her it was this guy that I know who is in drug treatment and I
made up some lie. I said it was his girlfriend calling me and they are all
worked up about him and all kinds of shit. I mean tonight is not a good
night. Any other night, like tomorrow night or something, I could say I
am going to…well, I am supposed to study with this guy tomorrow
night but…
R.	Well, just say you called and um…he wanted to study with
you a couple of hours tonight. Say you need some help on something. I
really need to talk with you.
M.	Shit.

R.	Come on. I really want to talk to you.

M.	I can't do it tonight. Just too much shit going on. My parents don't even want me to move in really, but I will. It would be a lot better if I could talk to you tomorrow, between my classes or before, or in the morning sometime.

R.	I know. It's just that it's not a good time for me.

M.	Why not?

R.	Because of having the jobs and all that kind of stuff.

M.	Do you got to go to work tomorrow?

R.	I'm supposed to.

M.	Where did you get a job at?

R.	Huh?

M.	Are you going to tell me where you got a job at?

R.	Uh…Pizza Hut.

M.	Oh really?

R.	Yeah.

M.	That's cool.

R.	Can't you just make up…I mean…can't you just spend ten minutes?

M.	No, I can't. Hell, I can't leave. I ain't going to. If I was at my house, I would be able to, but I can't here. I ain't going to do that. Fuck, I'll come back and…"Where have you been, nah, nah, nah. Hell, I've got to study anyway. I got about twenty more pages I got to study before tomorrow.

R.	Yeah, but it…I mean you could just tell them you were going to the store or something.

M.	I can't drive.

R.	What do you mean you can't drive? Oh, you can't drive a car?

M.	No. Hell, I didn't have a license in the first place. I've been driving under suspension too.

R.	Well, can't you meet me down the road? I mean they wouldn't even know you snuck out.

M.   No, I ain't doing that. I ain't going to do that. I don't…I'd rather meet you tomorrow. I'm not…I don't know. I still don't trust you that much.

R.   Oh, good grief. Not that again.

M.   You didn't tell anybody? You didn't tell the cops…

R.   I haven't…

M.   you were raped or anything, did you?

R.   I haven't told anybody anything.

M.   See, there is this girl raped over in that part of town (the newspaper article).

R.   Well, I ain't got anything to do with that.

M.   Okay. I'm just freaking out.

R.   No, that ain't got anything to do with me. I just wanted to talk to you.

M.   I didn't mean for it to be like it was. I guess I just don't know. I guess I forced myself on you, but I didn't…I mean I thought you were going along with me. I guess…

R.   No. I wasn't at the time. I mean I don't know what is going on with you. I just know I just like…you know…I just like you and everything and I just wanted to talk to you.

M.   Well, it's like…I mean…any night other than tonight is Okay.

R.   Yeah.

M.   Because you know I am moving out and we are breaking up and you know I want…

R.   Yeah, I understand.

M.   I want to have a friend, you know?

R.   Yeah. Well…I mean…I can be your friend you know. That was the whole reason I called is because the other night did kind of upset me and I kind of wanted to clear things up.

M.   Well, I am sorry about that. I guess I just figured…I don't know…you're a wild woman or something.

R.   No. (laugh) No. Not at all.

M.   Kind of weird. I guess I get turned on by people with accents.

R.   Oh. Well, um…so I can call you tomorrow?

M.   Well, I can meet you tomorrow.

R.   Okay.

M.   I'll be uh…I have a class at ten o'clock. I get out at eleven and then I have class at twelve o'clock. So I can see you either at…between eleven and twelve or I can see you like at nine in them morning before I go to my ten o'clock class. Either one of those and then after I get out of school at one o'clock, I got to go to work.

R.   Oh. Well as long as I…well…if I can see you by nine…I mean I'd at least get to see you for an hour.

M.   Okay.

R.   Talk to you.

M.   Where do you want to meet me at?

R.   Um…shhh…I don' know.

M.   Do you know where the ECU student union is?

R.   The student union?

M.   Yeah.

R.   Huh-uh.

The rest of the conversation was just me giving her directions to the student union where we were to meet in the morning. She was to meet me inside of the student union at nine in the morning.

Man! This is really getting weird, I thought. What is this girl's problem? I don't think I did those things she said, like ripping her shirt and being rough with her. Did I? Something is really fishy here. Why is she hassling me like this? I've got to keep alert tomorrow so her girlfriend doesn't shoot me or something.

Maybe I'm crazy? The valium, the cheating on Krissy, the car crash, the DUI, the ghost at the attic apartment, my brain. Nah! To heck with that! I remember that night as clear as day and so must she.

Chapter 3   She's Confused

I thought about how I should handle the meeting with Rita at ECU on Wednesday, March 27th. She was really getting on my nerves. My plan was to be calm and passive with her, offering my help wherever I could. What else can I do? Maybe she will figure it out and get on with her life and leave me to mine. If I upset her, with all of this talk about me assaulting her, she might go to the police or somebody, so I will tell her what she wants to hear and hope she will chill out and leave me alone.

We were to meet in the Student Union before my class at ten o'clock. I was on my guard, looking around for anything unusual. This whole thing was just not right. I was uncomfortable and suspicious. I waited for a while and then found her waiting outside instead. She was wired for sound and because of the wind, some of the conversation was inaudible.

R.   Hi.
M.   I thought you were going to meet me inside?
R.   Do what?
M.   I thought you were going to meet me inside?
R.   Oh, I didn't know if you wanted me to meet you inside or out here.
M.   Yeah, I said meet me inside, but that's Okay.
R.   Man, it's windy.
M.   So, what's up?
R.   Oh, not much.
M.   You cold? You got chill bumps.
R.   Just a little bit.
M.   The cops ain't coming after me, are they?
R.   Hell no.
M.   Shit, we could find some sun. You want to? Let's sit down there or something. Not much sun, but a little.
R.   All right.

M.	What time do you got to go to work?

R.	I'm supposed to go in at twelve.

M.	At Hardee's?

R.	Yeah.

M.	Let's go sit up there on that brick wall.

R.	Do what?

M.	Let's go sit on that brick wall over there. Where did you get that shirt?

R.	A friend of mine.

M.	Yep, no more car for me.

R.	Do what?

M.	I said no more car for me.

R.	Got to stick with the bicycle, huh?

M.	Yep. Stick with the bicycle a long time.

R.	Uh, at least we are in the sun now.

M.	What's up?

R.	Not a whole lot, just kind of wanted to talk to you.

M.	Yeah.

R.	I guess I can talk to you about it, not a hell of a lot of people around here. I don't know…I guess you might say I'm just…I'm just kind of sensitive you know. When it comes to guys and stuff…and it…you know…that night just kind of upset me quite a bit. I mean…I was even ripped, you know? That's how bad it was.

M.	Sorry…Damn.

R.	Yeah, that helps. I just…I don't know…it just really upset me, you know?

M.	You probably need to talk to some girl.

R.	Do what?

M.	You probably need to talk to some girl or something. I don't know that much about that kind of stuff.

R.	No. I mean…I just kind of wanted to talk about it, you know? I don't really…I don't really know anybody around here. I'm just sad, you know? I just moved here so I don't really know anybody. I don't know…you just…you kind of scared me really. Because…I don't know…when you dragged me in the car like that, you know?

M.   I didn't drag you in the car.

R.   Yeah, you did.

M.   More or less?

R.   Yep.

M.   I just kind of remember saying do you want to go drink some beer and you said yeah…

R.   No. And I just have been kind of hurting, especially physically, you know? Because I never…you know…I never had a guy force something like that on me. You know…I didn't even want anything like that.

M.   I don't know. Uh…maybe I got the wrong impression and scared you or something.

R.   Do what?

M.   Maybe you (inaudible) didn't do that, I hurt you or something. I wish it wasn't true, but I don't know if I can help you with that.

R.   Well, you…

M.   I must have scared you really bad for you to leave with me. I wish I would have seen that now. I didn't think that was how it was.

R.   I just kind of wanted to get things…you know…straight because it really hurt, you know? Yeah, I guess I was scared because it was hard for me to really say anything.

M.   That's what it was. You not saying anything, I figured that meant you were cool and calm and trying to act that way.

R.   Yeah. I was pretty scared. I mean I never had a guy force himself on me like that, you know, ripping my clothes and stuff like that.

M.   I don't remember that. I remember saying take your pants off.

R.   Well, you took them off. Then you ripped my shirt.

M.   How did I rip it?

R.   The strap on it.

M.   (inaudible)

R.   Well, I think…oh…no…I just felt like talking to you about it would…would help some. Because…I mean you really scared me. And yeah…you just went to pounding away…you know…and it…I remember kicking you once or trying to anyway.

M.   I can't believe…

R.   Then when you screwed me in the other place, you know, God that hurt.

M.   I'm sorry.

R.   I just didn't know why you did that.

M.   I was pretty loaded. I get loaded about two or three times a week.

R.   Yeah, you were pretty mean.

M.   I'm usually not that way. I'm usually more shy than anything else. I mean…I am still mean, but I'm not…I have feelings for other people.

R.   You didn't that night. It just kind of freaked me out when you forced me into the car. You know, I didn't really know what to think after that.

M.   That's all right. I asked you if you wanted to go drink some beer and you said Okay.

R.   No. That night was like a horror to me.

M.   Are you going to be Okay physically?

R.   Uh-huh. I only had one other person who would do me that way and that was my ex-husband.

M.   How old are you?

R.   27.

M.   I was loaded that night. I don't remember that night. I came in there and I remember seeing you sitting at that table and I said, well, I'm going to get something to eat and go sit by that girl.

R.   I remember going into Hardee's and when I came out, I went to go use the phone and I went to walking and that's when you got me in the car was right close to Hardee's.

M.   I sat there and ate…

R.   Right close to Hardee's…

M.   Food with you. Didn't I?

R.   Not with me.

M.   Yeah, I did.

R.	No, you didn't. Not that night. That night, I went out and got a soda, and I walked up to the pay phone and I used the phone. And I came walking back.

M.	At Hardee's?

R.	Right beside Hardee's.

M.	I sure don't remember. I remember…

R.	You must have been loaded.

M.	I remember some blonde in there and…

R.	Well, it wasn't me. I know…

M.	You didn't eat any french fries in there?

R.	I know you came in…No. I was in there a lot earlier. I went in there a lot earlier, went out and I went to use the pay phone.

M.	And I just picked you up?

R.	You were staggering…

M. Just a couple of beers…

R.	No. You were parked right in that…right next to…like it is in the middle of Taco Tico and Hardee's.

M.	That street?

R.	I know you were, you know…

M.	That street?

R.	Yeah, you were pretty…pretty loaded. I know that.

M.	Was I sitting there? And you came walking by?

R.	Uh-huh.

M.	I can understand it now. It must have been the valiums. See, that's why I was thinking it was a different thing because I can remember sitting there that night and talking to some blonde. I could have sworn it was you.

R.	Huh-uh.

M.	I could have sworn that I was talking…we were talking about your accent and everything else…

R.	No. The only thing that you talked about…you talked about something about the accent at that apartment. But there is more than one than one blonde girl that works in there. There is another one that has an accent.

M.	And you are from Boston, aren't you?

R.	Yeah.

M.	I thought that I…

R.	I had a piece of paper in something else in my pocket and I was wondering if you found it. At the apartment or anything?

M.	What did it say?

R.	It just had…it was a resume for Pizza Hut. I had to do all that thinking and write it all out and then I lost it.

M.	I think that place is open there. If you want, we can go by there and take a look around. Shit, I can't believe I did something like that.

R.	I couldn't either. I was just wondering, why me.

M.	You didn't report or anything, did you?

R.	No. I haven't talked to anybody about it. I have got to go to a doctor though.

M.	I'm sorry. I just can't believe it.

R.	It's something you can't go around doing.

M.	I could have sworn it was you I was talking to.

R.	Huh-uh.

M.	I remember sitting in that booth and talking to you. At least that is what I thought I…

R.	No. When I walked in there, there was a heck of a lot of kids in there. A lot. And then I went to use the pay phone.

M.	When I went in there…

R.	When I went in there it was packed. Every kid on earth I think was in there. When's your next class.

M.	Ten. What time is it?

R.	I don't know.

M.	It's probably 9:30 or so. I'm sorry Rita. I know it has to be hard on you.

R.	I'm crying about it.

M.	It's pretty much my fault, I guess. It's not your fault. You definitely didn't give me any indication you didn't want to. You sound like a smart girl. I just I just scared you and thought…well, I probably didn't know what to think.

R.	I didn't either.

M.   (Hey, what time is it?)
Fifteen till.
  (Thank you)
  Sorry I did this. I hope it doesn't mess you up in the head.
R.   Oh.
M.   Just don't feel guilty. I can't change anything that happened but it wasn't you. If you wouldn't have had that blonde hair, I wouldn't have stopped. Uh…you are pretty and all. Don't think that you are not. Don't let it be doing…anything to you. It was all me, you know? Anytime you want to talk to me just call, Okay? Do you feel any better now or worse?
R.   I just feel about the same. I just feel…hurt.
M.   I've got to go to class. Call me at home.
R.   I'll talk to you later.

Hopefully that did it. Maybe she will leave me alone now. Of course, looking back now, I realize what an idiot I was. That did it all right. She prodded and dug and worked hard, using lies and police psychology to get me to say what they were looking for. I was just saying whatever would get her off of my back, and that was what came to mind. Certainly, the last few minutes of the conversation really gave the police something to work with. Why did I say that stuff? Because I was an innocent mind just responding to her, looking to comfort her and get her off my back.

I didn't really know what I was "sorry" **about**, but I felt bad for her and wanted to make her feel better. Maybe I felt sorry for asking her back to the apartment, like it was my fault we had consensual sex. I thought that saying I was sorry would accomplish this, like taking the responsibility for something to make those with you feel comforted, like with a child. Heck, I actually felt embarrassed for what she was saying I did. But on the other hand, I knew I didn't do anything like that, that I could remember. My confusion was certainly growing at this point.

How easy it would be to turn these statements into words admitting guilt. From that point on, the police were building a reasonable case for

Peterson and Ross to give try. She called me again at work that afternoon.

M.   This is Matthew.
R.   Matthew?
M.   Yeah.
R.   This is Rita.
M.   What is going on?
R.   Not much. Sorry to bother you.
M.   That's Okay.
R.   But I really didn't have the chance to really talk to you that much at the college. I just had a couple of questions I wanted to ask you and I really couldn't ask them there.
M.   Okay.
R.   Do you remember…I mean…that night that happened. Do you remember ever having a knife?
M.   No. I didn't have a knife. I don't have a knife, except at home. Why?
R.   I was just wondering because I saw one, but…
M.   Why?
R.   Huh?
M.   Why?
R.   I don't know. That was just another thing that scared me.
M.   I didn't have a knife. I mean…I have one at home. I don't…you know…one that has been there for years. I don't carry one. It's not even a pocketknife. It's a fishing knife, a filleting knife.
R.   I guess just the main question I really wanted to ask you…it's just something that really has been bugging me and I don't really feel like I could put things behind me until I ask you.
M.   Yes.
R.   I was just wondering why did you rape me that night?
M.   Well, I didn't take it like that. Did you?
R.   Yes.
M.   I am busy right now.
R.   I mean…I am just…

M.	You trying to get me in trouble or something?

R.	No, I am not. It just hurt me. I don't want to go to anybody with this. I just wanted the question…you know…answered myself.

M.	Well, I am kind of busy right now. Can I…Jesus…somebody's waiting here on me. We're trying to work on something. But you can probably call back later.

R.	Okay.

M.	Okay?

R.	What time can I talk to you?

M.	Call back in a couple of hours.

R.	Okay.

M.	Okay.

R.	All right.

M.	All right.

R.	Bye bye.

M.	Bye.

M. This is Matthew.

R.	Matthew?

M.	Yes.

R.	This is Rita again. I am not going to call you anymore, Okay? I am just going to talk to you this one time. I don't want to call you back in two hours, because I am going to be like wicked busy. Uh…

M.	Are you at work?

R.	Do what?

M.	Are you at work?

R. No. Uh…I am going to put it to you real clear, Okay. Because my head is really screwed up right now especially after what happened, Okay. And all I want is just the question answered from you, Okay. Because if you don't I probably will go to the cops. I just want to know why you raped me, that's all I want. Just to clear my head up.

M.	Okay.

R.	I mean, I'm sorry it just…

M.   Okay. Well, shoot. I can't think of what it was. I thought in my own stupid mind that you left with me from Hardee's. I mean…I don't know. I remember picking you up at Hardee's…And I told you that today. I thought I said let's go get a beer.

R. No. You didn't say that to me at all.

M.   That is where my brain is messed up. I mean…what I did the night before screwed my brain up.

R.   I just want to know why you did it, that's all.

M.   I did it because I thought you were with me and you were consenting to me and you were wanting to be with me. If I thought any otherwise, I wouldn't have done it. I misunderstood from the very start what I was doing. Apparently, I was out of my own head. I wasn't thinking with my own mind. I mean…I don't even remember…you know…you tell me this and I don't even remember it. I was just out of my own head, not thinking what I was doing. I would never have even thought about that without…I mean…I'd never pick somebody up and take them somewhere and do that. I thought we were drinking beers together…you know…talking…and you're from Boston and I am from here and we are getting along…you know?

R.   No. It didn't go that way at all.

M.   But I want to talk to you some more if you want to.

R.   All right. I just wanted the question asked. Do you know what I am saying?

M.   Yeah.

R.   Cause it blows me away. You got to understand where I am coming from too.

M.   I can understand. I can understand exactly where you are coming from. I hope you…that you can understand where I am coming from, because I am telling you nothing but the honest truth. What went on in my head. What I was thinking at the time. That may sound like I am a stupid ass, but I guess I was. It wouldn't even…my brain was halfway working, I guess. I never even think about doing that to anyone, you know? Especially with someone you…you know…I mean…like you care now…who I normally respect and go out with…but I mean…I never do anything like that.

R.	The only thing is…I mean…I didn't even know you. You know? I had never even seen you.

M.	Yeah.

R.	You know. Well, we can talk about this another time.

M.	Well, you are not going to call the cops?

R.	No. I am not going to call you or…

M.	Do you want to meet me at school tomorrow? Because I feel bad for you…I mean…I am the one who did it. I am trying to make some kind of repair.

R.	I think another thing that really scared me is when you just made me get in the car. You know…I didn't even want to get in the car. I didn't even know who you were.

M.	See, I don't even remember that. I have no recollection of that. I thought maybe…I don't know…I went into Hardee's and got…I remember eating a ham & cheese. I remember sitting down with a girl who had blonde hair and was eating french fries. I could have sworn to God that that was you.

R.	No.

M.	And you wanted to go drink a beer…and that apparently wasn't you.

R.	No. That wasn't, because I was in Hardee's about…I guess it was about thirty minutes before that.

M.	I mean…it all clouded in my mind and I never even…I don't know what to do now after its happened. I don't know what I can do to help you. You know?

R.	Yes.

M.	I am sorry. I never do that. I wouldn't do that to you or anyone else. I've never done it before in my life. Where are you at now?

R.	At my friend's house.

M.	You are not at the cop's station?

R.	No. I am not and she is in the next room. She ain't hearing anything. I haven't even said anything to her.

M.	I am just a sorry motherfucker, I guess. I wouldn't ever do that. I can't believe I would. That doesn't sound like me at all. I mean…I believe you but that doesn't sound like me. It does because of what I did the night before, eating valiums. But that doesn't even sound like me…I mean…I would never drag anyone to the car. I don't know why…I mean…I have a girlfriend at home. It doesn't sound …why would I want to grab you and put you in the car and take you over there? I mean…I can remember at least talking to you…you know…but it doesn't sound…I can't believe I would do something like that.

R.   There wasn't much talking. But…

M.   It's my damn fault. It ain't you at all. I mean…you know that. I can't believe I did that. I have no recollection in my mind…picking you up. I still thought it was from Hardee's because you work there and that's what I remember.

R.   Yeah. I work there but I only went in there to get a soda. I was only in there about four minutes.

M.   Yeah, because I thought I met you there. And I remember we drank Bud Light is what I remembered.

R.   No. You were drinking beer, that's for sure.

M.   I mean if you want to talk to me again tomorrow, I will do that. I don't know…I want to do something to help you get over this. I don't know what that is. I just can't believe that I actually did that. I mean…I even thought about it the next day and told my best friend, "Yeah, I met this girl from Boston"…you know…"at Hardee's"…and I went by your house a couple of times to see if you were home to talk to you…you know…and let's go do something.

R.   No. I had never met you before.

M.   So, what do you suggest I do?

R.   I don't know. I just…

M.   You need to talk to…I guess you don't have any close friends.

R.   About the only thing besides…you know…you doing that there…I mean…what really hurt physically is…I mean…why did you do it to me in my rear end for?

M.   See, I don't remember that either.

R.   I mean that…

M.   I don't even remember that. I don't know why I did that. I can't even believe this is actually happening. I can't believe it actually happened. I mean…do you think you are going to be Okay physically?

R.   I don't know.

M.   I think you will…you'll…I think you will probably be Okay physically. I hope. Maybe if we can talk a couple of more times and get to know one another just a little bit better, maybe that can help you out mentally. I honestly…I can't believe all this…I mean, I believe you…but it's hard for me to believe all this. That I actually did all this. That this happened. Because in my mind I met you at Hardee's and we mutually consented to go drink some beer…find some place to drink some beer…

R.   No. Like I said, that was the first time I ever met you. I mean it really pisses me off, you know?

M.   Maybe if we can talk about it tomorrow…I guess at school or something…and do it for a couple of days, maybe that will help out. What do you think?

R.   I don't know. I am just pretty damn hurt right now.

M.   I am really sorry.

R.   Do what?

M.   I am really sorry. Do you want to see me tomorrow?

R.   I don't know.

M.   Are you going to work today? Did you not go?

R.   No. I didn't go.

M.   What can I do to help?

R.   There is nothing really you can do.

M.   I mean… would it help if we talked again?

R.   It might.

M.   I am deeply sorry Rita.

R.   I just…about the only thing…another thing boggling me is I just…I don't see how you got certain things in your head. It's like you're lying to me about it. That you don't remember this shit.

M.   Have you ever eaten valiums before?

R.   Huh?

M.   Have you ever eaten valiums?

R.	No. I have never eaten valiums.

M.	Well, they like make you forget stuff. I mean you take them and you don't remember a thing and that is what I did. I had been doing them for a week. I did them on Thursday night and…I guess that was Friday night…or…Friday night. I drank alcohol with them again…It was like I go into a black out where don't remember anything. You know I thought about it the next morning and everything and…well…what came up in my mind was that I went in there…because I did go in there…and I sat with some blonde girl and…I don't even remember. I thought that was you all along.

R.	No. I had never met you before.

M.	Okay. That is where my mind left me. I remember…I just…to me I went in there and I remember getting a ham & cheese and sitting by some girl eating french fries and talking to her and thinking it was you. I guess that just…I don't know…it sounds weird to me too because I think…because usually I can remember…I mean…I can honestly remember that I was sitting there talking to a blonde girl from Massachusetts with green eyes and she was eating french fries and she was talking in her accent and everything else. And then I remember that I said let's go drink some beer and we went and got some beer and I said do you want to go over here and…you know…

R.	Well, that wasn't me because when I went to Hardee's I got a soda and I walked straight out and I went and used the phone and I came walking back and you had beer in your car but it wasn't from taking me anywhere.

M.	I must have just left Hardee's and went and got that beer.

R.	God. When you get messed up like that, do you always pick up blondes? You know?

M.	No. I have never done that in my life. I don't know what was going through my head at the time. I guess I thought…

R.	I just…you know…I don't understand why you took me to that apartment and raped me. I just…I guess it just…

M.	I guess it didn't seem to me like it was raping because I thought I had met you.

R.	No. I mean…you ripped my clothes off and you stuck it in two different places and…I mean…you really hurt me.

M.	Do you want to talk to me again?

R.	I don't know. If I do, I will call tomorrow.

M.	You aren't going to call the police, are you?

R.	No. I just wanted to know really why you did it, you know? I guess it's just any question a girl would want to ask.

M.	Well, I want to talk to you if you want to talk to me again. Because I don't…I feel bad about it and I mean I was in a black out apparently. If I remember all his wild-ass story…you know…I guess that is how my own mind justified it at the time and maybe because I honestly do not remember. If you find any friends one of these days you ask them about valiums, what they do to you. They make you totally forget. You can go somewhere, meet somebody, do something that you would never forget and the next morning you won't remember a thing.

R.	Do you remember ever seeing that piece of paper that I had? I mean it was for a job interview.

M.	I remember you said that. I don't…no I didn't…I honestly don't.

R.	I wasn't in the car?

M.	I don't think so. That car is totaled now.

R.	The car is totaled?

M.	Yeah.

R.	Wow.

M.	I totaled it Saturday, broke a rib and it's a bunch of shit. Got a DUI. I am in a lot of trouble. But I don't…I mean there is no reason I would take that, you know? I don't remember seeing it or anything. An application?

R.	Huh?

M.	A Pizza Hut application?

R.	No. It wasn't an application. It was just like a resume type thing.

M.	Oh.

R.	So where did you wreck it?

M.	Out on…out by Francis. Northeast of town. I was driving in the morning, drunk, and got run off the road and ran into a steel fence…steel pole fence…and it totaled it.

R.	Oh.

M.	Busted my…well, I think I just bruised my ribs. I thought they were cracked, but I think they are just bruised. And scratched my face up. I don't know if you saw the scratch on my forehead.

R.	Yeah. Yeah, I saw it.

M.	I guess I am getting paid back for what I did, you know. I mean…it seems to happen to me. But I wish I could do something to get it out of your head or physical pain and everything else. But I want to talk to you. I do feel for you. I am not…I am not lying to you. All this stuff is honest truth. I mean why would I make up some stupid story like that…you know…if I intended to rape you that night, I wouldn't have told you my name, would I? I wouldn't have told you well I'm Matthew Thompson, you know? That doesn't sound right, does it?

R.	Well, when you looked down at me…I mean…right before you put it in like you did…all you said was I'm Matthew and that was it.

M.	I didn't tell you my last name?

R.	No. You didn't tell me your last name.

M.	How did…I told you where I worked or something?

R.	Do what?

M.	I told you where I worked?

R.	Yeah, you told me where you worked.

M.	Well, that is still too weird. Well, I have got to go, really.

R.	All right.

M.	Do you want to talk to me tomorrow?

R.	I don't know. I just want to sleep on it.

M.	Okay. Well, take you a nap or something.

R.	All right.

M.	Okay.

R.	Bye bye.

M.	Bye.

That was the last time I would talk to her. It is amazing what you can get people to say, especially the innocent. At this point, the whole deal was getting very serious and very confusing. After her call, I again thought about the possibility of this happening and could only convince myself ninety-nine percent that what I remembered was the truth. The weekend had already reduced my self-esteem to nothing and now I was not sure of my sanity. The next day the police came to speak with me.

It was Thursday, March 28th. I was doing just fine in my Intermediate Accounting II class, and always in attendance. I can still see Mr. Cowan, as he looked at the door window, paused his lecture and went to see who was motioning to him from outside the room. He opened the door, stuck his head out, and then looked back in at me.

"Matthew, someone needs to speak with you."

Butterflies. I gathered my stuff and walked out of the classroom. I was not really happy to see that an investigator for Pontotoc County, David Leewright, was the person wishing to talk with me.

"Matthew, we've got a situation here that we need to resolve. This woman came to us last night to report a misunderstanding between you and her. You are not under arrest. We would just like to know if you would like to give a statement as to what happened that night."

"Sure." I felt relief actually. With the confusion of the last couple of days, I was not under arrest but would get to give my version of the facts. The cops will help me straighten this out.

We walked together to his car, drove to the station and went downstairs to the basement. I was eager to tell them my story so they could investigate my side of the story.

Leewright and I sat in a small room and began to talk. I told him the truth of what happened. I found out later that they videotaped this conversation through a one-way mirror without my knowledge. It really didn't matter because I was only telling the truth of what happened, but I am sure they thought I was an arrogant smut telling them the details (the truth) of our sexual encounter.

At the end of the interview, I told Leewright that he needed to talk with the people who worked at Hardee's and the 24-hour Texaco that night. I foolishly believed that the police would help me clear this up and help find the truth. Sometime later in the day I called him at the station to tell him about me talking with my friend Leah.

That night I was scared. I didn't know why I was scared exactly, but I was. I tried to piece together events in my life to find some understanding. I have had some strange occurrences happen to me, and these were showing themselves in my thought processes as I continued to try and convince myself of my sanity, and my memory of that night.

I did find the focus to study for a business law test that was at noon tomorrow in the Administration building. And I eventually found sleep.

Chapter 4   Falsely arrested

I woke up early on Good Friday morning to study some more. It was March 29th, 1991. Easter came early that year. I still felt uneasy since waking up, but wanted to do well on the test.

When it was time to go to the college, I rode my bicycle up the hill to ECU, tackling the hills from my apartment on the south side to the top of the 14th Street hill that showcased ECU.

I left my bicycle just outside of the administration building, out of breath but focused on the test. I walked up the steps to the second floor with my mind on business law. I hurried up the hall to find a seat against the wall, hoping to have time to go over my notes one more time and to set my brain for the test.

There were a lot of the students from my class waiting outside, waiting for the class before us to finish taking the same test. I walked to a clear spot on the wall, turned around, leaned into it and slid down to a seat. I still had a few minutes to freshen my mind with my notes.

A quick double zip, I got out my notes and began to concentrate, staying in the mindset to do well on the test. The law of contracts, agreements between people. This stuff is really tricky, so many details to remember. My eyes and mind were on the notes, but suddenly my spirit felt a disturbance. Butterflies flew into my stomach and time slowed down as I spotted who was coming down the hall.

Detectives David Leewright and Tom Cosper had just turned the corner at the west end of the second-floor hallway and were looking right at me as they continued down the hallway. Leewright, the lead Pontotoc County detective in the case, was just not very friendly. He was heavy set, yet stumpy, kind of like Curley the stooge with a mustache. He was close to the end of his tenure with Pontotoc County. Mr. Cosper was younger, dark headed and slim.

As our eyes had met, I'd quickly realized that these detectives were not just strolling around the ECU campus, nor were they here to talk with any of these nice college students. They were here to talk to me. My instinct took over. I stood up and put my notes away in one motion, slung the bag over my shoulder and began walking toward them. My instinct…save embarrassment from the crowd of classmates.

As I approached them, looking right at them and their smug faces, my whole body was just sick. They weren't walking very fast, enjoying their position. I was almost to them, within about twenty-five feet of where the hall ends and splits to the left and right, when Detective Leewright, with one hand reaching to his gun holder, and cuffs out, spoke loudly:

"Matthew Thompson, you are under arrest for First Degree Rape and Sodomy-crime against nature."

What a terrible feeling it was, that came over me. I never hesitated. I kept walking and walked right by him.

"I'm walking around this corner before you cuff me."

They both looked at me with a look of confusion. I just kept walking and turned left around the corner, before I stopped. With noticeable anxiety, Detective Leewright hurried over, ready to take me into custody.

Of all the reactions I could have had to seeing those policemen, my primary instinct saw to it that I made it around the corner, just to save embarrassment in front of my classmates. That just took over, and I walked around the corner.

As he was locking the first handcuff, I took a deep breath and felt the seriousness of the charges. The clock in front of me grabbed my attention with its face and clicked, 12:00 o'clock noon.

I had to ask myself: Is this a dream? No. Why is this happening then? I didn't rape the girl. At least I don't remember it that way. Not at all. There must be a simple explanation for all of this. I'm sure that God will sort everything out and get me out of this. This is just a temporary misunderstanding.

We continued to the south stairs, went down and back north in the first-floor hall, to the central door. Before we went outside, he told an administrator, Mr. Snow, the reason for taking this student out of class. Can still see his face.

I saw my college roommate's mother leaving her work right there, going to lunch. Embarrassment found its way into my cheeks as I tried to hide behind my eyebrows.

The walk to the detective's waiting car was agonizing. I just wanted to get to the station so that we could straighten this out. Maybe I could be home this evening without having to tell any of my family. And besides, I've got to arrange to retake my test.

The drive to the station was uncomfortable and confusing. I was naively asking if I could speak with the girl and help her with her confusion. Or was it my confusion? I asked the detectives if they had investigated my story, as I voluntarily told to them yesterday. They said they had, but had found nothing to support it. I just didn't know what to say about that.

They lead me through the back door into the booking area and removed the handcuffs. Detective Leewright told the booking officer my bail amount and charges. He was trying to embarrass me again.

"Twenty-five thousand dollars for First Degree Rape and Sodomy-Crime against nature."

Twenty-five thousand dollars! Oh God. This can't be real. They can't be serious. What do they want from me? This was not a good day.

The officer began to collect my belongings and personal information. She was an attractive young woman.

"How tall are you?"

"Six feet."

"Weight"

"One eighty-five."

"Eyes?" She looked at me and answered her own question. "Green."

"Hair? Sandy blonde." Again, answering herself.

"Any scars, tattoos or distinguishing marks?"

"No."

She finished up the descriptive information and then looked at me with a look that drew nausea to my stomach. I didn't understand that look. She continued to fill out the form, looking at her watch to record the time and writing down information about my personal belongings that were being confiscated. I was allowed to keep my jeans and Marlboros and was given two books of matches. My shoes were handed back to me without laces.

Underwear, socks, a t-shirt, a towel, and a set of sheets were my outfitting by the jailer. I just couldn't believe the bail amount. That drove reality that much deeper into my confused soul. I was scared.

I actually asked to speak with the alleged victim, to try and straighten things out, but my requests were denied, with a laugh, I'm sure. I didn't feel that I needed an attorney for anything, so I didn't elect to call at that time. This surely must be some trick by the police. I mean, I am on felony probation for the OKC deal. I'll just wait to talk with them to see what they want me to do. There may be a way to get out of this.

With the sound of the "rattle" of the keys swinging in his hand, the jailer got my attention, and said, "This way Matthew."

He led me up the hall to a cell in the Ada city jail. I recognized, and sort of knew the jailer. Will was an older man, kind, calm, and fair with the prisoners. He was just looking toward retirement. We passed the small, dark kitchen on the left and the women's cells on the right, turned the corner and I was deposited into the first cell on the right. Just me in this cell. That's good. I entered, turned and watched him close the door and lock it with the key.

I inspected my two-man cell. I could almost reach from wall to wall, about seven feet wide. When I lay on the bunk and put my toes on the front bars, I was a little short from being able to touch the back wall. About nine feet, I guessed. There were two metal bunks attached to the wall, a sink and a toilet. Man, I hated being in jail.

I sat up on the bottom bunk to take stock of myself. I had cigarettes. I was alive and I wasn't accused of murder or anything. I still have a chance to get out today. Things were good except for the small detail of me possibly losing my mind. And these charges.

I knew that I would need something to read, so I began to look around the cell for magazines or books. I found some books under the mattress, some Louis L'Amour, and I found some magazines hidden within reach of the cell. These reading instruments I will ration like food so that I can have something to occupy my mind.

It was just after noon. What a bad day this was. I lit another cigarette, my only companion. I had to think.

I was really confused. I didn't understand why this was happening. I really believed that the police were setting me up with these charges for some reason. They must really want me to go to prison. And yet, with equal vigor, another part of me searched for the reality of today. I was desperately trying to remember.

I tried to piece together my thoughts. As a child, I'd had various head injuries that required stitches. I thought of my motorcycle wreck déjà vu in Stillwater a few years back. I'd had several seizures in my life caused by withdrawal from valium, usually coming a few days after taking the last of the pills. I remembered our ghost at the attic apartment, and the weird car wreck last Saturday. Is it possible that my brain and spirit have malfunctioned or something?

It felt like two separate people providing argument to support their respective positions. But I remembered what happened that night! It is reality. It is the truth! I've got to have confidence in myself! Surely the police are just playing games with me.

Doubt had been creeping into my mind since her first phone call, and I was now fueling it with past experiences in my life that had opened my mind to the ways of the world.

I'd lived in Stillwater, OK for a couple of years (1985-1987) while attending college there. One night when I was nineteen, after discussing motorcycles during the day with a close friend, I had a dream of me having a motorcycle wreck.

In the morning I remembered the dream just enough to remember that I had a dream about motorcycles. You know how dreams are. Two days later my dream came true in a déjà vu episode that lasted several minutes.

One of my friend Russell's friends, had a motorcycle, a Honda 650 street bike. He came over to Russell's house and I asked to ride his motorcycle and he let me.

It was a perfect day for riding around, seventy-five and sunny. After checking out the Boomer Lake crowd, I wound up in a residential neighborhood, testing my driving skills in and out of the ninety-degree corners. To my right I saw a girl washing her car in the driveway. She looked and smiled at me, so now I had to show off.

I went into the corner as fast as I could, then gave it the gas as I came out of it. At first glance upon straightening out from the corner, I could see the road continuing ahead. Fifty, sixty, seventy miles per hour. Man, I was cool.

I was almost out of street when I realized that the road came to a T and did not continue forward. There was a four-foot-wide drainage culvert that fed into a small pond about ten yards from the curb. The culvert had created an optical illusion to me upon my first glance. Instantly I knew that I couldn't stop in time to make the curve. Real cool.

I hit both brakes and tried my best to slow down, so that I could minimize damage to the bike. I had slowed to perhaps 20 mph as I approached the curb and the pond ten yards from the curb. I was ready to pull up on the handlebars as hard as I could to try to raise the front forks above the curb. Time had slowed considerably for me anyway, but as I approached the curb, it slowed even more. Right before I hit the curb, as I was pulling with all of my might on the handlebars, the dream of a couple of days earlier shot through my head in a microsecond. I was in déjà vu.

I pulled up as hard as I could and hit the curb. There were only a few yards left before the pond, but I knew from the dream that I wouldn't go in it. At that moment, my instinctual reflex laid the bike down on its side and I jumped off.

The right mirror had broken off and my sunglasses had flown off during the crash. I was fine physically. I looked to the right of the motorcycle and there was the mirror facing up and my sunglasses were resting on top of it, folded and looking like someone had placed them there. This image brought the "knowing" feeling as I viewed it, exactly as in the dream.

At the same time, I was crashing, the person who lived in the corner house at the T was arriving home. After I spotted the sunglasses, and put them on, I turned to see this car slowing and the passenger window coming down. I knew what to expect.

The driver asked if I was hurt and needed help. I motioned with my right hand and said that I was fine. As I looked at my hand and it waving, it was the déjà vu feeling, as in my dream.

I was really freaking out now. I looked down at the ground and remembered from the dream. I knew that a woman and her children would come out to ask me if I was hurt and if I needed to use the phone. Instant butterflies came to my stomach when I looked up and saw a woman and two boys walking around the perimeter of the pond, coming my way.

They reached me and asked if I was hurt. As she said this, her voice and the words brought the feeling again; exactly as in the dream. I began telling the woman the truth of what was happening to me. She actually understood and believed me, I think. She could see that I was not faking.

Her youngest son was exploring the motorcycle when his mother called to him.

"Matthew, get away from there." Her voice again brought the feeling with the words as she called HIS name.

I told her my name. Again, she acted like she really believed me as I told her about the dream, the sunglasses, mirror, the neighbor coming home and now her.

After a few more seconds of talking and disbelief by both of us, I knew it was time to go.

She said, "Do you need to use the phone?" Hearing her voice, once again, the knowing feeling, the dream.

"I knew that you were going to ask that," I said.

"I remember driving the bike away. Let me see if it will start."

I picked up the bike and inspected it for damage. The right handlebar was bent into the gas tank and caused a dent there. Other than that, the bike was fine. It was flooded, but I gassed it as I hit the electric start. It started and I looked at the woman with a smile.

She didn't know what to say, nor did I. I waved goodbye to her and the kids and drove over the curb onto the street. This was the last recognition from my dream, the knowing feeling as I drove over the curb onto the street. The ride home I didn't remember, from the dream, I mean.

I was not on any drugs that day, nor drunk. This event really screwed me up for a couple of months, gave me an excuse to drink more, I guess. I dropped out of school and got into more bad habits. Life is not just a linear, perfect world.

Krissy and I had some unexplained occurrences happen to us when we lived in the house at 907 E. 12th (the same house address (the main house) where Rita and I went that night) in 1990. We think a ghost lived there.

Our apartment was the attic of this large three-story house built in the early 1900's. The apartment Danny lived in, was just behind this house, a smaller "efficiency" dwelling.

From day one, I began to notice a "presence" with me as I was in the apartment. People have an energy they put off. Sometimes you can feel that. Say someone is sitting next to you, and you can feel his or her energy. Well, I was feeling this energy without a person being present. The feeling was not one of fear so I figured the ghost was friendly. I would try to sort of communicate with it. Its just one of those things.

Krissy had an occurrence where she saw an image in her vanity mirror. Once as Krissy and I were sitting on the couch watching TV, a light flashed in the bedroom that we have never been able to explain.

Anyway, I believe that the three-story house has a ghost or spirit living in it, although I have never felt fear for it. As a matter of fact, after I moved out, I talked with the girls who lived downstairs and asked if they knew the ghost. They were not surprised and related to me some strange occurrences of their own. I'll always wonder about this ghost and its possible presence with Rita and I that night.

Not so much now, do I believe in ghosts.

Back to reality in the jail cell. Soon my new friend Benny brought me some lunch and gave me the low down on the city jail's routine. I knew Benny's family. Benny was kind of the bad apple of the family, a little slow and underdeveloped in the mind. He assured me of three meals a day and three showers a week.

I sure hoped I could be out before dinner. I was just sick as I thought of my girlfriend and ten-month old son. Krissy was a loving, pretty girl, and deserved nothing like the horror of this. Josh was our new blue-eyed little boy. His father and her boyfriend had been arrested for rape and sodomy, but I knew that I didn't do anything wrong. I think.

Soon after I finished eating my bologna sandwich, again came the rattle of the jailer's keys as he walked down the hall. My thoughts were sure that he would be coming to let me go this minute, to tell me that the girl had confessed or something and everybody was sorry. My encounters with the police were situations that I wish had never happened. I never did anything to spite them or mock them. I just tried to live my life as best I could.

Will motioned for me to come to the front of the cell and whispered that the detectives wanted to talk with me down in the basement. I nodded. He unlocked the cell and escorted me to the basement.

I was taken to the same room as yesterday. Tom Cosper was the only person in the room. Yesterday, it was Detective Leewright who interviewed me. I went in, sat down and lit a cigarette. Except for an ashtray, an audiocassette recorder was all that was on the table in front of us. I didn't know what they would want of me, but here I was. I looked into Tom Cosper's eyes, eyes the color of the green crayon. Trustworthy eyes.

"Now Matthew, that wasn't exactly the truth that you told us yesterday, was it?"

"Yes, it was. Look, do you think that perhaps I could talk with the girl on the phone here at the station. I'm sure that we could straighten this out. Tom, I remember meeting the girl at Hardee's and she had a Boston accent and…"

"Matthew, do you think perhaps the drugs and alcohol have played a part in this incident?"

"Yeah, but I just wouldn't do something like this normally."

"Normally when you are off of drugs."

"Yeah. I am a good-natured person."

We paused a few seconds and my thoughts were racing to all parts of my life. I had come full circle now, sitting in this room for the second time. I looked at myself from the outside and summed it up as my fate. Two weekends earlier I had cheated with this girl at the house where the ghost was. Last weekend I totaled my girlfriend's car as I drove out to try to see another girl. But the other part of me didn't believe this, and knew the truth.

I had come to a point where I was not sure of the truth or of my own memory of what I remembered as the truth. The girl would not lie about something as serious as this, and the police and prosecutors believed her. Have I really lost my mind? They were serious about this, intensely serious. I was scared. That deep pit in my stomach made me think back to being a kid and being sure you're going to die or something. My fear mixed with the ultimate intellectual confusion, the doubting of my own sanity.

"Matthew, we want to try to figure this out and get you some help. You've got a chance here to straighten this thing out. We know that yesterday's statement wasn't the truth, and we are offering you the chance to provide a statement to please the district attorney about how this misunderstanding really happened. Then I'm sure we can get you some help and work something out."

I was looking into his eyes and the weight of this whole thing was bearing down on me. I felt comfort in him and his offer of help. He must be interested in the truth as well as I am. In time, the truth will prevail, right? I think I can trust him to continue to search for the truth.

"I can't say anything that I can't remember."

"Just describe how this situation might have happened. Okay? Perhaps the drugs made you misinterpret her signals to you. I'm going to start the audiocassette recorder now. The first thing I am going to ask you is to admit that yesterday's statement was not the truth. Then you just describe how this might have happened in a way different than what you have told us."

So that is what I prepared to do. I put on a fake voice and in confusion even doubled the number of drugs that I had bought and taken, placing the blame of my actions more squarely on the valium. He started the cassette recorder and we began to talk.

I was lost and confused. Never did the thought enter my mind that this was a statement that would be labeled a confession and used in my trial. I thought we were working things out, however that might be.

Never was the word "confession" used, nor did I sign anything labeled a confession, or write anything. I actually believed this would help me, cooperating with them.

In addition, at this point, realize that I knew nothing of her description of the person, her version of the events, the yellow car or the true nature of the charges against me. Only later in the day would that information cease my confusion.

Chapter 5   Make us a Confession

I.   Matthew, I need to talk to you but first I want to…you have already been read your rights…but I want to read them to you again, Okay?

M.   Okay.

I.   You do have the right to remain silent, anything you say can and will be used against you in a court of law. You have the right to talk to a lawyer and have him present with you while you are being questioned. If you cannot afford to hire a lawyer, one will be appointed to represent you for any questioning, if you wish one. If you do decide to make a statement, you may stop at any time. Okay. Do you understand each of these rights?

M.   Yes sir.

I.   Okay. I need for you to sign this right there. Okay. Also, the time of this interview is at 1:39 p.m. Matthew you were involved in an incident and we have been talking about it. You did give me a statement earlier, but which really is not going to be a true statement is it completely?

M.   No.

I.   What we need to do here Matthew…is like I told you…we need to get this thing straightened out. I feel that there are things that led up to this incident. You have been charged with rape and sodomy. I believe there are things that led up to this incident that you didn't elaborate on before. I think that there's things that happened, and what I need you to do, is I need you to tell the true story, and I don't want to put anything in your mouth that didn't happen, but we need to know the true story so that we can get this thing straightened up. If you have got a problem, we need to get you some help. And the only way we're going to be able to get you some help is to get this thing worked out. Tell me what you can remember about that night. Do you…did you know Rita's last name?

M.   No.

I.   The girl that you took to that apartment.

M.	I didn't even remember her first name.

I.	Tell me what had happened prior to this night. I think this took place…it was on a Saturday night.

M.	Saturday night.

I.	Do you remember what the date was on?

M.	No, it was almost two weeks ago.

I.	Okay.

M.	From today.

I.	Okay. It was on a Saturday night.

M.	Right.

I.	Can you kind of give me some background what had happened a little before this?

M.	No(?). Beginning the Saturday before I'd bought 50 yellow valiums and ate…Saturday I probably ate 10 or 15 and that was the beginning of my spring break where I didn't have to go to school. I had money from my job, so I had beer continually.

I.	Okay. You drank some beer along with the valiums.

M.	Yeah.

I.	Okay.

M.	And smoked marijuana and then every night that week up to Thursday night when I ran out of them. I would eat seven, six or seven a night and drink beer every night.

I.	So, you're talking about a week before this you had got some valiums and you had been more or less taking them for about a week.

M.	For the whole week and drinking beer every night and smoking pot.

I.	Up until that night you were taking them also… the night this happened.

M.	No sir. I ran out on Thursday night.

I.	Okay.

M.	There were so many in my system though…

I.	You were still under the effects though?

M.	Yeah, very much so.

I.	Okay. Were you also drinking alcohol?

M.	No. On that night I was drinking alcohol, so that brought back the effects of the valiums.

I.	Okay. What were you driving that night? Can you remember?

M.	I was driving a '85 Firebird, red Firebird.

I.	Okay. All right. This blonde, which her name is Rita, you know that now?

M.	Yeah.

I.	What…when did you first see her? Or when did you first think that you saw her earlier?

M.	I thought that I saw her in Hardee's, but now I believe that was somebody else.

I.	Okay. Somebody else that looked a lot like her.

M.	Yeah.

I.	Okay. Do you think that the drugs at that time had an effect on you to where you were?

M.	I was under the influence of them.

I.	Okay. What happened then?

M.	Well, I can remember being at the apartment…

I.	Okay. Do you remember picking Rita up?

M.	No sir, I don't.

I.	Okay. You remember no part of picking her up, where you picked her up or anything?

M.	No sir.

I.	Okay. Did you pick her up…Do you remember…was it after you left Hardee's? Were you at Hardee's?

M.	Yes.

I.	Okay. What did you do at Hardee's?

M.	I ate a ham & cheese sandwich.

I.	Okay. And you left Hardee's and then picked her up?

M.	Well, I think I must have gone and got some beer then.

I.	Okay. Where do you think you went to get beer?

M.	I went to Texaco.

I.	Okay. Would that be the old Fast Break?

M.	Yeah. The old Fast Break on 10th street.

I.	Okay. What happened then?

M.	Well, apparently, I picked her up…

I.	Okay. After you went and got beer at Fast Break.

M.	Right.

I.	Okay.

M.	And then I remember being at the apartment…

I.	Okay. What apartment are we talking about?

M.	It's 907 E. 12th, Apartment #7.

I.	Is that kinda in the back of…off of 12th?

M.	Yeah. It is in the back in the alley.

I.	Who…now there wasn't anybody actually living in that apartment at the time or had his stuff there didn't he?

M.	It was Danny, and he was in jail at the time. He's a friend of mine.

I.	Danny is a friend of yours?

M.	Yes.

I.	Okay. Did you know he was gone from the apartment at that time?

M.	No. At the time I didn't know that.

I.	Okay. You took Rita to this apartment then, right?

M.	Right.

I.	Tell me what you can remember from there.

M.	Well, I think that she was probably scared to death and I didn't realize that. I was…

I.	You think maybe the drugs had kept you from realizing that?

M.	Yeah. I guess I was thinking that she liked me or something, you know?

I.	Did you know…had you ever seen Rita before this night?

M.	No.

I.	You never seen her any place as far as you know?

M.	No.

I.	Okay. Go on…what you can remember.

M.	And…I can remember that we talked and I believe that we were talking like she liked me and I like her, but I now see that she was talking to me because she was scared to death, and…

I.   Can you remember anything that was said?

M.   Oh, just talking about her accent, being from Boston and that's really about all I can remember is that she had an accent, a Boston accent.

I.   Okay. What happened then?

M.   Well, we drank a couple of beers and then…

I.   She drank some beer with you?

M.   Yeah…and then we started kissing and stuff and to me it was…seemed like that was mutual but I don't believe it was. I think she did this so I wouldn't…I think she was scared to death.

I.   Do you think that maybe you had threatened her or something? Do you think maybe that drugs had…

M.   Well, they might have. I wouldn't do that. I mean I…

I.   Normally, you wouldn't do something like that?

M.   Normally, I wouldn't do it. I guess she would probably know if I threatened her or not… because I really don't…

I.   You don't remember is what you're saying?

M.   I don't remember.

I.   Okay.

M.   And then I remember I had her shirt off…

I.   Did you take her shirt off?

M.   I believe so.

I.   Okay.

M.   And I was like kissing on her breasts…

I.   Okay.

M.   And the whole time thinking that she was…liked me and was consenting to this. And then I remember I asked her to take her pants off and to me…

I.   Did she do that or did you take her pants off?

M.   I really can't remember.

I.   Okay.

M.   I think that I said that as…maybe I was trying to be sexy or something…I don't know…trying to tell her to take her pants off and by this time I had my shirt off and then once we had our clothes off, we started to have sex and I think now that she did that to not make me mad or something…you know…apparently, I put off an impression to her that I was not…you know…that I was intoxicated…

I.	Do you think she was afraid of you?

M.	Possibly. Afraid of me…

I.	Because of the drugs that changed your personality. Is that what you are saying?

M.	Right.

I.	Okay.

M.	And…

I.	Did she hit you or anything? Can you remember this?

M.	No…I…she was totally passive. Maybe that would have appeared to me…you know…that maybe she thought if she hit me, I would hit her back.

I.	Okay. Did you hit her?

M.	Not that I can remember. I don't think I had a reason to.

I.	Okay.

M.	And I just remember having sex with her and of course I thought she was enjoying it and that was the state of mind I was in that was not the truth.

I.	At that time…what you are saying is that you didn't actually feel…

M.	I didn't actually feel like I was…

I.	Was raping her at that time.

M.	No. I thought that…

I.	You thought she wanted you?

M.	Right.

I.	Okay.

M.	I was…

I.	What did she do to lead you to believe that though? Do you think it was your state of mind or do you think it was something that she did?

M.	I think it was my state of mind and I think she was just scared and didn't know what to do and so she didn't…

I.	So, what you are saying is that you don't remember her fighting back real hard?

M.   No. And now I think she did that out of fear.

I.   Okay.

M.   And I took that to be a passive sign.

I.   Took that to be that she probably wanted you. Is that what you're saying?

M.   Right. She wasn't saying anything back to me. And then I remember having sex with her and I honestly don't remember actually having intercourse with her in the butt, but I do remember when I was behind her putting my finger in there, thinking of course that she liked this.

I.   Okay. You don't remember putting your penis in her rectum?

M.   No sir, I don't.

I.   Okay.

M.   And then…

I.   How long…do you remember about what time? Can you remember the time that this was taking place probably?

M.   It was probably 3:00 or 2:45.

I.   3:00 in the morning.

M.   Yes sir.

I.   Okay. But you don't remember where you picked her up at actually?

M.   No, I don't.

I.   But you do…Do you remember arriving at the apartment?

M.   Yes.

I.   And being at the apartment?

M.   I remember arriving at the apartment and I had two six-packs of beer and I put one in the refrigerator and I dragged the carpet into a small room so we could have a place to sit on.

I.   Do you remember if you had a weapon of any kind, a knife or anything that night?

M.   I don't…

I.   I'm not…

M.   She said that, "Do I remember having a knife?" The only knife I have is a filleting knife and it's at home in my drawer.

I.	You think maybe it was a pocketknife or something there…maybe you would have said something to her with the knife. I am not saying you took and put it to her or anything, but did you maybe…did you mention a knife?

M.	I honestly do not remember anything about a knife.

I.	Okay. You say…where did ya'll do this?

M.	It was in the small room on the east side of the apartment and there were no curtains or anything.

I.	Was it in the front…that little front room?

M.	It was in the front part. Yeah.

I.	Okay. Okay. After this what happened?

M.	Well, of course I was thinking the whole time that she liked me and she told me her address. That's what I can remember.

I.	What did she tell you her address was?

M.	805 E. 12th Street.

I.	Okay.

M.	And then about all I can remember is taking her home and I didn't take her home to her house, I took her on across the street down by the…there's…two blocks on the west side of Mississippi on 12th Street.

I.	Okay.

M.	I think there is a rental place there and a TV repair place.

I.	You're talking about Ben's TV?

M.	Yeah.

I.	Okay.

M.	And I let her off right there and…

I.	Was it daylight at that time?

M.	No. It was around 4:30 or something…

I.	4:00 or 4:30 or so? How long do you figure you were at that apartment all together?

M.	Oh…probably an hour and fifteen minutes.

I.	Okay. What else…Can you remember anything else that night that comes into your mind that…

M.	Well, I went to the bar and drank…

I.	After that you went to the bar?

M.	No. I had been at the bar.

I.	You had been at the bar earlier. Okay. I was fixin' to say…it would be closed. This would actually be on Sunday morning, wouldn't it?

M.	Right.

I.	Okay. Where did you go after you let her out?

M.	I don't even remember. I figure I probably went home.

I.	Okay. Where were you living at that time?

M.	1100 S. Mississippi, Sanders Apartments.

I.	Okay. Are you living there at this time?

M.	No. Right now I moved back in with my parents.

I.	Okay. Whose car was that you were in that night?

M.	My girlfriend's.

I.	What's her name?

M.	Krissy.

I.	Krissy what?

M.	xxxxxxx

I.	xxxxxxx. Are ya'll still boyfriend and girlfriend?

M.	Well, we…at this time we were…

I.	Okay. But now you've kinda had problems?

M.	Problems. Yeah.

I.	So, you're living back with your parents now. Is that what you are saying?

M.	Right.

I.	At this time. Is there anything else you want to put on this statement?

M.	Well, that…my…every bit of trouble that I have been in has been drug and alcohol related, and it seems like everybody has seen that except me. I've seen it but I've…but I've really…because it was me…maybe if I had been on the outside looking at myself, you know, maybe I would have seen it, but…

I.	So, you think that…I mean you don't remember everything that night and you really …you really feel that normally you're not the normal type of guy that would rape a person?

M.	No.

I.   Do you feel like the drugs and stuff had the effect to make you do that that night?

M.   Very much so. They…

I.   They affected your memory and…

M.   The valiums effect my memory to where I can't remember sometimes…being blacked out…can't remember what happened the whole night, you know, people tell me stuff, and I'll say, "No, I wouldn't do that. That's not me."

I.   You mean this has happened before when you have done something?

M.   I have done something crazy and they say, "You did this." That is not in my character.

I.   Right. And you think that it is the drugs that caused it because you didn't remember it the next day?

M.   Yeah.

I.   You can't remember doing some things that you do?

M.   It's happened many times. I was eighteen when I first started doing valiums.

I.   Okay. I think we will go ahead and end this statement at this time. The time is 1:56 pm, same date.

*

I was returned to my cell after the meeting. I continued to hope for release, or talking to the girl on the phone or something. Maybe I'll go to a treatment center or detox. I was very confused. What a mess.

Again, I was weighing the State's side in my mind, continuing to chase the ghost rapist theory. From my memory, I'd play the consensual encounter over and over in my mind, trying to remember how I could have possibly gotten things so mixed up. I still couldn't remember having a knife or accosting her. My heart wanted to believe in my innocence, but my mind was evaluating other possibilities. I began to wish I hadn't given that statement to Cosper "to please the DA". I needed to call my attorney now. Maybe with his help I can get out of here today. There was no question who I would call.

I needed an attorney and a friend. That was Tommy. I always went to him with traffic tickets and legal advice. He was a friend of my grandfather Harvey Lambert, who was an attorney in Ada for almost 60 years. I called him from the phone that the jailer let me use. He said that he would be there in a few minutes.

I was only back in my cell for a few minutes when the jailer's keys again announced his entrance into the jail.

"Matthew, your attorney is here. I'm going to let you talk with him in one of the women's cells. There is no one there and that way you can have some privacy."

"Okay. Thanks."

He unlocked my cell and I saw Tommy as I turned the corner. Tommy was a guy that everybody liked. Personable, honest and well connected in Ada, he and his easy manner would win a lot of friends, even if it didn't win him a lot of cases.

"Hey Matthew. How are you doing, bud?"

"I'm Okay, I guess."

We followed Will and he locked us in one of the cells.

"Tommy, I didn't rape this girl. I swear I didn't."

"Okay. Slow down. Tell me what happened."

I began to tell him the truth of what had happened and what I felt needed to be investigated: the employees and patrons in Hardee's at the time in question and the employee at the Texaco (Fast Break) where I bought beer and cigarettes. It was now almost two weeks after the alleged incident, but the sooner we investigated, the better our chances of finding something favorable.

I asked Tommy to obtain the cash register tapes at Hardee's and the Texaco on 10th and Mississippi. These would back up my story of what we were eating and drinking at Hardee's and that I bought beer and cigarettes at the Texaco. Even though it had been two weeks, this was basic investigative work and it shouldn't be hard to find a good lead on who was in Hardee's that morning. The large majority of the people in Hardee's at that time would have just left the bars. I am relatively well known in Ada among this crowd, so I'm sure that a person could be found that remembered seeing me at Hardee's sitting and talking with this blonde girl.

I was shocked by my own feelings of embarrassment as I completed my story. He looked at me like I was a kid who just told him a tall tale. "He will believe me when he investigates," I thought. If he can find just one person that saw the girl and I together in Hardee's, this will show him the validity of my story.

I told him about the statement I had just given to the detectives and he was very worried about this. He was to meet with the district attorney in just a few minutes to find out the details of their case against me. I felt like the patient trusting in the surgeon with the scalpel in his hand, preparing the first incision.

We talked for about an hour. Again, I was worried by the look in his eyes as we parted. Was I crazy and telling him a memory that was just a figment of my imagination? Maybe. No! Shit!

Hope began with new vigor. Now that Tommy is on the case, I should be released pretty soon after he investigates.

"Matthew, I'll come see you after I talk with them. Hang in there, bud."

"See you later."

Will placed me back in my cell and Tommy went to talk with the district attorney.

Tommy spent a couple of hours with the district attorney, learning of their case against me. During these two hours I was in deep, deep thought. I was struggling with my own soul. I was torn between my memory and the collective opinion of the police, district attorney, and the girl. This was it. Was I to spend time in prison or in a mental institution?

Valium had always been bad news for me. I had continued to use valium even after having a seizure caused by withdrawal from it. Heck, I didn't take an unusually high dosage or anything. Why me? The seizures may have caused some permanent biological damage, and they were caused by the valium in the first place. Taking into account that I had taken valium the week leading up to the night in question, I may have been in a withdrawal type state because I had taken the last pill two nights earlier. It was certainly possible that some type of seizure weirdness could have occurred, but heck, you can't talk or think or move, just convulse.

All of these things coupled with the depth of my imagination made anything possible. God, I'm sorry. I didn't mean to hurt anyone. Right? You know that! You know the truth! Don't you? I met her at Hardee's and we went back to Danny's apartment and had consensual sex. You remember that, don't you? Please help me.

My soul continued to search for this horrible person within. My brain charged through all of its files, searching for a knife, an abduction into a car, seeing her on this street. I just can't find it anywhere. It can't be true. But she believes it is and so does everyone else. This has got to be a dream.

Tommy came back to see me at about five o'clock. He had reviewed the woman's statement to the police, as well as the detective and police reports. He had not yet gone to interview anyone, but the day was not over. Will let us talk out in the hall, without locking us in a cell.

My understanding of the charges against me was that she had complained of being abducted by a man in a car and taken to an apartment where she was beaten and raped. I always assumed that her story to the police included a description of my red car, a description of a man matching my features and a description of the apartment. I thought that it was understood that she lived in a bi-sexual relationship with a woman.

I assumed that the basic details of a rape case must be there for me to be arrested. In fact, I never even thought of any other possibility. I didn't waste my energy thinking that the State would arrest me without a complete case of my guilt. The truth is what matters, right?

Tommy related to me a short summary of the details of her statement to the police. She lived with her boyfriend, not a "girlfriend". She described the perpetrator: saying he had acne-scarred, pockmarked face, a ponytail or shoulder length hair, tattoos on his wrists and wearing cowboy boots. He was driving an old model yellow car that she had seen him in earlier in the day.

That was not me. I had a smooth complexion, short hair, no tattoos or markings on my hands or wrists, and would only wear cowboy boots once a year to the rodeo. I was driving my girlfriend's red Pontiac Firebird and had never seen this girl before meeting her in Hardee's.

She also said that I broke into her apartment a couple of nights after that, wielding a large knife. She said that she was able to take the knife away from me and that I then left. She said her boyfriend did not wake up during this and so could not testify to it. This part of the story was never brought up again by her or the State.

I was so relieved. It was like I had been in a power outage for a few hours and now the electricity was back on. My computer-brain was powered back up and operating well.

What a crazy situation this was. What a crazy girl! I almost couldn't believe it, but now everything made sense. But I realized it was hard to believe. The insanity and tragedy of it all was just hilarious. She's completely lying!

My confusion ended. I was not insane at all. For whatever reason, this woman had made up a boldface lie about me raping her. It was that simple. She had also lied about living with a woman and instead lived with a man.

I felt great ecstasy knowing that my brain was not hurt and was healthy. I was refreshed with self being back in good graces. At the same time, I envisioned a jury trial if the charges were not dropped. What a mess I had gotten myself into by not coming out and simply denying everything. They all tricked me. What a vulnerable dupe I am, like a little kid.

Chapter 6   I'm dreaming, right?

When Tommy and I finished talking, I was placed back in my cell. He said he would investigate as I requested. I knew now that I wouldn't be going home at least until Monday when I had an arraignment and bail reduction hearing. What a long weekend this would be.

I hoped that I could get out soon to complete the semester. There were only six weeks left and I had four classes: Intermediate Accounting II, Income Tax Accounting, Computer Accounting Systems and Business Law. If I couldn't complete them, then perhaps I would be allowed to withdraw. I'll tell Tommy to call someone at ECU.

The next thing I did was write letters to my parents and Krissy. I explained my innocence and the circumstances of it all. Will said that I could leave the letters with him and a member of my family could pick them up this evening.

While I was relieved to be sane, my heart was just sick because of these false charges and my arrest. While I knew I was innocent, I was in jail mistaken for a horrible rapist and sodomist. Nice.

I was mad at the district attorney whom I felt was smart enough to see the deceit of the girl. I was not really mad at the girl because I didn't understand her or her motive, but was deeply intrigued and puzzled as to why she was doing this to me, a man who treated her kindly.

Why did she give this description of another person? Is there a person that matches that description? What does he have to do with this? Did he meet her after I let her out? Did he give her the scratches and bruises? Maybe the boyfriend was involved. She might have gone home and got caught and he might have beaten her.

I was just nauseous and disheartened thinking about how Krissy and my family must be reacting to my arrest. Their anguish may be worse than mine because I have some control over how I handle this and I have comfort knowing the truth. They can do nothing but pray that I am truthful, sane, and that I will handle this with success.

The humor in this crazy mess was overpowering in the first few moments after Tommy returned my sanity to me. The craziness of it was tragically funny, but another aspect was funny too. The police, detectives, and prosecutors had been tricked also. They were spending so much time, money, energy and emotion on a wisp of smoke, which is what the girl and her story were. It reminded me of a Candid Camera episode where the audience knows the truth and laughs at the person on the other end of the camera, looking so foolish from our perspective, as they spend great energy and emotion on a trick. Like a cat chasing its tail.

Slowly the humor evolved into concentrated, serious thinking about my future and the meaning of this in my life. Was it Karma for breaking other laws? I needed to gather myself and gain some acceptance of where I was. I sat on my bunk, lit up a cigarette and began to think about how I wound up in this nightmare.

I fell asleep for a couple of hours after dinner and dreamed I was at a big party at the administration building. All the teachers and students were hanging out, drinking beer and partying. I was happy just walking around and people-watching.

Dinner was stew, cornbread, Jell-O, and Tang. I had an extra piece of cornbread that Benny gave me wrapped up in some toilet paper under the corner of the top bunk, so I got it to eat with some water from the sink. It was about eight o'clock. I asked myself again, "Is this just a dream?" Nope. Real.

Will let me use the phone earlier and I called Dad. There was not much to say, just that I had written a letter to them telling what had happened. They were just wondering if I was all right and if I would be able to see them Monday.

The weekend was spent working out a sanity saving routine to pass the time. I wrote a lot to Krissy, the letters full of emotion. Innocent or not, she's mad at me. Right now, I wished I didn't even have a girlfriend. It would be easier on my heart.

Monday morning, I was formally charged with the two crimes. My dream of an April fool's joke passed with a sigh. I was able to look Krissy in the eye when relating my innocence. She then knew for sure of it. My parents I wasn't so sure of. They believed me, but many thoughts and fears were showing themselves as they tried to deal with this. However, they were with me to the end.

I did my best to explain to my family how I had wound up in this mess. The letters had explained it, but it was just so extraordinary. There were so many factors involved. The ironies that I saw were just tripping me out.

Will locked me back down and wished me luck. Surely, he believes me. I got a drink from the sink, sat on my bunk and lit a Marlboro.

The mystery now, thank Jesus, is her, not me. I may be the only one that knows that, but that is just how it is. I am completely innocent. I finished the cigarette in deep thought, and then drifted into sleep trying to make sense of this senselessness.

This nightmare was currently reality in the city jail. My days and nights were spent dreaming of release by innocence, release by bail and the usual other daydreams. The rattle of the jailer's keys always got me up and alert, bringing a rush of thoughts of good visions and happy words out of Will's mouth. I have faith it will happen soon.

There were some characters in the city jail here with me. One girl was accused of hiring two men to shotgun kill her husband on a hunting trip. All three of them are in here. I saw her yesterday when I used the phone.

I know the guy in the cell to the right of me. He went to the hospital the other day for swallowing some razor blades or something. He is a little desperate I guess, facing 80 years.

Benny is a little too kooky (he has some learning disabilities) to be completely understood and trusted, but he likes me and is loyal. He is the cook so he gives me enough food and drink. He tells me he is innocent of his charges too. I think, Wow! Do you have a good lawyer?

I had been here for one week and one day. Today was Saturday April 6. Two young teenagers were put in the cell across from me. They were talking loudly into the vent, trying to communicate with a girl in the women's cells around the corner. Their "fall partner" I guess.

One of them was a ringer for Nirvana's lead singer, and the other kid looked Hispanic or Native American. I watched and listened as they got settled in.

"You got a light?" said the light-headed kid, with a cigarette hanging from his mouth.

"Yeah." I had some paper matches to spare. Grabbed a pack, walked to the front of the cell, stuck my arm through and pitched the book to him.

"You know how to tear them in half so they'll last longer?" He looked at me for a second, then took a match out and sat down on the bunk to tear it in half. Fascinating. His name was Johnny.

"What happened to ya'll?

"We were parked at Wintersmith Park, by the swings, smoking a joint and out of nowhere a cop is behind us and getting out of his car. The joint was fat and just smoking up a storm. I saw the cop in my mirror and whispered 'Put it out! Put it out! A cop! A cop!'"

The dark-haired kid jumped in.

"I didn't know what else to do but eat it. I had about a half a second to do something, and I knew that putting it out in the ashtray would be smoky, so I just ate it! I rolled a bunch of spit around the tip and then chewed it as fast as I could and swallowed it! It really didn't matter though because we forgot about the bag sitting wide open between us. Right then he said 'Everybody freeze where you are!'. So, I just froze."

We all laughed at his recollection of their tense moment.

"You froze when he said freeze?"

"Yeah."

These two and another girl had been arrested for possession of marijuana. Maybe other charges. They would be arraigned on Monday. As we talked more, Johnny and I found that we had a mutual friend whose name happened to be Matthew. There were a few more words between us over the weekend but not much. They all were released on Monday on their own recognizance.

I was moved next door, in with the guy who had to go to the hospital for eating razor blades, or was it broken light bulb? It was good that I had someone to talk to, as the days were getting longer, me waiting for my release. We played cards a lot and talked about who we knew and stuff.

On Thursday I was moved to the county jail across the street. The couple of minutes walking outside and across the street were the most exciting minutes in quite a few days. I was given a bunk in an eight-man "bullpen". Four bunks and a toilet on each side, with a central area and table. There was a TV here also. The man who was accused of shotgun killing the woman's husband was in my bullpen. He was a pretty nice guy. We played quite a few games of gin

I knew another one of the guys, Deano, as he was known. He had six months to do in the county and had done quite a bit of it already. My mind could not comprehend six months in this jail. That would be torture. He had accumulated quite a bit of personal belongings over the months, with letters and supplies from his supportive family, and had the bottom bunk with jail seniority. I was on the upper bunk.

I got comfortable in my new space. It was good to have some new books to read. The rattle of the keys was a different pattern but still the bare foundation of hope for me, waiting any day for my release.

I recognized a friend of mine, "Church", in the other bullpen. We talked for a while after dinner. He was in on a second-degree rape charge. I faintly remembered hearing something about it. He summed his case up in a word of warning to me, 'Don't sleep with the mayor's underage granddaughter.' I'll remember that one.

It was Friday, April 12th. I'd been in for two weeks. After breakfast and a couple of chapters of *Alive*, I fell asleep with my dreams.

"Matthew Thompson…Matthew Thompson." I heard my name being called but I was asleep so I didn't have to answer.

"Matthew Thompson made bail. Matthew Thompson, you made bail." That woke me up.

I still was incredulous coming out of my sleep to find I'd made bail.

"Grab your mattress and your stuff and come on." The trustee was apathetic to my release but I was filled with joy. Thank Goodness.

My father had been looking for my original stock certificate in OG&E. He found it, sold it, and we used the money for my bail.

I watched Josh take his first steps that day of my release on bail, walking across the carpet with a look like, "You had better catch me when I reach you Daddy! I'm trusting you!"

My parents and I discussed some things about the case and then Krissy and I talked when she got home from work.

"Why didn't you just say, 'I didn't do it,' and then call a lawyer?" Krissy was frustrated with how I could be so stupid, in giving the "confession".

"I thought if I talked with them that I could get out of jail. I don't know why I didn't just keep my mouth shut. Even though I was confused about it all, I didn't have anything to hide and wanted to cooperate. I really thought I might be insane and wanted some help. Only after Tommy told me about her version of the facts did I realize that I was not crazy. You said you believed me, Krissy. I need for you to continue to believe me. Look at me. I'm telling you again, I didn't rape her and I am not lying about any of this. Do you still believe me?"

She looked me straight in the eye as I bared my soul to her. Krissy was mad at me for cheating on her, and this had caused her pain in itself, but she realized that this was much more than that. She knew I needed her support and she offered it.

"I believe you Matthew. I know you better than anyone. When I saw your face at the arraignment and you told me you didn't do it, I looked into your eyes and knew you were telling the truth. That will never change. But what happens now?"

"I've got to go to trial."

"What happens if they find you guilty? How much time will you face in prison?"

"I won't be found guilty."

"What if you are?"

"I could get a life sentence."

Monday, I went to speak with Tommy at his office. Walking in the law office complex, I felt comfortable with the familiar surroundings. My grandfather and his partners had built this building. Growing up, my sister had a part-time job for a couple of years cleaning the offices at night. I usually went with her to help. This place was part of me.

"Hi Matthew. Go on in." His secretary was a familiar face and friend. I couldn't help notice her diverting her eyes from mine though. That was a little unsettling.

He was kicked back in his chair smoking, a large ashtray full of butts in front of him on his desk. I sat down, facing him. The energy was different today. This was not a traffic ticket. A question was sent to my thoughts, "Does he believe me?" How could he not, he knows I tell the truth and he has heard the ridiculous story by the girl.

After some small talk, he could tell that I was not in the mood to chat and we got down to business. He told me that the State was offering a plea bargain of ten years. They would drop the sodomy charge if I pled guilty to the rape charge. Tommy was always a good attorney for me because he had good relationships with the prosecutors and DA. He would help me.

"Tommy, I can't plead guilty. Even if they offered me one day, I can't spend the rest of my life explaining to people how I was so innocent of this crime but plead guilty to it for this reason or that. I've got to go to trial."

"Do you know that you will face a life sentence at trial?"

"Yes."

"Matthew, if you were my son and I was advising you what to do, I would say take the plea bargain."

I paused for a few seconds to take that in. I guess he didn't hear me. My mindset was focused on preparing a case for trial and had been for two weeks. I changed the subject with my natural diversion to this subject.

"Tommy, did you talk with anybody at Hardee's or Texaco?"

"No, I'll make a note to do that today." He scratched a note on his desk calendar.

"Like I told you, I bought a ham & cheese sandwich and water. She had something to eat also. She is an employee of Hardee's, so it is probable that she took her discount on that purchase of food. If we could get the cash register tapes to verify this order and then within a few minutes, an order for a ham & cheese and water, we could show that my story is true. The same logic will apply for the Texaco. If we can show that a few minutes after the Hardee's tapes, someone bought two six-packs of Bud Light on sale, then we can use that too."

"Okay, we'll see what we can find."

I left with hope that he would soon find the evidence that would lead to the charges being dismissed. Maybe even today!

He really didn't understand my position and probably never would. I had only one life and it was being screwed up with a false rape charge. There was no other option than for me to go to trial. I knew this from that first day after Tommy told me the girl's story. My lawyer needs to help me save my life.

He mentioned that the preliminary hearing was at the end of next month and that we may waive it. I didn't really know what went on at a preliminary hearing. I had always been guilty of what I was arrested for and had accepted any plea bargain offered. I would take Tommy's professional advice. In the pit of my stomach, I couldn't help but get the feeling that he was expecting me to take the plea bargain as I had always done.

I went to Danny's apartment to see if I could find the death threat that I had found and had thrown on the ground. I could not find it.

I set up an appointment to talk with the manager at the 24-hour Texaco. My friend Teri knew him. He told me that the police had come in but interviewed the wrong person. They interviewed the night shift employee, but not the one that worked that night.

Teri also happened to know a man who worked at Hardee's. Krissy and I met him one day at Taco Tico. He said he thought the girl was always on drugs, that her behavior after the alleged rape was not consistent with what he would expect from a rape victim, and that she always dressed sleazy.

A couple of weeks later, I talked to the man who worked that night at the Texaco but he did not recognize me. It had been about four weeks since that night and I really couldn't expect him to remember me.

I talked to the girls who lived in the apartment (Apt #1 on the first floor) across from Danny's. These girls had lived there when I lived in Apt. #6. I asked one of them if perhaps they had seen my familiar red car there on that night, or if anyone had heard any noises coming from Danny's house.

The girl said they had heard about the rape and had thought about what they were doing that night. She said they had a small party that night celebrating St. Patrick's Day and had about five people over but didn't remember seeing my red car or hearing any noises or anything. I planned to bring this up at trial to show that there were cars and people just a few yards away that could have been summoned by Rita were her story true.

I spoke with Danny and found that the police had wanted him to wear a wire and try to talk with me. He refused, not believing that I would do something like this. It sure would have helped if he would have told me this that Monday at the AA meeting.

I continued to proclaim my innocence to my attorney. He advised me to waive my preliminary hearing, which was May 29th. I took his advice because I trusted him and he **was** the attorney, not me.

As I found out later, the preliminary hearing is a "mini-trial" where each side presents the gist of their case to let the Judge then determine if the case has merit to be bound over for trial. Waiving this hearing was a terrible mistake because Rita had disappeared shortly after my arrest and could not be found. It is possible the case would have been dismissed at the preliminary hearing. It would have been better if my business law class had been a criminal law class. Maybe I would have made better decisions.

Tommy never investigated my side of the story. He didn't investigate one bit. The only evidence I ever saw in his possession was a copy of the medical report, which I haven't seen since.

I didn't know what to make of his decisions. Sadly, I reasoned that he didn't believe me and didn't think investigation would reveal anything. Actually, he probably just expected me to just take the plea bargain. I had always admitted my guilt to him in all of my arrests.

Always. I always considered myself a bad liar; it was just against my nature. I respected Tommy and his opinion, but he was wrong and I needed to find another attorney.

Finally, after two months of my repeated requests, he mentioned that he was not a trial attorney but that he could refer a good one to me. I thought all attorneys were trial attorneys?

Tommy's work for me was done. He referred me to another attorney, George Butner. I went to see him and liked him. He replaced Tommy as my attorney in the middle of August. We expected to go to trial on the fall docket.

I wanted to take a lie detector test. My repeated declarations of my innocence brought George to contact someone he knew in OKC to administer the test.

My Dad and I drove up one morning to the man's office. Before the test, the man and I talked. He probably could have cared less what I had to say at this point, in that he was just laying down the procedure that we would go through, but I began to defend myself, to explain myself. I mean, here he was looking at me like I was a violent rapist, right? Or maybe he wasn't.

I had smoked pot the night before and I told him that I had. I also told him what a naturally calm person I am and that I never panic. I felt he needed to understand my excellent cardiovascular condition, with a resting pulse around fifty.

How defensive I must have seemed. Before I even took the test, I was telling him how "cool" I was and seemed to be making excuses. As my parents and family knew, my "defensiveness" in confrontations had been a recurring response since I was a young child. Unfortunately, this guy didn't understand me to that level. I should not have said anything.

I passed the test with a +4 rating (on a scale that goes from -16 to +16). The man said I did not really show any response worth recording to the questions. He told me that I could take another test at no charge to be sure of the results. I was a bit frustrated, as I had just tried to be honest and stay relaxed.

I came back a week later and took another test. I stayed off pot and even took a urine analysis before and after the second test to show I wasn't trying to beat it by taking drugs, as my past raised that possibility. He told me the results were much the same and therefore were somewhat inconclusive.

Perhaps he believed I took drugs trying to beat the test, or at least was wary of me after I told him I had gotten high the night before. That's what trying to be honest gets me. That was exactly my point in explaining my possible galvanic response. If I was telling the truth, there shouldn't **be** a physiological response. It is when you lie that you get nervous and illicit a response.

In my opinion, this test was very subjective and I obviously was very unlucky to score as I did because I told the truth. My weirdness about explaining my physiology was probably misinterpreted or had a bad effect.

Back in Ada, we were told that the trial would be heard on the fall docket, in September or October. On August 13th, we had a hearing on some motions that my attorney had, just routine motions that needed to be heard. Krissy went with me to the hearing. After it was over, we were standing to leave.

"Your attorney didn't win any of the discussions. He sucks."

I was insulted but tried to explain.

"There is no win or lose in these arguments, they are just routine motions. We knew we wouldn't win these."

She looked at me without a change in her expression. She had the right intuition about George, while I was blind to see anything that I didn't want to see.

Chapter 7   Praying for truth and justice

In late August, George obtained copies of the tapes of Rita's story, of the phone calls and of my confession. After reviewing the tapes and especially her interview with police, I was astounded at the nonsense she was telling them. I found it unbelievably humorous because I knew the truth. It was funny that the police and the DA believed her! What dupes, just like me.

By chance, later that day, I called my friend, Matthew, and told him about the tapes and all. I told him of the description of the man, the car and the details of her statement that these guys had harassed her earlier in the day.

"That sounds like Johnny Conners (name changed)," Matthew said coolly and matter-of-factly. My whole body felt a rush of energy, and I stood up.

"WHAT?"

"You know Johnny, remember a couple of weeks ago…"

"Yeah, I met him in the city jail." A couple of weeks earlier I was at Matthew's house and Johnny was there, working on his car or something. We just kind of said hello and talked about jail or whatever.

"Johnny has a bright yellow older model Chevy Nova, and he has tattoos of crosses, I think, on his wrists or hands. He has acne scars, pockmarks from acne and long hair. I think he has a ponytail too. He wears cowboy boots all the time and that sounds like something they would do, harassing women or just messing with people, you know? Man, that's pretty weird, huh? I don't think he would rape anybody though. He's not like that. But that describes him perfectly."

I was so grateful to God for what I was hearing. My adrenaline revved up and I wanted to cry with joy. This must be the missing link. I called George and told him what I had found out.

Johnny was the teenager in the cell across from me in April! When the police book a man into jail, they record any scars, tattoos and distinguishing marks such as a pockmarked face. Johnny was in the yellow Chevrolet Nova when he was arrested. I always wonder if anyone in the police department took notice of him when he was arrested. Of course, they already had me as the suspect in the case.

After reviewing in detail her story to the police, I felt pretty fortunate that she gave this crazy statement. It reeked of deceit, confusion and inconsistency. If she had made her story include a true description of me, and of the actual car I was driving, I would really have been left without explanation as to my innocence. Whether I would be found innocent or not, I thanked God that for whatever reason, she made up her story this way.

My continuing puzzlement was why she gave such a description of the person and car. It told me that she wasn't concerned with punishing me personally, or she would have described her version of the incident using the true facts of my description, car, etc. She gave a description of someone else or made up a description. That was clear to me. Did her boyfriend catch her, and tell her to make up a rape story? Why would he do that?

Maybe she got scared that she would get caught when she got home, so she made up this story to provide explanation, yet did not want to implicate me directly? That made some sense, but then she picked me out of the yearbook, identifying me personally.

Perhaps she was actually raped by this person in the yellow car after I let her out. But that didn't really make sense either. What made sense was that the whole thing made no sense.

Five months after my arrest, in September, George hired private investigators to investigate our case in order to be ready for trial if they brought us up in the fall docket. Walter Buchanan and Pam Bond were going to work for us. Walter was an older gentleman, looking very much the part of an aging, Oklahoma lawman, complete with the boots and hat. Pam was a pretty Native woman with long black hair.

They were given Rita's present married name. She currently lived in Massachusetts so we would be unable to go there. We had no idea that Rita had been married twice before and grew up in Texas. Had they been provided this information; they could have discovered **a lot** more about Rita at this time.

They were also only given the name of the man living with Rita at the time of the alleged incident. We knew nothing else about him or where to find him. We weren't able to locate him until after my trial began.

Soon after Walter and Pam were hired and had done some work for us, I met with them at my parent's house to discuss what they had discovered about the girl. I was very anxious because I just **knew** they had found something in my favor.

They had attempted to find favorable evidence from the workers at Hardee's, even though it was now a little late. The manager of Hardee's said that Rita owed her money and owed some other people money as well. She said that Rita told her one day that the case would probably never go to trial because my parents had a lot of money and they would probably pay her off.

In addition, the four or five witnesses at Hardee's remembered her coming in by herself around 2:00 a.m. and when the bar crowd hit around 3:00 a.m. nobody remembers her leaving at all. They further indicated that she was dressed like a San Francisco hooker and that she continually walked the streets and came in late at night. She was consistently dressed in mini-skirts and tank tops and just came across as a person of low moral character.

One worker said that Rita came in Hardee's the day she was wired with the microphone before she was to meet me at ECU. She said she was joking around about being wired up and this woman thought it strange the way she was acting. I was **very** unlucky that no one saw her talking with me or saw her leave with me that night.

The landlord of her apartment said that the tenant next door to Rita claimed the police were called to her house several times on domestic violence calls. We were not able to obtain any police reports to back this claim up. A credit check showed that she owed over $6,000 to JC Penney's department store.

This is really all we found out about Rita at this time and by the time of the trial. Her being from out of state made it difficult to obtain information about her without actually going to Massachusetts.

Walter was confident that the case would never come to trial and if it did, I would surely be found innocent. Walter resigned himself from the case soon after his appearance because he felt a conflict of interest might arise because he worked part-time for the Sheriff's department delivering summons and such.

Pam found out where Johnny lived and took some pictures of his yellow car to possibly use in the trial. She also obtained some personal information, his birth date (11-4-72) and the location of his tattoos. He had a grim reaper on his right bicep, a cross (web) on his left hand and his initials on his right hand. He drove a bright yellow Chevrolet Nova and had shoulder length, sandy blonde hair. He would not talk to her about the case and denied he knew anything.

We were left off the fall trial docket and had information that the reason was that Rita had left Ada in April 1991 and no one could find her, although they believed her to be in Texas.

In February of 1992, we were told we would be on the March felony docket. At this time, the State lowered their plea bargain offer from ten to five years on the rape with the sodomy charge dropped, all to run concurrent with the OKC larceny charge. I of course refused the plea bargain. We were again left off the docket.

I want to include here the exact wording from a letter that George Butner sent to me, dated February 26, 1992, that recounts much of the information our investigators Walter and Pam had told to me in our face-to-face meeting as stated above:

February 26, 1992

Dear Matt:

Walter Buchanan, our investigator, contacted me concerning the alleged victim in this case. He has been unable to locate her and he has been unable to locate her boyfriend. He did learn from the manager at Hardee's that the victim after the incident told the manager that your family had money and they would probably pay everybody off. In other words, it seemed to the manager that she may be looking for a little bit of money.

In addition, the four or five witnesses at Hardee's remembered her coming in by herself around 2:00 o'clock A.M. and when the bar crowd hit around 3:00 o'clock A.M. nobody remembers her leaving at all. They further indicated that she was dressed like a San Francisco hooker and that she continually walked the streets. She was consistently dressed in mini-skirts and tank tops and just came across as a person of low moral character.

Mr. Buchanan has been able to trace her to Houston, Texas, through her last paycheck but has been unable to locate her in that city.

He is attempting to locate her now by locating her parents, but his impression of this young lady is that she may not be found. That is our prayer at this time. I will keep you posted as to all things that come to my attention and knowledge.

Cordially yours,
George W. Butner

*

In August of 1992, I enrolled in 12 hours at East Central for the fall semester. I assumed that if the case did come to trial, that I would be found innocent anyway, so I tried to move on with my life.

When I was in the city and county jail from March 29, 1991 to April 12, 1991, little did I know that the letters I wrote to my girlfriend proclaiming my innocence were being intercepted and read by the DA. Krissy kept all of these letters. In 1992, Pam asked to see them to have a handwriting expert analyze them. This expert said that in her opinion I did not commit these crimes and was telling the truth in the letters.

This is it. It's interesting, I guess:

~

"These are my findings according to the principles of Graphoanalysis, without prejudice or bias, and without liability to the analyst:

Background: The writer, "Matthew" is in jail at this time on a charge of rape. Matthew stated that he did not rape the girl who accused him. The analyst checked for wholesomeness of integrity and for possible violent tendencies in the personality of the writer, since rape is considered an act of violence.

Through careful analysis of Matthew's handwriting, no pattern of violent tendencies is revealed. There does not seem to be mental disturbance or a strong desire to control. The traits of temper and aggression are minimal or absent. His writing does not show signs of pent-up emotions, which could overrule his objectivity. The trait of resentment seems more confined to the area of not wanting to be told how and what to think, as opposed to carrying around "emotional baggage" that could produce grudges and outbursts. Irritability is strong at times, but this trait is a secondary one in light of the charge against him. The writer responds from an objective point of view and is not likely to act on impulse. This writer is impressionable. He is broad-minded and encompasses a permissive philosophy in life. Even though his mind is very sharp, he is unable to be discretionary in the area of weighing consequences. For whatever reason, he has either not learned wholesome values or simply has chosen not to embrace them. He has a lack of moral strength. His conscience has not been developed in a wholesome manner. This process has caused his integrity to disintegrate. When dealing with this individual, it is imperative to check his story from a second, and perhaps a third reliable party. The writer is an opportunist. His attitude is most likely to "play now and play later" instead of "play now and pay later". His commitment level appears low.

Conclusion: After careful evaluation of this handwriting, I would say that Matthew is not a violent type of person and it is unlikely that he did commit a crime of rape. He is insincere and sets his own rules (which are counter to tradition). It is highly likely that he listens to the wrong influences. When trouble arises, he depends on trying to talk his way out of the situation. He is likely to bend the truth and to withhold pertinent information. He is capable of trying to verbally manipulate others. Even though there is not "pat" criminal writing, and behavior cannot be predicted with Graphoanalysis, it is my finding that this individual is unlikely to have committed this particular crime. Matthew's strong tendency in dealing with life's problems is to escape rather than to strike out.

Incidentally, Matthew has a scientific mind, an excellent ability to organize and has a colorful imagination. Engineering aptitude is prevalent in his writing. Channeled properly, these traits could be utilized in a most positive way."

~

In September, we were told the trial would begin on Monday, November 2, 1992. The detectives for the State began to interview all of our witnesses on our witness list. Karla, my girlfriend's boss, told me that they were very rude to her. They asked her if she knew that I had "assaulted a woman in OKC" and was on probation for that charge, which was "larceny from a person".

They also used this credibility-damaging lie on at least two other witnesses on our list. One of them was one of the girls that lived in the apartment across from Danny's that I had asked if they could testify that they were awake and having a party that night. This girl did not know me well, so their statements did not help me.

Right around my twenty-first birthday, for about six months, my friends and I would drink and go to the bars, looking for fun. We always hoped for a woman, and some of us were feeling our oats for a few months and fighting was pretty exciting to us. We were testing our powers. We met all kinds of people, you know.

After this period came new thoughts of how to pass the time, which wasn't in good directions. Talk of larceny and robbery. Hey, it wasn't my idea, but I followed like a cow, I guess. In August (1988) after drinking all night, and taking Percocet, I stole a woman's purse in OKC. I reached in the passenger window of her car and grabbed her purse. I had all I needed except CASH, to get into the bar in Ada that night. You can see I needed some direction in my life. Yeah. Bad decisions. I didn't want to physically touch or hurt anyone. My intent was complete lack of physical contact, like stealing cigarettes or something. But no, I wasn't nice. For this stunt, I got seven dollars in cash and a couple of rings. I took one of the rings to a pawnshop and kept the pearl out of the other one. I was not a good criminal. I didn't really plan it, you know. She got my license number. I was caught. I admitted, without a second's hesitation, that I had done it.

As it turned out, the woman was super nice to me and wanted me to get probation. She asked if I could return her rings, as they were meaningful to her. I bought back the ring from the pawnshop and returned it and the pearl to her. She sat by me at the sentencing/court appearance. After five long days of punishment, in the OKC city jail, I had a 5-year deferred sentence. Probation. Of course, now the Pontotoc County officials would use this as evidence, of violence involving a woman, to validate/justify their filing the charges, and pushing it to trial.

My friend Chris, was the one who I ran around with, and talked with about these petty crimes. I learned that he continued his ways when I went to prison, and became much worse over the years supporting a drug habit that he had developed with harder drugs. He was just a kid without a chance in this life, brought up without much guidance. I never saw him alive again. He overdosed in the summer of 2000.

Chapter 8 Trial

The weekend before the trial began, we were told that the girl was in town and I just couldn't believe it. I just couldn't believe she would come back and lie to try to send me to prison. I was still waiting for my release from this nightmare.

Pam and some friends kept an eye on Rita, hoping for a chance to catch her alone to speak with her and try to pry a confession out of her. However, she was with her mother and so was never alone. She spent most of her time drinking in her hotel's bar. The hope to gain a confession died out.

We would have to make some decisions about how to prepare my case for trial. Because of all of my past crimes and misdemeanors, putting me on the stand would open up my credibility to all of these things. We knew that the larceny charge would look very bad in the eyes of the jury.

For twenty-one months now I had been waiting to go to trial. Krissy and I had since been married and were now headed for divorce, although we were still very close. We were just two kids living through a difficult situation.

I had worked at a BBQ place for quite a while, and currently was the night auditor at the Main and Mississippi convenience store, until my picture was in the Ada News, in the newsstand in the store, reporting the beginning of my jury trial on Monday. The manager couldn't believe it, an incredulous look on his face, as he "had to" fire me.

It was painful to see the looks on people's faces, scared of me. My deepest thoughts and receptions told me that I needed to take the witness stand to allow the jury the opportunity to look into my eyes, and study my mannerisms so that they could see that I was truthful. I had my own plan for the trial that I thought would work. I related it many times to my attorney over the phone and in notes and letters. I was confident that I would soon be cleared of these charges.

Day One

On Monday morning, November 2, 1992 I made my way up the stairs of the courthouse to the 3rd floor, nervous as heck. I had only one suit. Would swap out sport coat here and there, in the coming days.

I noticed a crowd of people, as I made it to the third floor, waiting around the courtroom doors. The jury pool. Can you imagine, you and your potential jurors just gather in the hall. 5-LIFE on two charges. I made my way to the vacant jury room in the back where I was to meet with George.

George looked a little nervous himself.

"Hey George. How are you?"

"Good Matthew." We shook hands.

"Matthew, you know that the plea bargain is still being offered."

"Yeah, I know. I mean I figured it would be."

The five years was still being offered on the rape with the sodomy dropped, but they said it would go to 15 years, once the trial began. This statement, first off, by my attorney, was frustrating for me at this moment. I felt he still wanted me to take the plea bargain. Much better would have been an expression of enthusiasm about trying the case.

Certainly, all the advice given to me was in my best interest, when facing two life sentences. I just was not able to take the plea bargain. We were all looking for the truth, and I think a bit shocked that the girl was there ready to testify. Problem was, they still weren't listening, because I told the truth from the start.

George explained what we would do today, which would probably be just picking the jury, and he expressed his fears and concerns about the case. If I didn't testify, the jury would never hear about my past or any of my arrests. However, if I testified, that would open the can of worms for the State to ask anything about my past. I told him that I felt that I would need to testify, but I understood his concerns.

After jury selection, the State would present their opening statement and we would have the opportunity to present ours after that. George felt that delaying his opening statement until the State rested their case was the best tactic. It was unorthodox but I heeded to his professional advice. As I look back in hindsight, it was unwise to waive our opening statement. There were two completely different stories. The jury needed our story in the beginning to be able to compare it to the State's case and to detect inconsistencies and lies in Rita's testimony. In the end, the jury was left confused. A confused mind says no.

We took our seats at our table as the slow jury selection process began. My yellow legal tablet and pen were ready for notes. I was out of my body in a way, as if this were a bad dream that would soon be over. I wouldn't believe Rita was here until I saw her. I could just feel the deep and puzzling thoughts about me resonating from all of the jury pool and audience. Yeah, this is pretty hilarious.

The jury was seated about 2:30 and the State completed its opening statement. The energies of all the eyes, thoughts and words thrown at me were paralyzing. Never had I felt more powerless, like a bound and gagged hostage. I could do nothing but sit there, monitoring my facial expressions and body postures to maintain an appearance of innocence. I still don't know what that is. It must be something guilty people portray.

As far as "my self" was concerned, we were temporarily invisible, none of this slander affixing to us. We looked ahead with hope to a strong presentation of our defense and a verdict of not guilty. Truth will prevail, faith be to God. Or to George?

The State's first witness was one of the women out walking that morning. She called 911 after encountering Rita downtown near the fire station. She recounted what her involvement was: that she encountered Rita, observed her to be upset, hysterical and claiming to have been raped, and that she called 911.

The next witness was police officer Lynn Haines, one of the many Ada Police Officers who responded to the 911 call. Things are kind of slow in a small town, so a rape victim gets a lot of attention. Probably half of the Ada Police Department responded to the call that morning, sirens blasting and tires screeching like there was an "all units" announcement of free coffee and donuts at the fire station. Officer Haines transported Rita to the hospital and testified as to his observing her to be upset and so hysterical that he could not understand much of what she said.

As the day ended, just before the Judge instructed the jury that we would resume tomorrow at ten o'clock in the morning, the State presented their first exhibit to the jury. The last thing the jurors saw that day in the courtroom, was a picture showing the "injuries" on Rita. They would stew on this overnight and Rita would be on the stand first thing tomorrow morning.

I was worn out emotionally but happy that the day was over. Tomorrow presented exciting opportunities with Rita on the stand. George should win the case for us tomorrow with a good plan of action to clearly point out all of her inconsistencies, lies and changing story.

Day Two

Election Day. I awoke a little disappointed that I had to awake at all. My dreams were free and uncomplicated. In those few seconds waiting to gain my bearings upon awakening, I was warm and comfortable. Consciousness brought instant butterflies as my mind found its gear. Jury trial. Rita today.

I drove myself to the courthouse, my mind a little fluttered and lacking clarity. As I shut my door and was walking to the east door, I looked ahead and saw one of the other Judges arriving at the courthouse. He looked me straight in the eye as he neared the door, nodding slightly. He found the door handle and pulled it open, presenting me with the open door.

"Thank you, sir."

As I passed him, our eyes met and I felt a bolt of comfort pass through me. His countenance was vigorously unassuming. A depth. We nodded again and went our ways. I had always liked and respected him. Yes, honor is alive and well.

George was a little preoccupied as we met in the back room. My questions about his plan for Rita's testimony were ducked, and kind of answered "while running the other way". I took a smoke break before we were to begin. At the only smoking area on this floor, me and some of my jurors were smoking butts in front of the courtroom when George motioned for me.

"Matthew, I have some things I need to discuss with you. We are going to go in the other courtroom for a few minutes."

"What is it?"

"Well, I just have some concerns I need to voice before the plea bargain offer is removed. When Rita takes the stand, the State will remove their plea bargain offer. I'll explain it in here. Come on." He placed his hand on my upper back, leading me to join him in the other courtroom.

The Judge, prosecutor, court reporter and my family went into the other courtroom to hear what George had to say. He was trying to get me to take a plea bargain.

George went on for ten minutes or more, trying to talk me into taking a plea bargain, which was now back up to 15 years on the rape with the sodomy charge dropped. I was disheartened with George's attitude. We'd known the difficulties of the case from the start and this decision was resolved long ago. There was zero interest in a plea bargain. I felt he wanted to go home and take a Jacuzzi or something. I needed him to focus all of his attention on questioning Rita on the stand. I would soon find out that he had no preparation for this.

He also brought up the fact of our investigator Pam finding the boyfriend just last night and our desire to put him on the stand.

When he finished, he took me aside like I was making a terrible mistake and asked me to take what time I needed to think about it to come to a decision. My family was caught up in it, looking at me with looks of helplessness, looks of fear for my future.

I understood the looks and concerns but they all had their sails pointed in a different direction than me. Had I not made clear our direction? What a waste of time this was.

It took me one second to answer, with the first half of that second spent realizing that he didn't believe in my innocence. He thought I was guilty or crazy or something. I answered him with a question.

"Are you ready to cross-examine Rita?"

For twenty-one months, my primary hope was that Rita would not be found and would not show up if a trial were held. She had in fact disappeared after my arrest and caused the State to postpone the trial due to her wanderings. This primary hope shattered loudly upon my heart when I saw her walk into the courtroom. She actually showed up.

Who was **this** girl? Her appearance had changed. Instead of bleached blonde hair and seductive clothes, she had brown curly hair like Little Orphan Annie and wore a plain "country girl" brown dress with pretty flowers on it. What an angel.

She took her seat at the witness chair, looked pleasantly at the jury, then at me with a look of fear and uneasiness. Her final cue was the look at the prosecutor to begin her part. What a devil.

I readied my yellow notepad to write down every contradiction and every question I wanted George to ask. I was sure that her testimony would be loaded with contradictions. Heck, she had even changed her original story in the last couple of days.

She changed her story upon returning to Ada to testify at trial. She said that she had forgotten to mention that, I HAD stopped by a convenience store (on 14th and Mississippi; Campus Corner) first, to buy some beer, before taking her to the apartment. The truth is that we went from Hardee's to a different store on 10th, and I walked in to buy beer and cigarettes. She said that I pointed my knife at her and told her to stay down, while I went in to buy some beer. I mean, does this even sound right? Pardon me while I take a break from this kidnapping, to go in and get a bottle o suds? A clerk was working at the store. It would be lit up and all she would have to do is get out of the car, yell, run to the clerk, etc.

She also said now, that she did not remember the footwear the man was wearing, even though she stated in her interview with police that her attacker wore cowboy boots and left them on during the ordeal.

Right at the end of the direct examination by the DA, she broke into tears and tried to gain sympathy. I felt like she deserved an Oscar.

She testified that she used the phone to call about the Pizza Hut job and then was walking back to Hardee's when abducted. The State was trying to use the fact of her having her job application with her, as to how I knew her name and where she lived. Here is the relevant testimony prosecutor Ross asks her about what happened from then on:

Q.	And what happened when you started to go back to Hardee's?

A.	I walked down the hill part. And there was an alley with the dumpster right there. And I didn't notice the car that was sitting there. He got out and met me.

Q.	Where did he meet you at?

A.	Right there.

Q.	By the alley?

A.	Yes.

Q.	And what if anything did he say to you?

A.	He told me, "You didn't think I would catch up with you bitch."

Q.	And had you…what did that bring to your mind?

A.	Earlier that day I was walking to Homeland grocery store after I got paid.

Q.	And what happened?

A.	Him and a couple of friends were in a car, a yellow car, and he scared me then…or one of his friends did. And I ran into…in front of someone's house.

Q.	Back in the alley after he said, "didn't think I would catch up with you", what else did he say?

A.	I'm sorry.

Q.	Take a few minutes.

A.	After that he started acting like I was a friend of his from way, way back. And I told him I did not know him. I had never seen him except for earlier that day.

Q.	And then what happened?

A.	He took me by the back of the head and he pushed me in his car.

Q.	When he pushed you in his car what door did you go through?

A.	His side.

Q.	Driver's side. Was there anyone else in the car?

A.	No, there wasn't.

Q.	What happened after he pushed you into the car?

A.	He told me to keep my head down and I was very scared. I didn't know if he was going to kill me or what. And he drove and it was real short drive and he stopped.

Q.	Did he say anything to you?

A.	He told me to stay right there or he would kill me.

Q.	And what happened next?

A.	He got out of the car. I kept my head down. I looked up to see if I could make eye contact with anybody that could have been around, there was nothing. I kept my head down because I didn't know if he was in back of the car or front of the car or what.

Q.	When you raised your head up could you tell where you were?

A.	I just saw windows. I knew I was at some type of little store or something.

Q.	And you said you put your head back down. What happened then?

A.	He got in the car and he threw a paper sack right beside my feet.

Q.	What was in it?

A.	Well, I didn't know what was in it at first.

Q.	Did you find out later?

A.	Yes, it was beer.

Q.	What happened after he got back in the car?

A.	Got back in the car and it felt like a real rough type road and then we stopped.

Q.	And what happened after you stopped?

A.	He got me out of the car and with his foot he banged in a door.

Q.	A door of what?

A.	I didn't know what it was at first. It was just a little bitty building, little bitty place. Then when I got in I saw that it was…it was a little apartment.

Q.	Did it appear to be occupied?

A.	No.

Q.	Was there any furniture inside?

A.   No.

Q.   Any lights?

A.   No.

Q.   Was there any natural lighting?

A.   Yes.

Q.   And could you tell the jury what that was?

A.   It was through the window. There was light through the window because there weren't any curtains or anything on it.

Q.   And did you have a feel when you saw that for where you were or what area of town?

A.   When I looked up through the window all I saw was a big brown building. There was a clock…I noticed there was a clock on one of them.

Q.   And what happened after you got inside the apartment?

A.   He pushed me down.

Q.   Were you able to tell what kind of…what you were pushed down onto?

A.   I'm pushed down on a crumpled-up piece of carpet.

Q.   Were you face down or face up?

A.   I was face down.

Q.   And what happened then?

A.   He took my clothes off. He ripped my shirt off.

Q.   Rita, let me hand you what has been marked for purposes of identification only as State's Exhibit No. 2. I ask you if you can identify what this is?

A.   Yes, it was the shirt.

Q.   Is that the shirt you had on that night?

A.   Yes.

Q.   Rita, after he ripped your shirt off what happened?

A.   He pulled my pants down.

Q.   Were you completely naked?

A.   Yes.

Q.   What happened after he took all your clothes off?

A.   He pulled his pants down.

Q.   And then what?

A.   He put his penis inside of me.
Q.   Penis inside your vagina?
A.   Yes.
Q.   Did he begin to have sex?
A.   No, it wasn't sex.
Q.   Did he penetrate your vagina?
A.   Yes.
Q.   During this time did you ever see any type of weapon?
A.   Yes, I did.
Q.   Would you tell the jury what that was?
A.   It was a knife.
Q.   And what did he do with it?
A.   He ran it along my chest.
Q.   Did he make threats to you during this time?
(Objection)
Q.   Did he say anything to you during this time?
A.   He just kept threatening me not to go to the police.
Q.   Did you try to resist him?
A.   Yes, I did.
Q.   What did you try to do?
A.   I kicked him and I scratched his arm.
Q.   Did you make any attempt to draw attention?
A.   Yes, I did. I screamed.
Q.   What happened when you screamed?
A.   He hit me.
Q.   Where did he hit you?
A.   He hit me in the face.
Q.   What else did he do to you?
A.   He scratched me. He just kept scratching me.
Q.   Where?
A.   In the chest.
Q.   Rita, let me hand you what has been marked State's Exhibit
No. 3 and ask if you can look at that and tell me what that is?
A.   Yes, scratch marks.
Q.   Would you tell the jurors what happened next?

A.   He took his penis out and he put it in the anal part.

Q.   What position were you in at this time?

A.   What?

Q.   Were you still face up?

A.   No.

Q.   When did you change position?

A.   In between it he turned me over and that's when he started scratching me. And he turned me back over.

Q.   You said that he put it in the anal part?

A.   Yes.

Q.   I know it's hard, could you be more specific. Could you tell the jurors using terms of anatomy what he did?

A.   Took his penis out of my vagina and put it in the anal and then he took it back out. After a while he put it back in my vagina again.

Q.   Did he penetrate your anus with his penis?

A.   Yes, he did.

Q.   And what happened after that?

A.   Seemed like a long time we were in there. And after he was done, he put my clothes on, put his on, and he took me out and he put me back in the car the same way he put me in before. Put me in on the other side.

Q.   Passenger side?

A.   Yes.

Q.   What happened then?

A.   He just kept threatening me the whole way that I better not go to the cops or tell anybody at Hardee's about it. And I was scared he was going to kill me. I thought he was going to take me out somewhere and kill me then.

Q.   What happened then?

A.   We drove and he kept telling me to open the door and we were still moving. And he kept telling me to open the door and I couldn't get the door open. It was frustrating him. I was afraid he was going to kill me if I didn't get the door open and I couldn't get it open.

Q.   And what happened?

A.   Then he slowed down and he opened the door and he threw me out.

Q.   Did you know where you were?

A.   No.

Q.   And it was still dark?

A.   Yes.

Q.   What did you do?

A.   I lay there until I made sure that he drove off.

Q.   Did he say anything to you when he threw you out before he left?

A.   He just kept telling me I better not go to the cops.

Q.   What happened after you lay there for a while?

A.   After I lay there for a while and I realized that he may not come back I tried getting up and I started walking.

When the DA passed the witness to George for him to cross-examine, George got that look of preoccupation again. He approached the bench and stated to the Judge that he wasn't prepared to cross-examine her. He had planned to prepare during the lunch hour. A conference was held at the bench outside the hearing of the jury.

The Judge gave him fifteen minutes. I didn't know what to say to him, figuring he would know how to figure this one out. I took a smoke break once again… with some of the jurors.

George began his cross-examination by more or less apologizing to Rita, saying he realized this was a very difficult situation for her. He might as well have moved over to the prosecution's table.

He basically did a bad job. Her contradictions were as plain as day to me and I wrote down each one. He refused, however, to look at my notes and did things his own way, which was very poor.

There was a big difference in her demeanor when George questioned her. Her crying had completely stopped, and she was very attentive and concentrating very hard to keep from contradicting herself.

His cross-examination didn't take more than one hour, and prosecutor Ross was allowed his re-direct examination and wrapped it up right before lunch, giving the State the advantage of presenting more pictures of Rita's injuries to the jury before they went to lunch. If you didn't know which lawyer was questioning Rita, I don't think you could tell from the transcripts that George Butner, and his questions, were FOR the defense.

In summary of how her testimony went, instead of laying out word for word all of the transcribed testimony, I'll use a summarization of her contradictions that I would eventually present to an appeals court:

1. In her initial statement to the police on the morning of March 17, 1991, she said he took her out of the car at the apartment. At trial, under cross-examination, she said she got out of the passenger side and he got out on the driver's side. A few minutes later under cross-examination she said he pushed her out the passenger door and then followed her through the same door.

2. In her statement to the police, she said she first saw the knife in the apartment. At trial she said she first saw the knife in the car before they got to the apartment.

3. In her statement to the police, she said the attacker said, "You thought you could get away from me before, didn't you bitch?" At trial she said he said, "You didn't think I would catch up with you bitch?"

4. In her statement to the police, she said he wore cowboy boots and left them on during the alleged rape. At trial she said she didn't remember his footwear.

5. The first recorded phone call she made to Thompson, their first conversation since the night in question nine days earlier, shows logical evidence of previous mutual conversation and friendship. Matthew asks her if her girlfriend sent the death threats to him. This statement would make no sense in the State's version of the facts, but makes sense in that Thompson said that Rita told him of a lesbian lover. You would expect the initial contact to be much different were Rita's version of the facts true.

6. She said that she left her apartment at about 2:45 a.m., immediately after waking up, yet the State's own witness, Greg Frazier, said that he saw her in Hardee's at about 2:00 a.m., before the bar crowd came in.

7. She said that earlier that day, in the middle of the day in the middle of town, she ran in fright from the alleged group of men in the yellow car, yet later, at 2:45 a.m., she says she APPROACHED the yellow car in a dark alley instead of fleeing to the safety of the convenience store less than fifty feet away.

The State's next witness after lunch was a man who had worked at Hardee's that night, Greg Frazier. His testimony related to the timing of when Rita was in Hardee's. He said that she had been in to get a soda some time before the bar crowd arrived. The bars closed at 2:00 am. Unfortunately, he didn't see her later on, eating food and talking with me.

Detective C. David Leewright had resigned before my trial due to some personal problems. Detective Cosper took the stand next as the lead detective in the case. He testified about his involvement in the case. I must say, he was mistaken about some of the stuff.

As I said, her story was changing when she came back for trial. Cosper told about how he and Rita had driven around the previous weekend and determined which convenience store it was that we had stopped at to buy beer. They believed it to be the Campus Corner on 14th and Mississippi. The Campus Corner was the other direction from Hardee's from where we actually went, the Texaco on 10th and Mississippi.

The State rested their case and we adjourned for the day. They had introduced no medical evidence to support rape, only pictures of the injuries. The medical report I saw in Tommy's office was not used to support their case. Only these pictures of scratches and redness. Tomorrow, Wednesday, November 4, 1992, we would begin OUR case. I could possibly testify tomorrow.

Dad and I went to vote for the president of the country. I voted for the guy who played the saxophone (Bill Clinton).

Later that night, I was thinking about the Campus Corner store and remembered a friend who used to work there. I remembered that Krissy and I met him one Saturday night after he got off work and he gave me a joint of Hawaiian. The store closed at two in the morning then! I picked up the phone and called the store.

The worker I talked with said that they used to close at two o'clock on weekends but now closed at midnight on both nights. Either way it was impossible for me to buy beer at a store that wasn't possibly open! I was excited and called George immediately.

"Hello."

"George, this is Matthew."

"Hi Matthew, how are you?"

"Good. I was just thinking about Cosper's testimony today, saying that he and Rita had determined the store to be Campus Corner, and I remembered a friend of mine who used to work there. One night I went by to talk with him after he got off of work on a Friday or Saturday night, and… that store closes at 2:00! There is no way I could have bought beer at that store."

"Hmmm."

"I called the store and talked with an employee, he called the owner and he said that it was true. In fact, the store closes now at midnight on weekends. So, we can show that as totally untrue! We can put her back on the stand to answer this impossibility, and have the manager of the store testify to the time that the store closes!"

"Well. Matthew, I'm not sure that we want to put the girl on the stand again. We don't want to give her another chance to gain sympathy from the jury."

"Don't you think we need to point out that this new change in her story is not possibly true?"

"Well, I am not sure it will help."

"What if we put Cosper on the stand again to have him answer to it?"

"Matthew, it just isn't good practice to put witnesses back on the stand. I think we are doing pretty well. Our defense starts tomorrow and we will be able to put reasonable doubt in the jury's minds. We don't want to swim upstream, you know?"

"Then we can just have the manager of the Campus Corner testify for us."

"I just don't think it is that strong Matthew. I think our best chance is to go on with our defense and get the case to the jury. There is reasonable doubt in this case. We don't want to confuse the jury. Matthew, I'll see you in the morning and we'll make our final decision then. Okay?"

"Should I call the manager and tell him that we might possibly call him to testify tomorrow?"

"No. Don't you call him again. I'll think about it and we can do that tomorrow if we need to. You get some rest, Buddy. I'll see you in the morning."

"Okay."

"Bye."

He thinks it isn't worth putting either the girl or the detective on the stand again, that we are sitting well. I didn't know what to say about this. Is this not an important issue? I'm confused again.

Rita had been in town since the Saturday before and Pam had been interested in giving it one last try to find some evidence that might help us. Late Tuesday evening, Pam discovered that the boyfriend Mike was staying at his mother's house in Gerty, OK. She went there late in the evening to interview him and I had heard nothing from her as I left for the courthouse the next morning.

Chapter 9   Innocent but guilty

Day Three

According to Pam's gathered information on Johnny Conners, November 4th just happened to be his birthday. Today was Wednesday, November 4, 1992. What a memorable day it would be.

As I reached the third floor of the courthouse, I recognized some of our witnesses from Hardee's, waiting outside the courtroom with the smoking jurors. I learned that Mike was also there and had spoken to the prosecutor and George. As I walked into the judge's office where George was, the phone rang. The secretary handed the phone to George.

"This is George."

"George, it is Pam." He mouthed her name to me. I watched his face for a good sign. I didn't know what he knew about what the boyfriend said last night. He listened unexcitedly for a minute and then gave me the phone.

"Hello Pam."

"Hi Matthew. Did George talk to you about my conversation with Mike last night?"

"No, I just got here when you called. What did he say?"

"I interviewed him at his mother's house in Gerty, late last night. I found out that he had been out of town, actually out of the country for a period of time since your arrest. Did you know that his mother is married to detective Cosper's cousin? The DA had to have known where Mike was the whole time."

"What did he say?"

"Willie and I interviewed him and his parents were in the room with us. I think that he knows more than he is saying, Matthew. He just seemed uncomfortable talking about it and maybe he didn't want to say something in front of his parents. Basically, he said that he and Rita drank a twelve-pack of beer and played cards that night until both of them fell asleep about midnight. He remembers her leaving to go get cigarettes at some point but that he fell back asleep until the police woke him up in the morning to tell him Rita was at the hospital. That's really about it. I think if you put him on the stand, you might get him to say more."

Pam would continue to work hard in the last few minutes, but I was disheartened that the boyfriend was not helping us solve this misunderstanding. We next were to meet with the judge and DA about allowing the boyfriend to testify.

Confident that the boyfriend would help me on this day, George and I met with the prosecutor in the Judge's chamber to discuss this "surprise" witness. To my disbelief, the Judge was not going to allow us to put Mike on the stand, saying his testimony was different than what we initially told the DA he would testify to (that he beat her up, put the marks and bruises on her, and/or coerced her to report a rape to the police). We argued that we could only guess what he would testify to. We had never been able to find him until last night.

During this conference, the prosecution admitted that they knew where Mike was all the time, but that my attorney never asked. However, we were still not allowed to put him on the stand. George and I had to make a decision to come to a stipulation about what part of Mike's testimony we would use, or preserve the Judge's decision as a ground for appeal.

A stipulation can be used by one of the parties in a trial when a witness can't testify. The Judge reads a statement to the jury as to "what the witness would testify to" if he were allowed to testify.

George filled me in on Mike's story. He basically said that he met her at a drug treatment center in Texas, with them moving to Ada and sharing an apartment after that. His story of that night was that they drank a few beers, played some cards and went to bed. He remembered her leaving to go get some cigarettes but fell asleep before being woken up early in the morning by the police saying she was at the hospital.

How disappointing to not have such a key witness take the stand. We didn't mean for it to be a surprise. We just could never find him, to depose his testimony. We decided to agree to the stipulation.

The Judge read the stipulation to the jury upon our return to courtroom number one, and soon after we announced the beginning of our defense.

It seemed like forever since Rita had been on the stand. George gave his opening statement and I had hope that we were going to present a good case. Although he was typically uninformed of the exact details, he did a good job opening our defense.

"Now we are going somewhere," I thought. With all of the witnesses outside and me testifying, we will be able to present a fair defense. He called my girlfriend as his first witness and asked her just a few questions about her red Firebird and her giving me the keys that night. Ross didn't ask her any questions.

His next witness was my mother to testify about the death threat note she found at her door. Ross didn't ask her any questions either and we broke for lunch. Our first two witnesses' testimony didn't last ten minutes.

An attorney friend of ours, Barney Ward, had been letting us use his office as a base of operations. Dad and I picked up a Folger's burger and went to wait for George to discuss our game plan. He arrived and we waited for him to speak to us.

"Matthew, I don't think you should testify. Of course, the final decision is yours, but I feel that we have created enough reasonable doubt with the description of you and the car that the jury will find you not guilty."

It was no different now than before. We knew that if I took the stand, my past would become fair game. I was a little unsettled as he continued to talk me out of testifying. He stated again his feeling that with all of the inconsistencies in the description and all, the jury had no other choice but to find me not guilty. That was a certain reasonable doubt, right?

Ultimately it was my decision. It would take courage to take the stand and I certainly felt fear. I also felt my attorney was looking at me, unprepared, pressuring me into agreeing with him. This whole darn mess just wasn't right.

What a decision. After knowing for a year and a half that I **must** testify so the jurors could look into my eyes and observe my truth, I felt cheated as I made the final decision to not take the stand. They didn't want me to screw it up again. Neither did I.

We only had a few minutes left for lunch when I remembered about the other witnesses that had been waiting to testify. George said in his running away manner that he felt we should get the case to the jury and not waste time on these witnesses. Waste time? I didn't know what to say about this.

We walked back to the courthouse, up the steps, past the smoking jurors and into our places. Never had I felt more guilty than when George stood and announced, "The defense rests," without me testifying. There was our defense, maybe a quarter hour total.

George did a pretty good job in his closing argument with the sodomy issue and the complete lack of evidence, especially the absence of any medical report or rape kit. He should have argued the same with the rape charge. However, during his closing argument, he paused, came over to me and whispered in my ear.

"What was I just saying? I lost my train of thought."

Not good. I had to think hard through my own frustration and pressure from this, but remembered and gave him his way again.

The State always has the final say. Ross painted a picture of me as a "chameleon" in his closing statements, as a rapist who changed his personality and story to fit the situation. How funny and ironic, if only to me. SHE is the chameleon, and so good at it. I was just a confused and innocent kid, trying to search for answers. He completes his closing statement asking the jury for guilty verdicts and time in prison:

"I ask you to find him guilty on both charges and to return a verdict on the charge of rape of guilty and sentence of not less than thirty years. And a sentence and verdict on the charge of sodomy of guilty and a sentence of ten years. Rita is credible. She was raped. She was sodomized. And this man right here, he deserves to pay. And we ask you to make him pay. Thank you."

*

After the prosecutor showed the Judge which jury instructions to read, the case was handed to the jury. It was 3:08 pm. These people would decide my fate.

Time was at a standstill. We retreated to base camp Barney Ward's office, to wait it out. There were all speculations among us but I was just in a trance, waiting for the words that I expected to hear, "not guilty". Sadly, George seemed proud of his performance as he drank what he said was a trial lawyer's reward, Diet Coke.

At 4:50 pm, the jury had a question. We returned to the courthouse to see what it was.

JURY FOREMAN: "We would like to know if we would be able to review them tapes again. The main ones we want to review is the one…the last one before the video, the video and the one after the video."

The jury was excused and there were arguments. George objected to the jury being allowed to review only part of the tapes. He said it would be unfair and that they should review all of the tapes or none of them. Our objection was overruled (as were 99% of our objections). They were allowed to review any and all of the tapes that they needed to review.

At 6:10 pm, the phone rang and we were informed that they had reached a verdict. The butterflies took their places, excited and ready for the action. I could only imagine a not guilty verdict.

We took our places and the jury filed in to take their seats. One of the jurors, a woman, was just crying away, which was odd.

Upon seeing some of their faces, George leaned to whisper in my ear.

"We lost. They aren't looking at us."

Not what I wanted to hear George. Surely not.

Time was slow and painful. The butterflies were a bit strong for comfort. My hands were in front of me, back in their not guilty pose, whatever that was.

The foreman of the jury handed the sentence to the bailiff. Finally, the judge was to read the verdict:

"In the District Court in and for Pontotoc County, State of Oklahoma. The State of Oklahoma versus Matthew Lambert Thompson, case number CRF-91-51, verdicts from. We the jury drawn, empanelled and sworn in the above-entitled cause do upon our oaths find the defendant **guilty** of the crime of Rape in the First Degree as charged in Count I of the Information and assess his punishment at **fifteen** years. Signed, Vernon E. Hendren, Foreman."

Guilty? As the word "guilty" was read, I dropped my head into my hands in despair, feeling my face flush with blood. I couldn't believe it. That **was** fifteen years and NOT fifty, right? Now the second verdict:

"In the District Court in and for Pontotoc County, State of Oklahoma. The State of Oklahoma versus Matthew Lambert Thompson, case number CRF-91-51, verdicts from. We the jury drawn, empaneled and sworn in the above-entitled cause do upon our oaths find the defendant **not guilty** of the crime of Sodomy as charged in Count II of the information. Signed, Vernon E. Hendren, Foreman.

Thank Gosh for acquittal on that charge. I had to refocus my thoughts and emotions again with my face in my hands. These people have convicted an innocent man. Thoughts of Australia and suicide showed themselves in my head. Could I finish this semester? I listened to the background sounds, a family member crying, hell…the juror was still crying. Someone calmly asked George what he thought went wrong. This was all so surreal.

I looked up and scanned the jury, trying to make eye contact with each one. Most would not look at me, as if ashamed or afraid of me. The jury was released and a few matters about my bail and sentencing date were discussed. I would be allowed to remain free until 4:00 pm on December 8th.

My family and I stayed around the courthouse for a few more minutes, stunned by the verdict. The women were crying: Mom, Krissy, my sister and Krissy's mom, and her sisters. We were all just stunned. We asked George what he thought a fifteen-year sentence would mean in actual time. He thought I would be able to get out in about three years.

"Three years?" My mother's face was full of tears.

"Mom, I will be OK. I'm not going to let them ruin my life."

My dad didn't know what to say, but held my shoulders in support.

"Son, I'm sorry. I love you and believe in you. Are you going to be Okay?"

"Yeah. Just kind of shocked, you know?"

Being on trial had to be the most frustrating and humiliating experience of my life. I felt like a fool anyway for being duped by her and the police, and then felt like a freak sitting there in the courtroom like a knot on a log. Everyone's looking at you, their imaginations putting together all kinds of scenarios and you don't get to do anything except sit there. What a powerless feeling that was.

We all returned to my parent's house in shock. Sadness, anger at George, anger at the girl, fear and despair were just some of the emotions. How would I ever prove my innocence?

While everyone tried to find answers looking back at the past, I began to focus on my future. What direction would I take now? Whatever it was, I was not going to let these punks ruin my life.

What happened God? I've been asking for justice, just simple justice, for twenty-one months and now I'm going to prison for something you know I didn't do. What's up with that? Maybe I wasted my time praying and hoping. I had strong faith that I would be acquitted.

After a long, nearly sleepless night, I awoke to find reality still cruelly laughing at me and slapping me around. The day before my sentencing date, on December 7th, I wrote my first narrative in freehand, about ten pages long. Even if the conviction remained, a book would allow me to get my story to the public's collective common sense. This is America, right?

It didn't take me long to realize that I couldn't finish the semester. Innocent or not, I would be recognized and probably feared, sitting there in class. Uncomfortable. I've had enough of those vibes already. And heck, what do I care about school. I'm a convicted felon.

Chapter 10   Prison

My girlfriend Krissy and I had been on and off since my arrest.
However, we were married the previous year on December 8, 1991. The
one-year anniversary would turn out to be my sentencing date in 1992.
We were expecting this mistake to go away. We had sort of broken up
by the time my trial came around, so really that was kind of good for
both of us. Just to not have to deal with heartbreak too, as I go away to
prison.

On December 8, 1992, I was formally sentenced to fifteen years and
turned over to the custody of the sheriff. This date had come up ten
years earlier too. December 8, 1982, was the day of the murder of
Debbie Carter, the girl in Ada in John Grisham's book, *THE
INNOCENT MAN*.

All of my thoughts and fears were with me this day as I lost my
freedom. I didn't know how I would ever prove my innocence.
Although depressed, I would never take my own life or try to escape. I
just wanted to do my time and carry on a normal life when I was
released. If I left the country or escaped, I might never see my son or
family again.

My dad went with me as I turned myself in to the Sherriff's office.
Fortunately, one of the deputies knew me and gave me a bunk up front
as a trustee. Was relieved about that. Certainly, better than a bunk in the
bullpen as before.

Only she and I really knew that I was truly innocent, but my mother
and father were there, ready to fight for me, ready to continue to support
and love me. They were hurt too, perhaps more than I.

I asked my father when he left, to bring me a journal to record my
days. Dad was a big journal keeper. I was just sure that I needed to keep
track of this part of my life.

So, the rest of the book is a little different. The actual (for the most
part) journal entries over the years, help me tell you the rest of the story
of my days in prison and fighting with my appeal. I sort of jump around,
explaining or adding to a journal entry, summarizing at each year end,

and just mixing in with the journal entries, but I think its manageable. Thank you.

Hope you can relate to some of the personal, human details as similar to your own, and I believe the actual journal entries help express the emotions of the times.

Wednesday, December 16, 1992

I talked to Mom and Dad. The Barker's wrote (or called) and said good things. Mick Cowan sent Mom a gift. That means so much to me, and it touches the bottom of my heart. I'm doing pretty well, no real depression. I wrote Unsolved Mysteries yesterday. I hope for the best. I miss Josh.

Saturday, December 19, 1992

Dad got the report from the handwriting expert. He's still working on getting everything together. Someone brought a bunch of chocolate chip cookies to Mom and Dad and they brought them here. Meatballs for dinner tonight. I've broken off contact with Krissy, easier on my heart. Talked to Josh. He sounds older. I miss him.

Wednesday, December 23, 1992

Merry Christmas! Today has been screwed up already and its only 10:00 am. Our hotheaded cook is the most racist, violent, hot-tempered man I've ever met. I think he might kill someone someday. If I can deal with him, I can deal with anyone.

A guy I used to know came in last night and he's going to try to help me. He played football for ECU and has an older teammate who is a lawyer.

I've been doing pretty well. I don't allow myself to get depressed or think about the future. I just try to stay stress free.

I made a little Christmas present for Josh (some candy and a card). I miss him. God help me in this case.

I talked to Bob Gray today. He told me what I already know, that I must show remorse and admit to doing it in order to gain an early release. Oh well.

Friday, January 8, 1993

Today was my court date in OKC to revoke my probation on the larceny charge. I haven't found out yet what my sentence is, but I didn't have to appear so maybe it went well.

My lawyer didn't even know that my court date was today when we called him Monday. Typical of him. I think every day about how lame a job he did in my trial. We presented nothing and never put the true story (all we knew) in the juror's minds. Oh well.

Krissy and Josh came to see me Wednesday. She loves me and feels for me. I've gotten over her completely. I still think about her and her new relationship but there is no pain anymore.

Monday, January 11, 1993

I talked to Dad today and he said George had arranged to get a concurrent sentence on the OKC charge. Good news, I guess.

I found out that I go to Lexington on January 21st. Good news or bad news? I still have delusions of the girl calling the DA and confessing. Sometimes when someone comes in the jail, I dream that they release me and tell me that the girl felt guilty and admitted to her crime against me.

Last night a guy in one of the solitary cells fell off of the top bunk and busted his teeth out. I woke up when he hit the floor, wondering what the loud noise was. Ouch!

Sunday I'll be 26 years old.

Tuesday, January 19, 1993

Not much change here. My 26th birthday was Sunday. Mom and Dad came to visit. They seem to be having a harder time with this than me. They are worried about sexual assaults in prison. Too much TV.

Krissy and Josh came also but came late so I only got ten minutes with them. Josh pulls the love from my heart. I hope he is doing Okay. Krissy looked pretty and smelled good.

I wrote a long letter to Rita last week and mailed it to Pam to try and mail. I hope she receives it.

My days at the Pontotoc County jail were numbered now. I would leave Thursday. Heck, I was ready to get to prison and its relatively wide-open spaces compared with this jail. I missed the sun.

I thought about how people must think the same thing when they can't make bail. That must be a prime tactic for the district attorney getting prisoners to accept plea bargains. The longer you are in here, the more likely you are to accept a plea bargain just to get out of here.

My days were spent doing trustee duties, reading and watching television. The laundry room had a bar where I would do pull-ups. I was practicing self-defense tactics to prepare for any fights I may have to endure. I had always heard that you would be tested at first. I needed to be in decent shape.

One prisoner there, Shawn, was another one besides the cook that I kept my eyes on. He was in for stabbing someone. Tried to kill him. Just plain mean.

He was big and strong too, about six foot two and muscular. Eyes as green as grass. One day he walked into the laundry room and shut the door as I was doing my trustee duties, the laundry. I was poised and ready, not knowing what to expect. He sat on the dryer and lit a joint.

"You smoke?"

"Yeah, but I'm laying off so I can pass a UA when I get to Lexington."

I felt him lose trust in me, thinking I was a square. He looked me in the eye, sizing me up.

"Screw them and their UA. Can you hold your mud?" He was asking if I could keep my mouth shut about the weed. I looked him in the eye and said I would.

"So, you raped some gal, huh?" Now he was fronting me up, testing my reaction, watching me.

"Believe it or not, I'm innocent. If I had done it, I would have admitted it and taken the plea bargain long ago. That's just how it is."

I talked with him about some of the details as he listened and smoked his joint. We talked more about the people we knew and then he went his own way, having a little more respect for me knowing that I claimed innocence and, moreover, went to trial to prove it.

Thursday, January 21, 1993

I arrived at Lexington Assessment and Reception Center (LARC) today at about 1:30 pm. I got my head completely shaved into a burr. The cells are rather bare, but c'est la vie. There are some strange looking people here. My roommate however, is a good person. I hope I get out of here ASAP.

Wednesday, January 27, 1993

Just got a tetanus shot, TB test and dental exam. Dentist said I have good teeth. I got my number last night, #162066. This place really sucks. I called home last night and Dad said the sex offender program is one year and there is a waiting list. Hopefully I get in ASAP. What a nightmare.

Thursday, February 4, 1993

Well, I may leave today but I guess I'll know within a couple of hours. I'm kind of nervous knowing that I'm going to a medium security prison, but I guess I'll feel more comfortable when I get there.

That lady who classified me yesterday is a real snot. She must really have a sorry life. She has to get her self-esteem from talking tough and disrespectful to prisoners.

My roommate finally left on Tuesday. He spent twenty-seven days here. He said there is a chance his case may be overturned. I gave him Mom's address to write if it does.

One guy in here got eight life sentences, two without parole. He said he had 384 pounds of marijuana, $18,000 and some guns. He said only 304 pounds and $10,000 were turned in, and a few guns were missing. That's about par for the course. Hope I see Josh soon. Later.

Thursday, February 11, 1993

I saw a young man have a seizure last night. It was a very strange thing. I had a very weird feeling in my stomach. It's a good thing that we knew what to do, because the guards didn't help much. I can understand how people long ago thought the devil caused these. The feeling I got watching it was scary and strange.

Karla Fischer wrote me a letter saying that Ginny Simone from Channel 4 wanted to talk to me about my case. Karla is cool! She is a good one and cares about my ordeal. I'll try to call Ms. Simone tonight but I won't say much over the phone.

Mom and Dad say Josh is very quiet. I hope he's just going thru a phase. Josh is going to make it. I know he will because I will be his driving force and inspiration. He is only thirty-three months old, just a pup.

Tuesday, February 16, 1993

I moved to Joseph Harp last Friday. The first movie I watched was *The Outlaw Josey Wales*, one of my favorites. *Chitty, Chitty, Bang-Bang* came on after it.

It's not bad here at all. My cellmate is an eye doctor who was convicted of trying to have his ex-wife murdered for abusing his son. He got 45 years. It is an easy description in manner and looks for Doc: (actor) Harrison Ford.

Food is about the same, but plentiful. Today I got my property and tomorrow is orientation. I had good visits on Saturday and Monday. Josh is a different boy around Mom and Dad. He is so shy. He is so outgoing around Krissy.

*

I spent twenty-two days in the LARC. I was transported up the road to Joseph Harp Correctional Center on Friday, February 12, 1993. My time had been spent reading the Old Testament and thinking. I was delighted to see the Dallas Cowboys win the Super Bowl. We used to have season tickets. I quit smoking cigarettes that day also (wouldn't last).

I was surprised to see how Joseph Harp looked. Maybe I was expecting rows of cells like in *Escape from Alcatraz*. These were more like dorm rooms, except smaller.

There were inmates of all types, some the stereotypical tattooed cons but others looking like anything but criminals. My friend "Church" was here, on E-unit, the sex offender unit.

A friend of ours was familiar with the sex offender unit at Joseph Harp. He had been on the Board of Corrections. When I was at LARC, I was told by him to try to get to Joseph Harp to take the one-year program. I was thinking a couple of meetings a week or something. Then it was believed that I could make parole soon after that.

Again, I had to sell my soul to get to Harp. On the form at LARC to request the sex offender program I wrote, "raped an adult woman" on the question about my crime. You had to admit to it, especially in the classification review by that case manager lady, and she had to make sure I was classified correctly. Maybe I should forgive here. Does it matter now anyway?

When I was on E-unit, every Wednesday the whole unit had like a Sex Offender Anonymous meeting, where everyone introduced themselves like at an AA meeting (Matthew, alcoholic). But you say your name and then the crime or "what you were". One guy seemed to take half an hour to list all his crimes, charges, etc. From day one, at that meeting, I always just said, "Matthew, rape." Just say the name, say the charge.

On the bus ride from LARC to Joseph Harp Correctional Center, which is just down the road, I remember a Vince Gill song playing on the bus radio: "Don't let our love start slipping away". I was put in a holding cell with one other man, a 50-year-old black man. He got his time was for selling heroin. He was friendly. We stood up on the bunk and looked out of the small window onto the yard.

Within an hour, I went to B-unit. My first cell was with the doctor on B-unit, and then I moved to D-unit. I was happy to be able to run and lift weights. There was a nice running track. Another advantage of Joseph Harp was the talkback TV college program. My plan was to continue my education, stay in shape and stay off of pot so I wouldn't get positive UA's (urine analysis).

The OKC larceny charge was dropped (wouldn't last) for the State's failure to appear at the hearing.

I moved from B-unit to D-unit, which is for people with special needs: Mentally retarded, illiterate, non-English speakers and inmates on psychosomatic drugs. My roommate on D-unit was serving a life sentence for stabbing and killing someone during a manic episode. He was a little strange. He would listen to music and look out the window all day and most of the night, especially on nights with lightning and storms. The majority of the people were on drugs to control their imbalances.

I was moved to E-unit (sex offender unit) on Friday, February 26. I was very much on my guard. I met quite a few inmates that day as my roommate introduced me to a lot of people. I noticed that a good majority of the people I met that day had blue eyes. My roommate is a large (fat) man with blue eyes. One of his eyes is closed halfway and reminds me of a childhood friend. I still don't know what crime he is here for.

The serial rapist from OKC, William Coakley, is here. The lawyer Carroll Gregg is here. Two brothers from Tulsa, the Burgers, supposedly the "Southside Stalkers" are here. Even though many of these people have severe sexual problems, this unit is the cleanest, quietest and most mature of all. Ninety percent of the people are well mannered and polite.

Friday night "Kenny" came to orientate me about the unit and program. He eventually told me that he is a child molester and has over fifty victims. I hate to say it, but I would kill him if he even looked at my child in the wrong way. He makes me sick.

A lot of the people express a noticeable weakness of self-confidence and esteem. I would categorize the people as either mean cold-blooded rapists/molesters or weak, powerless men envious of women. Some are here for statutory rape (Church) and I believe some men are probably innocent as I am.

Last night this big fat guy with the personality of a child came by my cell and knocked. He said he was just looking for something to do. He came in and I ignored him. After about ten seconds he realized I didn't want him around and he said he was sorry for bothering me and left. I think he's gay and I want nothing to do with him.

Friday, March 12, 1993

Today I had a meeting with three counselors called an intake. I had planned on what to say in order to stay here, but I ended up telling them I was not guilty and they said they would ship me. They said they would give me a couple of days to think about it.

About two hours later (after talking with Church) I had another meeting scheduled and said I was in denial and my ego got in the way. I will get to stay.

I hope to finish Vo-Tech (eight months long), which I should start within a month, before I am asked to begin the program. At that point I will try to get into the Lifeline drug program on C-unit. There is absolutely no way I can go through this sexual program by faking it.

I received my narrative and transcripts Tuesday. I have to add a few things and get the girl's interview from George before I send it off to Channel 4. I talked to Stormy (the girl I was seeing that broke Krissy and I up) yesterday. She was glad to hear from me. I wish I could get a hold of Teri. I'm worried about her.

Sunday, March 21, 1993

Dad went to an OKC hospital for something wrong with his stomach. I don't know any more than that. I was just thinking. I had just talked to a man who is religious and my attitude of God turning his back on me came through, but in reality, maybe unconsciously, I still try to let God run my life and let things fall where they may.

I think a lot about the day I get out and where I'll find work. Most of my thoughts are about work and grasping and holding on to good ideas. I have confidence in my own ideas, judgment and intelligence to succeed in whatever I do even though it will take more work and dedication than I can imagine right now.

I wonder why this has happened to me and what purpose it will serve in future events.

Saturday, April 24, 1993

I just watched the sun set out the west window. It reminds me of being at the Cloister's in Florida. The counselors had everyone go out on the dock and not say a word while the sun set. It was and is a very relaxing and fulfilling experience, very serene.

I have so many thoughts and ideas coming and going. I think up a handful of poems every day about life and looking at life from inside of a prison.

"Smoke" is gone, lowering my stress level. Smoke was a black man who worked in the unit serving line with me. We didn't get along from the start, and I imagined many times how I would whip him in a fight, but of course I didn't want to fight if I didn't have to, because I would lose good time if caught.

Thursday, May 13, 1993

I moved in with Church today. He is from Ada. I feel very good about the move. We talk a lot and are friends, not just cellmates. It's good to get away from Lee. I lived in my own world in that cell.

Today was a wonderful day, clear skies and seventy-five. I'm going to call Dad and talk to Josh. Mom is at Special Olympics. I started Vo-Tech May 3rd. It is going well. I aced the math test and the instructor said that my reading test score was the highest score he had seen and higher than he got and he has a master's degree! It made me feel good. I got my IRS check in and will get my guitar soon!

*

Church was in the Pontotoc County jail when I was, after my arrest. We had a good friendship. He is part Mexican, and looks sort of like the actor Andy Garcia.

Tuesday, May 18, 1993

Well today is Josh's birthday. Three years old! I love that boy very much and think of him many times every day. It hurts to think too much about him and how I'm not there for him, so I cut my thoughts short in order to stay emotionally stable.

I think about Krissy a lot too and I love her. I feel that she will soon stop corresponding with me and coming to see me. She has her own life to live and when someone is in jail, they're really in another world. It's easy to forget and slip away.

I'm not afraid of being in here a long time. I'm going to better myself while I'm here and I can't speed up the time. But look out when I'm released!

I obtained my public defender yesterday and I sent a reply to him today. His name is Thomas Purcell and God help him on my appeal.

Also, today I sent a copy of my 1992 tax return to the federal IRS investigator who took it last week. I am ready for my money.

Saturday night, May 22, 1993

I just thought I would write. I'm outside; it's about 11:00 pm. I sat in the room most of the night listening to music and thinking. I think about all different kinds of things, from the days with Krissy to my growing up days to Josh and my being in here.

I sometimes feel so angry for being in here on this crime that I get manic and have to mentally calm down. I get depressed when I have visits. Dad was telling me in the county jail that he wanted to have me out by next Christmas. Now he's talking of my pre-parole date in September 1996, but I'm thinking of having our friend get me up in two or two and a half years. I feel helpless with no one on the outside working for me. I wish God could put some love in that girl's heart. The IRS agent OK'd my check and I should get it Monday.

Tuesday, June 8, 1993

I watched *DayOne* on ABC last night. It told about some guys who were framed for something that they were totally innocent of. One guy who had very good character and didn't do drugs said he knew he didn't do it but was confused and thought maybe he had a split personality and his other half did it. Sounds familiar! I hope to use this to my advantage someday in showing that other people can relate to my story.

I got *The Dreams of Ada* today thru interlibrary loan. I read the first few chapters. I was feeling uptight tonight anyway and couldn't sleep. Every so often that happens and I get really isolated and my mind goes somewhere else. I think it's a combination of depression, loneliness, anger, and being sick of prison.

I was just trying to go to sleep and I remembered laying in a strange bed and thinking like this when I was in treatment in Florida in 1988-89. I was in treatment and halfway houses for nine months total! That seemed like so long and it really was. Now as I lay here, I can't see daylight for three to five years and it blows my mind!

Reality sunk in about March that I was going to be in prison awhile, but the whole incident happening to **me** still is bewildering. I hope to have the answer or the truth to this matter clearly and completely discovered one of these days.

God bless Josh, my flesh and blood, my son, to whom I am only a weekend visit or phone call. Daddy! Why? When? How? I know he must think.

Krissy, Matt, Josh: Aug. 1993

July 29, 1993

Well, there's not a whole lot to write about. It is very hot here at Joseph Harp. It was 105 degrees today! And humid too. I'm working on getting over to C-unit before the end of the year. I am going to see if our friend can help. I am also going to see if Bob Peed can help me with a smooth transition.

I miss my son, and Krissy too, but I'm doing fine. I'm gaining some muscle, mainly in my shoulders.

August 18, 1993

Still hot here. It has been 100 degrees for the past two weeks. I am moving to C-unit around September 1st. I had a hard time today. I am letting prison get to me a little. It is hard not to have a bad day every now and then and think about outside. I think about sweet little Krissy. I am really missing Josh. He is in another world than I am. Tod Carter was found dead this weekend. I feel for the family. Well, I wish I were out of here. I need some love.

September 28, 1993

Well today went pretty well. Almost. I learned that I'm next in line to go to C-unit and I am anxious to move. At about 5:15 pm I got word that I have a court appearance in OKC tomorrow. I guess they have re-filed the larceny charge.

I leave tomorrow at 7:30 am to face my fate. I of course hope for the best. It scares me though to think of the possibility of more time added on to this bogus fifteen. Oh well.

*

I was placed in a single cell in the new OKC county jail and was there for two weeks. Days were spent playing cards in the common area with three other kids that couldn't have been eighteen. One of them, in fact the frailest looking one, was charged with first-degree murder of an acquaintance. Books were also important. My dad in fact dropped off some magazines and books for me.

I almost made a big mistake one afternoon by standing up for a small white kid, when some blacks traded candy bars but kept his. I got the candy bar for the kid with just a pleasant request, but tension was evident afterward. I would have been in big trouble had a fight started.

A visit across town one day to the fourth floor of the ancient county jail resulted in a five-year sentence for attempted larceny, which would run concurrently. There was a large holding cell like area, with multiple cells and area of bunks where we waited for court. Well, there was an air conditioner vent just blasting cold air, and there were no blankets. Everyone was wrapping the green mattresses around them, but that was minimally effective. Pretty sure we were in there for a few hours. Certainly, no guards bringing blankets.

It was so cold in this old jail that when I was taken in for the plea bargain, I was shivering the whole time, waiting for my case to be called. There were probably 10-12 inmates and cases. They had a public defender there, just to assist with the process; and I talked with him about it, as he watched me shiver. Afterwards, we were back at the main county jail. I'm sure I was hypothermic in that courtroom.

When I was returned to Joseph Harp, I was given a bunk on C-unit where I would participate in the Lifeline drug program. I lost about ten pounds while in the OKC county jail. They've got to keep up the plea bargains, I guess.

The first night back I was moved in with a kid named Jason Davis. Jason had been in for second-degree murder since he was sixteen. He was now twenty-two but would get out soon. He was a neat kid and a respected convict. We talked a lot that first night. He was adopted as I was. It was funny to hear and feel his honesty when he thought about and anticipated his first woman. Just a few weeks later Jason died.

He and a black guy had gotten into an argument over a volleyball call, talking smack to each other and preparing for a fight afterwards. They went to the back "yard" to fight. The black guy went for the kill, and Jason got hit in the neck. For a couple of weeks after that, he was down and didn't feel well. When he finally decided to go to the hospital, an infection that began in the throat area had spread into the chest cavity. He died soon after arriving at the hospital. Never got to express his love for a woman. God bless his soul.

Christmas Night, 1993

Today really didn't seem like Christmas. The emotion just wasn't there. It seemed we built up for a month with lights and painting the units and all, and now it's just over. It was depressing but I still had a good day.

I talked to Benny and Lefty in the chapel. They were both nice.

I got my legal briefs back this week and hope for the best. I'm going to write the story about Kenny Boutwell tomorrow.

*

My first year had been interesting. Not knowing what to expect, I went in with a sort of gladiator mentality, which most people do. That first year I almost got into three fights. "Smoke" was a guy on E-unit that I worked with on the serving line until I started Vo-Tech. He just liked to push my buttons and piss me off. I must have dreamed a dozen times of how I would whip him (he'd probably killed me), but we never got to that point. The other two times had been on the softball field, just regular arguments between cons trying to act tough (me included).

I played softball for an E-unit team that summer. Of course, everyone knew that E-unit was the sex offender's unit. Many of the convicts were horribly tough on some of the guys, the weaker ones. I never had any problem in that respect.

I typed my narrative on a word processor in the library early in 1993. I had no proof other than the craziness of the evidence at this point but needed to be able to communicate my truth. From the very start after my conviction, I was determined to get my story to the public through some media. I knew the public's common sense would help me, either by pressuring the courts in some way or having an individual, "champion" my cause.

Church helped me adjust during my first year. His best friends were the Burger boys; both smart, funny and personable. Both insisted that the real "southside stalker" was their cousin and that they just made bad decisions in going along with him on a single night. Their cousin was shot and killed by the Tulsa police while robbing a Wendy's before the Burger boys' arrest.

In a fenced-in section right across from E-unit was "fantasy island", the mental illness unit. While D-unit was also mentally ill, this unit was for the unmanageable and such. They had four-point restraint beds and one man told me his experience in being strapped down for a couple of days. If you weren't nuts before that, you would run the risk of being insane if locked down like that for too many days.

Joseph Harp had many programs that weren't found at other prisons. I joined the drama club and had a great time preparing and putting on plays over the next couple of years. We traveled to Mabel Bassett prison once and put on Stalag 17 for the women. I played one of the lead roles, as Sefton.

Joseph Harp was at its peak as a nationally recognized "progressive" prison. It was geared toward positive thinking, programs, privileges and working hard to improve oneself. Warden Jack Cowley was its inspiration. I was fortunate for the synergy of this prison with my own focused determination.

Needless to say, the seven months spent on E-unit were insightful. I soon learned that the program itself was about 30 months long and you spent twenty-four hours a day admitting and working on your criminal sexual behavior. I didn't have any to admit to that I knew of. Maybe that is the wrong choice of words. I remembered everything that **actually happened** and even today it still reverberates from that space-time web of a couple of hours on March 17, 1991. Its energy is forever there. Illusions have no place to call home.

I did hear a lot of sickening stories and there were some really disturbed people there, but there were also some gentlemen who deserved to be given a second chance in society, and probably one or two who were completely innocent.

Joseph Harp was a haven for the most publicized molesters and sex offenders. E-unit was isolated from the other units and no doubt saved lives within the prison system. Some men would never leave the unit, as food at this time was served in each unit's private dining hall.

I know that rape charges are very dangerous and powerful tools that can be used by society to destroy the very soul of a man and his family.

I was obviously very humiliated to be on this unit but I kind of created a "don't give a hoot what other people think" attitude because I knew in my heart what the truth was. I had some earlier experience with this attitude anyway in Ada.

Chapter 11   New evidence!

I had done well staying off of pot for the first year, until I moved to C-unit to take the Lifeline drug program. There were plenty of drugs here, but there were also people totally involved in working themselves away from drugs, and learning why they did drugs in the first place.

After the one night in Jason's cell, I moved upstairs with a Hispanic for a couple of months. He had a marijuana connection and would light up two or three times a day. I couldn't resist. I love Marlboro reds and good bud. God help me, I would think. I had been UA'd only once, in March of 1993 when I lived with Lee and was not smoking pot. Even after quitting smoking cigarettes on Super Bowl Sunday, I picked them up again the first night at JHCC, watching *The Outlaw Josey Wales* with Doc, then quit again soon after, then started back in July.

The Hispanic also made some "homebrew" out of peaches, sugar, and yeast obtained from bread rolls. After a week, it was ready and we drank a half-gallon between us and smoked a couple of caps. "Caps" are a Chapstick cap worth of pot. That much was about eight dollars, usually paid in Marlboro or other name brand cigarettes. I began to look for another cell and moved after we about came to blows one night. We maintained respect for one another but our energies just clashed.

My public defender filed my direct appeal in December 1993. I had been spending a lot of time in the law library during the year, trying to understand the legal specifics of criminal law, and searching for a solution.

I moved into another cell in January of 1994. My cellmate Robert was blond-headed and we got along well. He was full of youthful energy and only had a short sentence. He hustled a living out of the kitchen; we sold hamburger sandwiches on the unit at night for a while. I had begun the Lifeline program in October, and was now doing a good job staying away from pot. I got a job as an inventory clerk at the Modular Furniture factory in January. On my twenty-seventh birthday, there was quite a stir in Northridge, California (January 17th).

My mother, father, Krissy and Josh would visit about every two or three weeks. My pastor Bill would come to see me, as would members of Krissy's family. There were food visits allowed at JHCC, so these were good therapeutic visits and the visiting yard was spacious.

The move to C-unit had been a breath of fresh air and was a good change for me. There were guys that I could relate to, similar in background, education and interests. I made quite a few friends and had a lot of activities: softball, running, lifting, Lifeline meetings and classes, drama club twice a week, work, walking the track with my friend James. James was forty-four, played a classical guitar, and a self-professed "cocksman" with the ladies. The guy got sixty years for being entrapped into buying 1.5 pounds of marijuana. His mistake: he chose to claim entrapment, and took it to trial. Jury gave him 60 years.

Larry was an artist I met in Vo-Tech class when I came back from the Oklahoma County jail to finish Vo-tech in December 1993. He carved tattoos, but I was not really with that, and knew I would be the last to ever have one. Larry taught himself the craft in prison and I appreciated his work, which included a lot of colors and deep psychological cartoons and characters. He also was an interesting fellow anyway, a Basque-American with salt and peppered hair, kind of a cross between George Clooney and Billy Bob Thornton.

One guy had Larry cut a green dragon on his stomach. It scared me when thoughts of me getting a tattoo entered my mind. A Skoal can size peace sign on my upper back using that green color began to formulate in my mind.

I finally decided on a more sentimental peace sign, the one with the American flag within, that was popular in the late 1960's and 1970's. In fact, the Thompson family put a peace sign in Christmas lights on top of their house in 1975.

He estimated it would take two hours. We met on the unit and headed for his cell. One of the inmates on the unit, a young kid, said something to Larry as he walked past, admiring and praising Larry.

"Fans. Gotta luv em." He joked. "But Matthew, I'm only as good as my next tattoo." He said that with conviction. How true when placing a permanent mark on a body. That was a good philosophy. Concentrate on the now. The now creates the future.

With a hair dryer motor, scotch tape, wires, a brand-new unwound bass string that I supplied, cut and sharpened for a needle, a touch of mechanical engineering to create a rapid up and down motion with the needle, the boiled and bleached toothpaste cap holders of the colors, and his coffee, cigarettes and sense of humor, he carved his masterpiece into me.

Saturday, June 4, 1994

Krissy came up again Memorial Day, May 30th. She had just got back from Palm Springs. She had a great time and met some different and interesting people. Good for her. She said Kyle moved out and that she was wanting to be by herself for a while. I wish her only good, positive and progressive things. I wrote her a letter last night about my week.

I talked to Ms. Johnson about being a truck rider (prison job) and she basically told me she wouldn't recommend me because I've got a rape conviction and haven't taken the E-unit program. It pissed me off and I told her she was correct when she said she didn't know the facts of my case. After a few hours I realized it was more of a political, Joseph Harp, DOC thing.

I start my humanities class Monday. I'm not sure if Pell Grant will be available to prisoners in the fall. I guess I'll know then.

Dad is going to copy my transcripts so I can begin to work on my post-conviction assuming the direct appeal is affirmed. I need some relief! A five-year time cut would be bearable.

I've given up on writing the news magazines. I've gotten no reply in the year that I've been writing. My fifteen years would seem only a minor inconvenience to them anyway.

These days are really hard on a man trying to get out of prison. The whole nation is really mad at criminals. The "three strikes you're out" law and the truth-in-sentencing law they are trying to get passed here. The public really has a distorted view of who prisoners really are and the prison world. They think violent criminals do one or two years on a twenty-year sentence. Wrong! The very earliest a person could discharge a violent twenty would be eight years.

Wednesday, June 15, 1994

A Presbyterian minister was killed at Granite. He was convicted of child molestation. He must have said the wrong thing to somebody. He should have come to Harp.

*

Monday, July 11, 1994

Today I received "the letter" from a lawyer in Massachusetts representing a man accused of raping Rita. He wants to talk to me because he believes his client is innocent. I have high hopes for this development. I still can't believe it actually happened.

*

It seemed like any other Monday since I had been in. I was walking after work to get my mail with other inmates. Was talking with Randy, a law clerk. Randy had a life sentence, been in over fifteen years, and after years of fights, conflicts with staff, and being a "convict", had turned himself around a few years earlier with the help of exercise, clean living and the Bible. Were he not in prison, I could picture him as a trout-fishing guide or something of the sort. I had been telling him about my case and he was going to take a look at my transcripts to see if he could find anything to help. We also talked about nutrition and running. He jogged on the track, a long way, almost every day, in his prison issue brogan boots.

"I'll talk to you later, Randy." I said, turning to get in line for mail at the mail window. The mail lady, Rose, knew one thousand inmates by face.

"Matthew, was your name marked for legal mail?"

"No, just regular mail."

"It seems like I remember you having legal mail. Let's see. Yes."

She found that I did have legal mail but it had not been marked on the mail list. I stood wondering a hundred miles an hour while she opened the mail and prepared the book for me to sign. Surely my appeal has not been heard already. I always get nervous when I get legal mail.

After checking the letter for a bomb, she laid the letter face up before me and placed the "sign here for legal mail" book by my right hand. My stomach went into cartwheels when I saw that the return address for the attorney was Massachusetts. Great! She is suing me now or something (we knew she lived in MA).

I thanked Rose, took my mail and began walking, fishing the letter out of the envelope and preparing to read it. I took a deep breath, gaining some patience and tolerance for more persecution. The words paralyzed me as I read them. I had been in for 19 months.

*

July 8, 1994

Dear Mr. Thompson,

I have learned through investigation that you are serving a 15-year sentence for the "alleged rape" of Rita Gasteau.

Currently, I represent an individual who has also been accused of committing crimes against Rita Gasteau. My investigation has revealed that she is not truthful concerning the allegations made in Massachusetts.

I would like to speak with you concerning Rita Gasteau. Please contact my office by calling collect at your earliest convenience.

I have attempted to speak with Attorney Butner concerning this matter and hope he will return my telephone calls in the near future.

Thank you for your anticipated cooperation in this matter.

Very truly yours,
John W. Brien

*

As I read the letter, my whole body started to tingle as my nervous system was injected with the sweet flow of joy and hope. And some validation too, you know? Like, "Yeah, I told y'all from the start…".

This was unbelievable, in itself! GOOD news, for a change. Certainly, finding this information and continuing with more investigation from here, was monumental to me as a person, being able to say, "Here, here is the beginning, of showing, that I'm innocent of this crime". Thus began the quest with newly discovered evidence, to "race it around"[1].

I almost couldn't move as I reread and reread the letter. Then I know I yelled, "Yes", or something, right there! Man, what a moment.

I just **knew** that the girl was crazy or something! Randy was talking with someone by the law library. Going a million miles an hour, I motioned to him and ran to show him the letter.

Immediately I went to the unit and called my dad. He called my public defender and the attorney in Massachusetts. I called Pam and told her the good news. I have received a little hope now of being able to clear my name.

Things have certainly changed for the better. How lucky I am for this to have occurred. Before today, I was the only one who really believed in me. Now I am not alone anymore. See, she has lied again!

Our family had been the "prayer family of the week" at our church in Ada. Maybe some were answered? On Sunday I had seen a snow-white dove as I walked to the unit. It was in the middle of the day, not at sunrise or sunset or anything spectacular, but I had remarked to myself at its beauty.

What a day for me. The letter arrived on a Monday. It was Monday, July 11, 1994. I wrote the attorney in MA back, in a few days:

*

July 15, 1994

Mr. Brien,

I cannot gather the words to describe my emotions when I received your letter. I have real hope of justice now.

I am thinking about sending you a copy of a narrative that I wrote about this situation. I hand wrote it the day before my sentencing date and refined and typed it when I came to prison. It explains my thoughts and feelings about the allegations and it came straight from my heart.

---

[1] Lyrics from Foo Fighters song, HERO.

On my word as a gentleman, I tell you I absolutely did not rape Rita Gasteau and my story is the complete and 100% truth.

People in backasswards Oklahoma think in very simple terms and this case is a handful of many different complexities that eventually led to my being convicted.   I have high hopes for the future and I thank you from the bottom of my heart.

Sincerely, Matthew Thompson

Friday, July 15, 1994

We found out from the lawyer in Massachusetts some of the facts about the allegations. She has accused her ex-husband (Rick) of breaking into her home and raping her twice. She also accused him of raping their seven-year-old son. This whole situation seems to revolve around their separation and his wanting custody of the children (a twelve-year-old girl and the boy). They want to see the results from the lie detector tests I took and are planning on sending a man down to give me another one. My public defender has said things look pretty good. Tomorrow is the Gospel Fest, Krissy and Josh will be up.

*

Rita has accused her ex-husband of raping and beating her. She said he broke into her apartment on two occasions, threatened her with a knife, cut her shirt with the knife and threatened to kill her. Sounds familiar!

The ex has passed a lie detector test on two occasions and has witnesses to his whereabouts on at least one of the nights in question. Right after he passed these polygraph tests, she brought the allegation that he also molested their seven-year-old son.

The attorney gives us all that he has at this time. He provides us with affidavits from six people who lived in the same apartment complex as Rita which describe her unusual behavior, a police incident report on one of the nights Rita accused him, and an arrest report of Rita for disorderly conduct.

As I review each piece of evidence, I'm just struck with the intensity of it all. I feel fortunate, and comforted by the new evidence. What if it

151

were a murder case instead and I had a life sentence or were on death row?

I am reinvigorated as I read these amazing documents. They're unbelievable, surreal even to me. Stephen King couldn't outdo this. Truth is stranger than fiction. I began to have the "anticipation" again when I would hear the rattle of keys, thinking they're coming to let me go home.

Massachusetts Affidavits

#1 - Joanne

Interviewed at 4:15 pm on September 7, 1994 (by this investigator) while she was cutting hedges in front of 200 Parker St., Lawrence (MA) where she resides and where she is the property manager. She declined to sign a voluntary statement form, saying she did not want to get involved with anything concerning Rita Gasteau. But she told this investigator:

"She's a whore, a junkie and an alcoholic and I don't want to have anything to do with her. Right after she moved in, she said her husband shot her. Her left leg was bandaged. I felt bad for her. I loaned her a cane. The next day she went down the stairs in high heels, no bandage, no cane. She's a prostitute. She jumped from one guy's room here to another in here. I could see her from the laundry-mat across the street (where Joanne works) when she came home from Wendy's in her uniform. She'd go right down the street to the package store without changing her uniform and not go back to work."

She could not recall the dates when Rita moved in and moved out.

The other five did sign affidavits for the investigator:

#2 - Gary

On July 3, 1994, while in the hall outside Rita's door, I heard a cat cry. I went into the bathroom and saw a cat in the toilet-bowl with blood in it. I called Ray. He called the police. They said no one was available. The cat was Rita's pet. It was black. Later I heard Ed say he took the cat out of the bowl. He said it to me. Photos were taken of the cat and the hallway. There was writing on the hallway wall. It looked like blood. When Rita came back home, close to dark, she was freaking out. She said she didn't know who Ed was. I called the ambulance. The police came and she was yelling that her ex-husband raped her little boy. She freaked out for a half hour and when the ambulance and police took off, she went upstairs. She refused to go to the hospital. Later that night she claimed her husband had a key to get into this building. On July 8, 1994 Rita showed Ray and I a newspaper clipping. On it in pencil was a threat of some kind, written in pencil. She said it had been left in her mailbox. She said, "Rick did this. He's coming for me."

#3 - Arline
On July 3, a Sunday, about two o'clock I was in my apartment on the first floor, Apt. #2. A woman I know only as Cindy knocked on my door and said Rita needed an ambulance because her husband beat her up. I hadn't heard anything from upstairs. I saw Rita come down, holding her stomach. There was blood on her white blouse. I had already called the ambulance. She walked down the street to the package store. She had a bag the size of two six-packs. She went back upstairs. She had gone to the package store as the ambulance was coming. I told the ambulance crew, "There she goes right there." She just kept going and they left. They only man I ever saw her with was Eddie.

#4 - Elaine
On July 3, 1994 I was in the yard in the evening when Rita came walking up the alley with a beer can in her hand. It was Budweiser. She was crying and saying Rick had beaten her up. I saw her put the beer can inside her shorts, red ones. She was flipping out. She said her husband had shoved the beer can up her front. Ed, her boyfriend, removed the beer can and threw it over the fence. Ray called the police and she mouthed off to the cops.

On July 8, I went to Daigle's lounge about 10:30-11:00 (pm). When I went in, she was dancing up close to a Jamaican named John. She was coming on to him and he was trying to push her away. She was intoxicated; could hardly stand up. I sat at a table with two friends. She sat nearby. A man brought her over a bottle of Budweiser, touched her on the shoulder and was trying to get her attention. She flipped out. She grabbed me and said, "That's my husband. That's Rick. Get him away from me." The guy didn't seem to know what was happening. I grabbed him by the shirt and he said, "I don't even know her." Five or ten minutes later, Rita and I left. She said, "Please stick up for me, that wasn't Rick." We walked up Broadway. At the Windsor House, she went into the doorway, pulled her pants down and urinated. That's when she asked me to stick up for her. A friend saw me standing there and came over to walk us home. My mother and stepfather were in the yard. My Mom asked what happened. I told her that Rick had beaten her up. Then I went back to Daigle's. The next morning, I came downstairs to talk with my mother and Ray. I told them I had told them a bunch of lies. That it wasn't true about her husband. Ray called Rita's boyfriend, Eddie down and told him the same thing. He started crying and went back upstairs. Later that day she called me a liar.

When Rita asked me to lie for her, she said to tell my mother and Ray that it was Rick who hit her. She said if anyone asked to tell them Rick beat her up. She didn't give me any reason. In the lounge I got a good look at her. There was nothing wrong with her face. When she was going to the bathroom in the doorway, I saw her pinching her cheeks.

#5 - Ray

I have known Rita Gasteau since January 4, 1994 when she and her boyfriend, Eddie moved in the room #7 at 257 Broadway where I am the manager. I have had conversations with her on a number of occasions until she moved out about the middle of July. The owner of the property, John DeCesare, ordered them out because of complaints of domestic violence. For example, on a Sunday morning in July, around 4 am, she yelled out the window for me to call the police. I did and they made her boyfriend take a walk. A couple of dozen times while they were there, I heard fighting.

On July 3, 1994 I was playing a guitar at the (unintelligible) in Methuen. I got through at 5 pm and got home at twenty minutes to six. With me at the time were Charlene, her daughter, Elaine, Gary, Lionel and his son Lionel, Jr. We were all in the apartment building at that time. I was inside my first-floor apartment. Elaine came from the second floor with a door lock and said she had found it on the floor outside Rita's apartment. I took the lock upstairs and knocked on Rita's door. She came to the door holding her stomach. I asked what was wrong. A few minutes later she said, "Rick came and beat me up." I offered to call her boyfriend, Eddie, at work. I called him from my phone downstairs. Then I went back upstairs to tell her he was on his way. I knocked at the door and there was no answer. Gary called me and told me he found a cat that was bleeding. He said he found it in the toilet-bowl in the toilet three to four feet outside Rita's room. It is the toilet she uses. I called animal control. Rita had left her room and I didn't know where she went until Dennis, a tenant, told me he saw her at the Garron's package store on Broadway. I saw her come home about 9:30 (pm) or a quarter to ten. She was crying. She sat on the ground in the backyard and said, "He got me again. Rick got me. He pulled me into the car and took me to the boatyard." Ed asked her if her raped her and she said yes. At one point, Rita asked Charlene to help her. I saw Charlene remove a closed can of beer from Rita's waistband. I called an ambulance and Rita refused to go with the paramedics. Rita and Ed then went upstairs. Rita had told me, Ed and Charlene that Rick kicked in her door, punched her, stabbed the cat and said, "This is what is going to happen to you next." She said Rick forced her to go to the boatyard in his car.

On the night of July 8, 1994 Rita came downstairs about 7:30 or 8:00 pm and said she wanted to talk to me and Gary. Charlene also was there. We went upstairs and she showed us a newspaper clipping which I recognized from the Lawrence Tribune. Written in pencil was "I'm going to kill you" or "I'm going to get you again." She said she found it in her mailbox. Around eight o'clock, I was in my driveway and I heard her crying and saying something like, "Please leave me alone. Don't do it again." I heard a door slam and I saw her come out alone and walk toward Essex Street. She went out the front and didn't say anything. I didn't see her again until about 12:30 the next morning when she came back home with Elaine and a man I don't know. Rita was with them. Elaine told me she saw Rick beating Rita up outside Daigle's lounge. The next morning about 11:30 or noon, Elaine came into my apartment and told me and Charlene that Rick wasn't even at Daigle's. She said she was leaving the lounge and asked Elaine to walk her home. Elaine said Rita had asked her to lie about it because she had been dancing and wanted to explain why she was so late. She didn't want Ed to know what she had been doing. Ed, who had gone out to look for her when he got home from work about 10:30 Friday night, was upstairs when Rita, Elaine and the fellow arrived. Rita told him, "Rick beat me up again outside Daigle's." Ed left saying he was going to go find Rick. He came back in twenty to twenty-five minutes and said he didn't see Rick. I didn't see any sign of injuries on her.

That night, Rita talked to me and Charlene until about four in the morning. I knew she had been drinking because I could smell alcohol on her breath. Ed was there too. She talked about her marriage to Rick. She claimed that on the day of her marriage, Rick made her dance in a circle and drink blood and that during a pregnancy Rick cut the baby out of her and made her drink its blood. That night, when Rita, Elaine and the man, whose name I don't know, got back to 257 Broadway, Rita painted a red mask on her face and told me, Ed, and Charlene that Rick had beaten her up outside Daigle's.

On Saturday morning, when Elaine said she had lied for Rita, she said she arrived at Daigle's at 10:30 pm or a quarter to eleven and saw Rita dance with some Jamaican and was drinking there.

#6 – Charlene

On July 3, 1994 I arrived home with Ray, Lionel, Lionel Jr., Kathy of Lynn, my daughter Elaine and Gary, and arrived home between 5:30 to 6:00 pm. We were home about ten minutes when I heard Rita yelling from a second-floor window, "Call the police. Rick beat me up." Ray called the cops. They came, talked with her and then left. I didn't see any sign of Rick. I've lived here seven years. I've never seen Rick. I wouldn't know him if I tripped over him. Sometime after the police left,

Gary and Lionel Jr. came out to the back yard and said there was a horrible smell in the second-floor hallway. Ray went up with Gary and Lionel Jr. and there was a cat in the toilet. It was brought down and Lionel Jr. and Kathy took pictures of it.

Later that night, about 8:00 pm, I went upstairs to check the hallway and saw writing on the wall right across from Rita's door. Something like "I love you." The previous time I was up there was earlier that day when I was upstairs to check on one of our tenants. There was not writing on the wall then.

About 10:30 that night, Rita came out to the back stairs and said Rick had killed her cat and was out to kill her too. "He got the cat and now he's going to get me." She said. We came in the house and she went upstairs.

One evening after the cat incident, we were in the yard and Rita said that as she was coming back from the store Rick picked her up and took her to the boatyard, raped her twice and then dropped her off on Broadway and she walked home. That was July 3rd. She was sitting on the ground and crying. She was holding her crotch saying, "Rick got me again. No one's going to touch me down here anymore. I have to keep it on ice for Rick." I saw a lump in the front of her shorts and Ed, her boyfriend said, "I'll kill the bastard." He reached down and pulled out a can of Budweiser from beneath her underwear and threw it over the fence. She had been drinking. I could smell it. I've been a bartender for years and I know. She and Ed went upstairs. I followed behind Ed because he said he couldn't control her. As soon as we got in the room, she pulled her pants down, leaned over the bed and asked me to check her, saying, "This is where Rick put it." I told her I wasn't a doctor. I called the women's resource center for her but here was no answer. I suggested she go to the hospital and she told me to forget it. Ray called the ambulance but she refused to go with them.

On July 8th, late at night, Rita arrived home with my daughter, Elaine and her friend. We were sitting in the yard, Ray, me, and Arline, who was living here then. Elaine told me that Rita had been "all over" some guy at Daigle's. Rita said, "No, I wasn't." Rita said she was outside of Daigle's and that Rick was outside too and he slapped her around. Later we went upstairs on the (unintelligible). Ray and I and Rita were there with Ed and she talked about her wedding ritual. She claimed Rick's family was in a cult, that she and Rick had to share glasses of blood, and that she had to have sex with other members of the cult before she went on her honeymoon. She said Rick's mother made her wedding cult dress with an opening at her private areas. She showed me a small teddy bear. She said Eddie had given it to her and that it reminded her of Rick and she kept it between her legs to remind her of Rick when he was good.

The next morning, my daughter Elaine came downstairs and told me and Ray that Rita had told her to lie for her about Rick beating her the night before. She said Rita wanted her to lie so Eddie wouldn't beat her up for being out drinking.

*

One of the nights in question was August 22, 1993. Officers Hidish and Beck described their involvement on the incident report, including the story Rita gave to them:

Witness #1- Rita Gasteau will testify that she was on the couch sleeping. And her husband came into the house by opening the door. He then grabbed her by the neck and pulled out a knife, stating to her that she had a short time to live. And then the man cut her shirt with the knife. He then started throwing things around and breaking furniture and stereo equipment and various other items. And before he left, he stated that he would be back to finish the job.

Witness #2- Officer Victor A. Hidish will testify that on August 23rd at approximately 12:30 am was detailed to 123 Emmett St. along with officer Beck. On arrival was met by Mrs. Gasteau. She related that her husband came into her home by opening the door of her house that was locked, that he came over to her choking her, pulling out a knife and making threats that he would kill her. She showed us her shirt that was cut by her husband. She also showed us the house with furniture thrown around, furniture damaged and stereo equipment broken. Mrs. Gasteau also stated that she was assaulted by her husband two days ago. Mrs.

Gasteau was advised a warrant would be requested for his arrest. A restraining order was also shown to us.

*

Attorney Brien soon sent us a copy of an arrest report of Rita. In June of 1993, Rita was arrested for disorderly conduct. On the incident report, Officer John Fornesi described his recollection of the incident:

Witness #1- Officer Fornesi will testify to the above date and time was detailed to Riverside Dr. regarding a girl screaming. Upon arrival, I observed the defendant crying on the grass. I approached the defendant who refused to give her name and was intoxicated being loud and abusive. At this time, I offered the defendant a ride home. This officer then stated to the defendant if she didn't leave, she would be arrested. The defendant began to call the police "f------ police". At this time the defendant refused a ride. I placed the defendant under arrest and transported to the station to be (unintelligible) by Lt. Baker.

*

Mr. Brien included a copy of Rick's suit for divorce from Rita. He was alleging that their marriage was void, as she had lied under oath on her third marriage agreement, saying that she was legally divorced from her second husband at the time. She was still legally married to her second husband when she and Rick married.

Finally, Attorney Brien faxed us a copy of the polygraph examiner's summary, as well as a summary of his own involvement in the case:

I, John W. Brien, depose and state the following:

1.   I am an attorney with law offices located at 170 Common Street, Lawrence, Massachusetts;

2.   Prior to becoming an attorney, I was a Trooper with the Massachusetts State Police from 1974-1985;

3.   On August 23rd, 1993 at approximately 12:30 am, Rita Gasteau, who was residing at 123 Emmett Street, Lawrence, MA told Lawrence Police Officers that her estranged husband, Rick, broke into her home some two hours earlier, pulled a knife on her, cut her shirt, choked her and made threats that he would be back to kill her;

4.   Police sought complaints against Rick for the following charges:

A.   Violation of a protective order;

B.   Assault and Battery by Dangerous Weapon

C.   Breaking and Entering in the Night Time with the Intent to Commit a Felony; and

D.   Malicious Destruction of Property.

5.   On September 16, 1994, I was retained to represent Rick in this matter.

6.   I soon learned that the children were taken by the Commonwealth of Massachusetts and placed in foster care due to allegations that Rick and Rita were unfit parents back in January, 1993.

7.   As of this date, the children remain in foster care and the parents are embroiled in care and protection proceedings in the Lawrence District court.

8.   After I determined that Rick had what seemed to be an airtight alibi, I recommended that he take the polygraph.

9.   Rick took the polygraph and passed the test, which was administered by Attorney James Johnson, Ret. Lt. Colonel, USAF.

10. On November 1, 1994, all charges against Rick were dismissed at the Newburyport District court Jury Session, Newburyport, MA, due to the fact that Rita failed to appear as a witness.

11. Present at court were numerous defense witnesses who were prepared to testify to collateral false allegations made by Rita against Rick. Also present was an alibi witness who put Rick at home in bed when these offenses were alleged to have occurred.

12. A short time after Rita learned that Rick had passed the polygraph, new charges surfaced alleging that Rick had sodomized his son. These accusations are being made by Rick's seven-year-old son.

13. Based on the evidence that I have seen to date, it is my opinion that Matthew Thompson is the victim of a miscarriage of justice.

August 22, 1994

Lots of developments in my case. I won't go into all of them, but today I learned of the statement Mike Bryan (the boyfriend) just made to Pam and John Brien. Also, Mark (my brother; listed as M. Thompson in the Ada directory) got a phone call from a woman on his answering machine. It went as follow: Ms. Thompson, Ms. Thompson, Matthew, Matthew, Matthew… After this recording, another call from someone calling him collect. I am anxious to get out of this place. I hope the small-town politics don't play into it.

August 26, 1994

Pam is preparing an affidavit for Mike Bryan. She is a good woman and shows real concern for my situation. She also talked to Mike Bryan's mother. She said Rita told her someone in a pickup picked her up, gagged her and bound her hands. Then took her and raped her "all night", dropping her off at dawn. Also, her ex-husband said that she told him she was walking home from work one night and was raped. So that makes four different stories she has told. I wrote the ACLU a letter this week and will have Pam call them next week to try and interest them in my case.

I got an A in my humanities class and have a Business Law class and a Management Information Systems class this fall. Also, Rita has been married two times previously. We hope to be able to contact these two men and hope that they can give us some helpful information about her.

Tuesday, September 6, 1994

Last weekend was Labor Day weekend. Saw Krissy, Josh, Mom, and Dad on Sunday. A very good spirited visit. Krissy is looking very well.

Last week the supervisor at Data Entry (where I worked) found out someone was tapping into the system and changing files and accessing the inmate's "days remaining" files. Whoever did this used my password and login. So, I was the initial prime suspect. They eventually found out who did it. I'm anxious to find out who.

September 21, 1994

Last night Fred and I went to the sweat lodge. This one wasn't as hot. It was more enjoyable. The moon was full and the color of golden wheat or something. It was really calming.

Also, I talked to Pam yesterday. She said Mike told of how Rita liked rough sex, and that they had rough sex that night about 9:00 pm. She always wanted anal sex too. He said he might have slapped her around and he knew that she had rug burns on her knees before she was with me.

Saturday night Stanton and I were talking about my case and I thought a lot about it. I stayed up to about 3:00 am, thinking.

*

Mike Bryan's (the boyfriend) Recantation

It seemed every time I called Pam, something new had been uncovered about Rita. Pam located the boyfriend Mike in Rome, Georgia. She called him up one day prepared to tell him about the new developments in Massachusetts. Mike told her, right then, that he had been thinking about me ever since the trial and that he knew I was innocent. He then told Pam the truth about his relationship with Rita and agreed to sign an affidavit stating these facts:

****

I, Mike Bryan, do freely give this statement of facts as I know them, to Pam, a private investigator working for Matthew Thompson.

I met Rita in the latter part of 1990 at the Terrell State Hospital in Terrell County, Texas. Rita and I were both in Terrell State recovering from substance abuse.

During my stay at the hospital, I talked frequently with Rita about her stay at Terrell and why she was there. Rita stated that she was there to overcome her abuse of alcohol so that she could gain custody of their children back from her ex-husband. She often talked of her stint in the Air Force as a flight simulator technician. These were the two main topics of her conversation with me during our stay at Terrell.

As time went by our relationship turned from one of friendship to a more physical one in nature. I had decided that upon my release from

162

Terrell, I would return to Oklahoma to find employment and straighten my life out. Rita decided that she wanted to live with me and go to Oklahoma also and together find employment.

After arriving in Ada, Oklahoma, we located a house on East 12th street. The house was approximately two blocks east of Mississippi, a main street in Ada. After a short period, Rita found employment at Hardee's. Hardee's was located on the corner of 12th and Mississippi. This worked out perfect for us as we had no vehicle and had to walk to all destinations. Therefore, her walk to work was only two blocks from the house.

Not long after we had moved to Ada, Rita told me of a female friend of which Rita had bisexual relations with. She said that the girl did not live far from where we were currently residing. At that point Rita then began to tell me of the details in full of the sex that they had together.

The sexual relationship that Rita and I had was extremely rough. This type of sex was requested by Rita and I went along with it. To put it simply, Rita liked to simulate a "rape" situation before and during sex where she was the "victim". It would not at all be unusual for her to want me to throw her to the ground, rip off her clothes, slap her around and she frequently requested that I "spank" her buttocks. In fact, the above was quite the norm.

At times the spankings were hard enough to cause bruising on her buttocks. Her face, elbows and knees have many times been hurt from rug burns caused by rough sex on the apartment's carpeted floor. During the sex act, anal intercourse was always a part of it and at times sex was exclusively anal.

On March 16, 1991, Rita was going to walk to the grocery store to purchase food. The store was "Homeland" and was located approximately eight blocks to the east of our house on 12th street. When she returned, she told me that three white males in an old yellow Nova had harassed her. They had made catcalls and wolf whistles to her. She did not act upset about the incident and, in fact, soon left the house again to walk to the convenience store to purchase beer and cigarettes.

Around dinnertime of the same evening, we began to drink the beer. I would estimate that Rita drank six beers and that I drank the other six.

Around 9:00 pm Rita and I had sexual relations in the living room. It is possible that I ripped her shirt in the scuffle that occurred during the initial part of foreplay. I do definitely remember that I spanked her buttocks and that the ensuing sex was very rough. So rough in fact that her face, elbows and knees were becoming red from carpet burns. Because of the burns we moved to the couch. We did have anal sex and although I don't distinctively remember, I believe that we had vaginal intercourse. I recall having sex with Rita as she was on her back and as she was on her hands and knees.

After we had sex, I went to sleep on the couch and Rita went into the bedroom to sleep. I remember her wearing a t-shirt and panties as that is all she ever wore to sleep in. I next remember Rita waking me around midnight. She wanted me to go to the store with her because she was out of cigarettes. I remember that She was wearing a tank top, blue jeans short and pink and white LA Gear tennis shoes. I don't remember if she wore a jacket. She carried only her cigarette case that was a combination coin purse.

That was a stupid reason to leave in the middle of the night in my opinion and I told her so. This made her mad and she left the house mad at me over my words. I waited on her a while and when she did not come back, I figured that she was staying out to make me angry. Therefore, I went back to sleep. I do not remember anything else until the Ada police knocked on my door around 6:30 in the morning and told me that Rita was in the emergency room and that she had been raped.

I do not recall anything particularly unusual about her when I saw her at the hospital. She was possibly a little withdrawn. I was quite hung over myself that morning and so it was impossible for me to tell whether or not she had been drinking recently.

We left the hospital and were taken to the police department so that Rita could give them her statement of what had happened. After that was over the police drove us home.

At the hospital Rita briefly told me what had happened. Rita told me that she had left the house and walked to the convenience store to buy cigarettes. As she approached the store, she saw the guy that was in the yellow Nova standing beside his car in the store parking lot. This was the same guy and car that had harassed her earlier in the day. Rita said, "He was at the store waiting for me. It's as if he was psychic and knew that I'd be there. He knew who I was." She said he then forced her into the car and raped her. She described him to be bigger than me. That was all that she told me of the incident.

In the following days, Rita, Detective Tommy Cosper (whom coincidentally is my cousin by marriage) and Detective David Leewright, began to work on taping phone calls of someone and they also wired Rita with a microphone. I was deliberately left out of all of this and felt as if the police did not want me to know any details of what was being done. This was all fine with me as I really did not believe that Rita had been raped and I was happy to be left out of it all.

There were lots of little discrepancies in Rita's story as she would tell it over time and I began to believe that it was not true and so did my mother. We talked of it and I guess compared what had been said to each of us individually by Rita. When things did not come close to matching, I began to disbelieve what Rita had told me. I don't know explicitly what discrepancy was uncovered that led to my disbelief yet I know that it occurred.

Less than a week before this occurred, I became suspicious of Rita and followed her when she was going to the grocery store. As I went around the block, I observed Rita get into a large older brown car with an older man driving. Rita was gone for two to three hours. I observed her come back in the same car and the man let her out around the corner from our house. She had been to the store at some point as she had groceries in her hands. I confronted her about the man driving her home but did not say that I had seen him pick her up. She told me that she had just bummed a ride home from the grocery store. I never did confront her with the truth of what I had seen. I never told her I not only saw him take her home but also pick her up.

At an earlier time, Rita had told me that she had been assaulted in the past by an ex-boyfriend or possibly an ex-spouse. I guess I did not pay much attention because discrepancies in her story made it unbelievable and I tuned her out.

About a month after the incident that occurred on March 17, 1991, I decided to take a job with a company I had previously worked for. This job would take me out of the USA and would station me in Japan. I took the job not only for financial gain but to also get away from Rita and the situation here in Ada. So, I left in April of 1991 and did not return until February 17, 1992. I returned and stayed with my mother and my stepfather who lived in Gerty, Oklahoma. I then moved to McAlester for a few weeks and then moved back in with my mother. From there I moved to Corpus Christie for several months, then returned to my mother's. I then moved to Coalgate (OK) and had two residences there before I moved in with my mother once again in November of 1992.

The last part of my statement is an apology. When confronted by Pam Bond prior to Matthew Thompson's trial in Ada, I did not tell her the whole truth as I knew it. I was embarrassed to tell of the details of our sex life with my parents there and still felt some odd sense of loyalty to Rita. Therefore, I did not tell all that I could. I do believe that an innocent man is in jail and I am willing to tell what I know as facts to do what I can. I did not tell anyone what I have just stated. Not even Ada Police. They did not ask and I did not offer any information.

Further, affiant saith not. Mike Bryan.

****

First of all, I'm so embarrassed for the crudeness of it all, but that is how I read it for the first time, too.

Was just further amazed. Wow! I digested that affidavit for days and days, blown away by the vitality and animation of it all. It all fit.

Mike's story corroborates my version of the facts. I said "she had told me she was bisexual and wanted me to have sex with her anally". Mike explains her red marks, rug burns, and slap marks. He said he might have ripped her shirt that night. He also discredits her story of what happened earlier in the day and that night, and provides an example of her promiscuity. And lies.

I was learning more about Rita and her behavior. She was mentally ill, one way or another. As I look back, I was filled with joy in these weeks, in prison or not. I was faithful that I would soon be sent home, after only a short time in prison, and was so grateful for the turnaround of my life, and the case.

In an extreme way, this had been a search for myself and I was now finding validation for thoughts that had tempted me over the years, thoughts of who I was, my big dreams and the path for my life. I was ready to be released.

Thursday, October 6, 1994

A prominent OKC attorney agreed to take on my case last Tuesday when Dad talked to him. I talked to him today on the phone. He sure sounded like a scrappy old man. He was cussing and everything. He seemed pretty pissed at George and thinks he did a bad job. I hear he is pretty good. I don't know how Dad will ever pay him though.

Haven't heard from Pam in about ten days. I sure hope she is Okay and working on my case. She really is almost finished with the investigation but we need the affidavits that she has.

Sunday, October 23, 1994

Garvin Isaacs took my case last Thursday for $10,000. He wants to file a motion for a new trial next Wednesday. Got affidavit from Mike signed and sent back. He thinks it looks good for me.

Finally, I was able to get computer assignments done for MIS. What a dilemma.

Sunday, November 5, 1994

Last Tuesday, November 1st, Rick was to begin his trial in Massachusetts but Rita didn't show up so they dismissed the charges against him, but the molestation charges are still pending. John Brien sent Isaacs an affidavit about how the situation ended up. Garvin is trying to complete the brief and will include an ineffective counsel motion in it.

Chapter 12 Expecting release soon

After finding out from Rick, Rita's previous married names, Pam set out to find the first two husbands. We knew they had lived in Texas while married to Rita.

Pam made contact with Rita's first husband and talked to him on the phone. He told her that Rita had accused him once of beating her. He said she went to the hospital claiming to have been beaten, but the doctor who examined her told he and his mother that he found nothing wrong with her and that they should be wary of her. He said he was asleep when his mother came and woke him up to tell him Rita was in the hospital claiming to have been beaten by him. He had no idea she had done this.

Pam also talked to the second husband. He told her a lot about Rita and her lies and all. We were not able at this point to obtain a written affidavit from either the first or second husband.

Thanksgiving Day, 1994

Today we had the usual T-day lunch. Not too bad for being in prison. I did a lot of thinking about past Thanksgivings and what people would be doing today. It's a little depressing but I've gotten used to it after two years.

Last week I gave an ultimatum that I didn't want the brief filed without the first husband's affidavit or at least his mother's. Garvin shot a certified letter to her immediately. I was impressed and relieved by that. I called yesterday and Garvin's paralegal said they had heard from the woman and she was going to send an affidavit. So, after we get that, the brief can be put together and filed. After four months, now I just have to sit back and wait for the court's ruling.

December 7, 1994

Got my new job at Data Entry, a clerk for Sharon. Took a lot of stress off of me.

Still waiting for Garvin to file my brief. Not much change in the last two weeks. Trying to get an affidavit from the first husband.

Looking forward to Christmas. I'm going to give Josh some presents in the visiting room. That should be rewarding.

*

The first husband would not sign an affidavit for us. He seemed hesitant to possibly piss off Rita. However, his mother provided an affidavit:

*

I, Betty _______, state that Rita:

1.	Claimed she was hit by a truck at a station while getting gas. She said the truck ran over her. She came to my door not hurt, but all upset.

2.	Once claimed Jeff was drinking and beat her up. Parkland Hospital said she was fine. I found my son in bed sound asleep.

3.	Everything I've heard about her is not good, the poor girl needs help.

4.	She did not get a divorce before she married Kevin.

I am very sorry to do this but I feel very sorry for the man and his family she got into trouble.

*

What good this statement would do was questionable but we included it. The affidavit didn't include everything that the woman had talked to Pam about over the phone, but she was probably in a hurry to get it done and over with when she prepared it.

Saturday, December 17, 1994

Today was a beautiful day, sunny and 55-60 degrees. Love this Oklahoma weather.

Thursday Garvin filed his supplement. Last Friday, December 9, my direct appeal was "submitted for cause". I expect next week to get a copy of the supplement. Then I'll just wait and hope the court can see the injustice.

December 20, 1994

Yesterday I received a copy of Garvin's brief. It looked strong but had some sloppy mistakes. It is ironic that December 19th is Rita's birthday. I hope for the best.

I had Josh's presents sent here so I could give them to him personally.

My new job as clerk is going really well. It takes a lot of stress off of me.

Friday, December 23, 1994

Josh, Mom and Dad came up Friday night. I gave him his presents and felt good being able to do that. I called after they got home and Mom said Papa (her father) had died. I think it may have been a relief more than anything. I am glad his suffering is over.

Not much happening here. Kind of depressing.

*

1994 had been a memorable year. The letter in July had changed my life for the better. I finished the Lifeline drug program in October and didn't smoke much marijuana this year. As I look back on it, it was a fulfilling year. I learned a lot about myself and in dealing with life. The "reality therapy" classes provided a good framework for understanding my needs and feelings.

Robert got into trouble in the spring and my buddy Fred moved in. Compatibility with my cellmate was an important consideration to me. I was lucky to have Church that first year and then Robert and now Fred. Church and Robert were like brothers and Fred was well traveled and very intelligent.

Fred worked in the clay shop and was never in the cell, which was good for both of our personal space needs. However, I always would speak with him and at night we would have discussions before going to sleep. I appreciated conversing with he and James.

I continued to run, lift weights, play softball, take college talkback TV classes, and participate in the drama club. We put on an anti-drug-message play, Sticks and Stones, for over three hundred people in the Joseph Harp visiting room. KOCO-TV, channel 5, out of OKC, filmed it. I WON the yard's arm-wrestling tournament! Beat Pat Hines in the final. Heavyweight! He is, like, 230lbs. I was 185 or so. I sent the trophy to Josh. Good things were happening to me.

My life was a waiting game like it had been from the start, from the day of my arrest. I was waiting for my release, confident that all of the new evidence would clearly show the injustice done. Still, haunting questions floated in and simmered for days. Why didn't Tommy or George investigate Rita's background? Would it have been difficult to find her two previous married names, her maiden name and that she grew up in Texas? I wonder what information we could find if we really investigated her past?

I was very disappointed that the first two husbands were not willing to cooperate. I felt that we should completely investigate her Texas past, but money was tight and we were sure that we had enough for a reversal. We called the polygraph examiner in OKC who had given me my test, but he did not have my results in his files anymore.

My friend James and I walked a couple of miles almost every day. We would talk about life, loves and our problems. He was in the federal court with his appeal and was pessimistic about my chances, even though he clearly believed that I was innocent and was impressed with the new evidence.

I was involved in a Christmas play for the drama club. I played a surfer dude who babysits a kid and tells him the miraculous story of Jesus' birth using a surfer dude accent.

I continued to take what classes applied to my major, still accounting.

My friend Skip and I had classes together. He was an exuberant guy who I liked to talk with. Smart, funny and sociable, Skip was fun to be around and hung out with a lot of the people I did. Didn't smoke pot. He had accidentally shot and killed someone with a shotgun in Stillwater and had a 20-year sentence for second-degree murder. We had a class together with an older man who had two life sentences for two murders in 1969.

Ron was schizophrenic and had been locked up since 1970 and was on psychotropic medication. He was harmless in manner and appearance like Brooks on *The Shawshank Redemption,* yet was mentally ill. One night, in the talk-back-tv room, he told us about the murders and his mindset.

He began to tell us about his life and the voices that he had begun to hear in early adulthood. He told the story like a grandfather would tell the grandkids a cute little story about his life on the farm. He was happy to have us listen and was very calm. He began explaining his home life and his job at the time washing dishes at a local restaurant.

Skip was being cute and smart aleck with him but I was totally enthralled with his story and his attitude. Skip would always mess with him about his medication, asking him the name and watching Ron respond with his institutionalized enthusiasm. Every brick of his measly foundation relied on his medication. At eight o'clock, Ron would birddog it to the pill line for his medication. That is what he looked forward to. I admit it was funny to see him get excited when it was pill line time. He would come back and be sleepy within an hour. Ron was very happy with his latest medication. It suited him well he said.

Anyway, his voices identified themselves as holy and told him it was necessary to "slay" two people. He was sent to find these two people, and stumbled by pure chance upon the victims that fate would have him kill, a single mother and her child. With his instructions to slay these people in the name of God, he broke in a window to find the child sleeping on the couch directly below the window. He plunged his chosen weapon, a paring knife, into the child's heart and broke it off.

My eyes were on Ron's face, which looked like the face of a boy who was telling the story of when he missed the game-saving fly ball. Not a good thing, but certainly emotional and life changing. He changed expressions and became visibly excited when he continued.

He said he heard a sound from the back and knew that it must be his next victim, the mother. Needing a weapon, he went to the kitchen and was brandishing a huge knife as the mother came into the living room, screaming. Attacking her, she backed up into the bedroom, screaming all the time, where she fell on her back on the bed, pleading for her life.

I was unable to move or speak, my stomach feeling the black grease viscosity of this revitalized episode. Skip was feeling it too, looking at me with that "get him" look, and having fun with it.

Ron's eyes became deep to a point I didn't understand. He grew intoxicated as he brought the story to its peak. He stabbed the woman repeatedly in the rib cage and his knife became stuck between the woman's ribs. He described how he recovered it by twisting it to one side, as if retrieving a fallen wrench or tool from a tricky spot, and continued with his mission of slaying the second person. My God. I won't ask Ron so many questions anymore.

Mental illness. That was pure fear, pure horror and evil. I am not this. Maybe Ron really did not know what he did was wrong at the time, although he does now. That is schizophrenia. I feel like I was whipped around in Rita's schizophrenic lasso for a few days, and it made me a little temporarily crazy.

My days and nights were filed with dreams of release in 1995. I thought about men locked away, who might read my book and recognize Rita as their accuser. I picture a man in his cell, reading the book. I see, feel and understand him deeply at the moment he recognizes his Lamia. His body floods with joy, as mine did when I read the letter on July 11, 1994. His life has hope. Right at this moment, today, somewhere, he bleeds for help and understanding, just like I do. For this reason alone, I must write a book.

Monday, February 6, 1995

Pretty good day today. On nice days the yard comes alive, with everyone happy and in good spirits. These days help everyone. I got a new cellie a couple of weeks ago. Fred moved to another unit. Fred's a good dude.

I have my Real Estate principles class tonight. I am enjoying my classes.

Haven't heard anything on my case yet. I will write Garvin and ask about how long the State has to respond. I feel a good feeling about it today after reading the decisions the courts are coming to.

I am ready to leave prison. I probably won't go to a minimum anytime soon depending on how the legislative session goes.

Thursday, February 17, 1995

We got locked down from 8:30 pm Wednesday to 5:15 pm today. There was a fight and some beer found on the unit last night.

I called Dad tonight and he had been wanting to talk with me. My appeal was affirmed (denied relief) this week but no mention was made of the motion for a new trial (new evidence supplement). I am somewhat bewildered right now as to why. I will call Garvin tomorrow. He is going to file a petition for re-hearing. I'll find out more when I talk to Garvin. I wish for the best.

*

My direct appeal, filed the year before by the public defender Thomas Purcell, was set for hearing December 9th, 1994. Garvin filed the supplement motion for new trial based on newly discovered evidence on December 15th, so we were cramping the court's style from the start at this critical juncture in my appeal.

Garvin didn't feel he needed to file an entry of appearance into the case, even though I mentioned this to him in one of my letters. An entry of appearance is one of those detailed legal requirements, although minor, that is required for the orderly functioning of the court of appeals.

The Oklahoma Court of Criminal Appeals ruled on February 14, 1995, that Garvin failed to file an entry of appearance, therefore all of the new evidence in the supplemental motion for a new trial was not considered because he was not my attorney of record. Thomas Purcell was. Nevertheless, the court ruled that even with Garvin's failure to enter an appearance notice, it was more than one year after my judgment and sentence date, and therefore this new evidence needed to be filed in the original trial court. Purcell's brief with the original appeal was also denied. We filed a petition for rehearing. If that failed, then it would mean filing to the court in Ada.

Soon after the court's ruling, another piece of information arose from Massachusetts. John Brien and the attorney who was handling Rick's ongoing molestation charges informed us of Rita's arrest for arson. They faxed us a copy of the newspaper article from the Lawrence, MA-*The Eagle-Tribune* of Tuesday, February 21, 1995 that detailed the incident:

Woman charged with setting rooming house fire:
LAWRENCE – A woman was arrested early Sunday morning after witnesses told Arson Task Force investigators, she set fires in a South Union Street rooming house.

Fire Lt. John Burton said two separate fires were set Sunday morning on the second floor at Valley Lodging, 77 S. Union St., one in a hallway and the second in a bathroom.

Firefighters were sent to the rooming house and quickly doused the blaze, keeping the damage to a minimum.

Following an investigation, Lt. Burton and Patrolman Timothy Levesque arrested Rita Gasteau, 31, who was staying at the rooming house when the fires were set.

She was charged with arson of a dwelling.

The investigation into the incident is continuing, Lt. Burton said.

*

Man, this has got to be enough for a Judge or court to see the girl's mental instability. However, this was not any proof about anything of the morning of March 17, 1991, so we were limited in its legal application. Yeah, but we can take it to the media, I thought. It helps show my innocence. My emotions were seeing the big picture of the conviction. Does that not matter?

Tuesday, February 28, 1995
We've got a petition for re-hearing in the works and will include the new information about the arson.

Dad has finally come to the realization that we need to get some media exposure in order to bring the truth out in the open. I got the phone number for the Jenny Jones talk show and will give it to him tonight.

April 4, 1995

Our petition for rehearing was denied on March 14, because it wasn't filed within one year of my judgment & sentence. Garvin is finishing up a trial in Waco and hopefully we'll have the post-conviction (to the Pontotoc County District Court in Ada) filed soon.

*

Garvin was on the Larry King Live show on CNN on Friday, March 31, 1995. His good friend, Gerry Spence, was the moderator of the show that night and a panel of defense attorneys and prosecutors were discussing the O.J. trial and justice in America. I didn't see the show, as we had Headline News and not CNN, but my father and brother saw it.

Towards the end of the program, the panel was asked if they believed there were innocent men in prison. Garvin vehemently replied that his client, Matthew Thompson, was an innocent man currently imprisoned for rape in Oklahoma. This made me feel pretty good. International television! I'll be out soon for sure now!

Monday, April 10, 1995

I met Garvin for the first time today. I was nervous but excited. He is going to go to the DA and talk to him. He said he got six to ten calls about the CNN show. One was KXII-12 in Ardmore.

Tuesday, April 11, 1995

A man named Eric wanted a phone interview with me today. He is from Ch. 12. We are telling him we'll contact him in a couple of weeks.

Tuesday, May 2, 1995

Garvin met with Chris Ross & Bill Peterson today. It did not go well. They believed Mike Bryan was a liar and that Rita's antics in Massachusetts were caused by my "assault on her" and her continuing trauma. They painted a picture of me as having a reputation for beating up women (I have **never**!). They asked Garvin if he wanted to recant his statements on CNN. They apparently were trying to change Garvin's mind about me. They said they would also charge me with rape by instrumentation if I were tried again. Garvin is going to try to get an interview with Rita in Massachusetts.

We thought that the DA was a reasonable man. Garvin was very disappointed and frustrated with the DA's attitude, as was I. He is a typical DA, playing games and lying to better his conviction ratio. And he can always hide behind his "duty as district attorney". Imagine the psychology of a person that could take away a person's liberty as a common joke? Isn't that what a cold-blooded murderer does?

I had moved to a new cell on C-unit in March. My cellmate was scoring ounces of weed and keeping it in the cell. The heat was too much for me so I moved in with another man for the summer. That went sour quickly due to his daily, continual release of flatulence and also because he ratted on me for smoking weed. By that time, I was looking for another cell, but didn't feel I deserved more prison time for smoking pot. If I were caught with a dirty UA, I would do about six more months in prison for smoking pot. I was UA'd once in May and beat it. I was again UA'd in August and beat that one.

May 15, 1995
Garvin and John Brien are working to talk to the girl or give Mike Bryan a polygraph. The Ebola virus has been going for about a week.

May 21, 1995
This weekend was the 2nd annual drug-free softball tournament. We came in second. Fun weekend.

Garvin has been making progress since the meeting with the DA. I am impressed and feel good about it considering the laziness of my former attorneys. I hope to get word soon from Pam about the addresses and phone numbers of the first two husbands.

August 2, 1995

Haven't heard from Garvin in a couple of months. He supposedly is waiting for Rita's trial in Massachusetts on the arson. I haven't heard from him.

August 5, 1995

Garvin left a message on Dad's voice mail. He said he is getting affidavits from local attorneys supporting our claim of ineffective counsel.

I had a hard week. Very lonely and depressed but feel better now that I've started back working.

*

In August I moved to the other side of C-unit. For a few days, my cellmate was an older man who had, a few years earlier, hit Tommy Ward (*Dream's of Ada*) in the head with a steel pipe. He and his son were both in prison, and I think had the same name. In September, my friend Albert moved in, and that would be my last cell and cellmate, at Joseph Harp.

Garvin sort of disappeared. The petition for rehearing had been denied in May soon after his failed meeting with the prosecutors, yet we had not moved on to file our evidence in the district court in Ada, our next step.

I keystroked some as a clerk at Data Entry, but in July I resigned to keystroke fulltime on Sharon's line. The inmates enter via 10-key all of the citizens of the state of Oklahoma's taxable income information, food stamp information, Department of Wildlife data like deer kills, etc., and other stuff. It was a cool job and I was happy with it. I was really accurate and in the top ten fastest. I would go to work, throw on the headphones with the KATT and before I knew it, it was three o'clock and time to go. Good money too, for prison.

I continued to have a need to run and stay in shape. I love to run and could say I ran the half-mile track at Harp as fast as anyone ever had. That is what the old hardcore runners said. My old cellie Fred was a jogger, and ran forty-two miles in the run against child abuse run in

1994. He won a pair of shoes for most miles run. I think I set an all-time personal record of seven miles.

Jeff was a strong distance runner nearing fifty, an eccentric guy who ran every day, and really pushed me on the half mile. I'll never forget the mile I ran with him once. God, thank you for seeing me to the end of that one, too far for me. There were a few delightfully dedicated runners at Harp. It was a good spirit there.

Jeffrey Todd Pierce, who was released from a rape conviction in 2001 from Harp, worked with the other Jeff, as a garden maintenance worker and I would see him on the weight pile and in the visiting room, usually with his brother.

There was a guy in for arson from Ada. He always came by to talk and smoke his weed with me, when he would have some. I say he came by to talk, but not really. He was deaf. He carried a little pad and pencil, and would go to my unit, write my name and cell number or something, and ask someone to holler at me. He had known my mom, a special education teacher, and heard I was here. It's funny…he was in drama club with us, and had parts.

However, the drama club had fallen into dormancy and I began to have a lot of free time. I walked a lot with James; he continuing to badmouth the appeals system, and me with my positive thinking. As fall approached, I grew impatient and started to slip into isolation and withdraw from all of the positive things.

I had some close friends, good people, all over the yard, but my pot dealing friends began to be the only people I talked to. I was getting into one of my moods, searching for a direction. Two of my new friends that I really thought were cool were really getting into Lifeline, sobriety and education about it all. I stopped going to meetings, stopped talking to people for enjoyment and was again idling. I was frustrated.

Sunday, September 10, 1995

The heat finally broke last week. This summer was the hottest yet. I started school August 26th. I have a TBTV class and a correspondence class.

I talked to Dad Friday night and he said he had finally talked to Pam about getting the Texas addresses. He also said to call him tonight and he would tell me what they found out, so I will.

September 16, 1995
Dad hired the investigator in Belton, TX to search for quality information from the first two husbands in Texas. We hope for the information within a couple of weeks.

*

We knew we couldn't live with ourselves without investigating Rita's background in Texas and the first two husbands. With the intensity of such relationships, there was bound to be more evidence of her insane behavior.

October 3, 1995
O.J. was acquitted today. I actually felt relieved for him. I don't wish anybody to prison. He'll reap what he has sown anyway. After it sank in, I was mad at my jury. Here I sit in this darn place.

Dad should talk to the P.I. tomorrow. He has a tape-recorded conversation with Kevin (the second husband) and has talked to some high school classmates who said she accused someone of rape back then.

Wednesday, October 18, 1995
Last night Dad told me that Thomas Vannoy had found a man who was a Baptist Director of Music who was the one Rita accused of sexual assault. I think he's the one back in high school. What a huge relief! I was engulfed in serenity after hearing this. Now if we can get the first husband to talk. We'll have the bases loaded for Garvin.

Wednesday, November 1, 1995
I received a summary that Thomas Vannoy sent Dad. I found one statement particularly interesting. The second husband's brother thinks "she is schizophrenic", that she is the only person he has ever known in his whole life who really has two personalities. He thinks she has a

mental problem and that on occasions as he and his wife were talking to her that she would change personalities and become a different person, even changing her voice. I KNEW IT!

Matt and Fred, circa 1995

Chapter 13   Texas Investigation

Investigator Thomas Vannoy was a professional. In October and November, he dug into Rita's past in Texas with vigor and efficiency. My logical requests were implemented with speed and enthusiasm; he prepared quality affidavits and letters of inquiry for the witnesses even though some would not sign, and he gave us summaries at the end of each month. God bless him.

He first made contact with the first husband's mother, Betty, concerning her son Jeff's marriage to Rita.

*Contacted Betty, concerning her son, Jeff, who was married to Rita.

Jeff ______ was her first husband but only married three months. His attorney was Randle Thompson.

The mother refused to provide an address or phone number for her son. She didn't want to damage their relationship.

She said that her son didn't want to get involved as he is now remarried and has a family.

I did ask her to give my name and phone number to her son and ask him to call. I don't believe she will do it.

She did remark that Rita was a funny person in her actions, and noticed little things about her, which made her think Rita was in need of medical help.

She said, "that Rita made false allegations against her son. Once she alleged that he beat her and pulled a knife on her." That Rita went to Parkland Hospital and when she and Jeff arrived, they were told by the doctor that he didn't believe Rita's story.

She said, "Rita would do strange things such as: sitting up in bed fully dressed, trying to look sexy in a dress, and red shoes."

When Rita got out of Terrell State Hospital, she came to take the little girl with her to Oklahoma. She said "that her son still grieves over the little girl, which is supposed to be his child." Betty has some doubts about the child being her son's and no blood testing was done.

Betty said they "are church people and didn't like what Rita had done to their son."

She said, "The girl is sick and will do worse than she has done if someone doesn't help her, that others can go to prison but Rita gets away with everything."

Betty believed that Matthew Thompson was out of jail and surprised to hear that he wasn't. She feels that someone should get Rita some help but refused to offer assistance.

Betty wouldn't talk to me in person or provide another statement or contact her son at my request. Protective of son.

The PD showed no record on calls to the residence involving Rita or Jeff ______.

*Contacted Troy (Rita's uncle).

Troy stated, "that Rita had stayed with he and his wife for about six weeks after her family moved to Dallas, then moved out before completing high school."

He said Rita and her family had lived here for about ten years and that her dad became very ill and they moved to Dallas. Her mother worked for Lone Star Gas Co.

He said, "that Rita and her brother were adopted when small babies."

He stated, "that Rita had problems in school. She was involved in drugs and alcohol but was never arrested."

He said, "that in her last year of high school he thought that she had reported a rape and he thought the charge had been dropped after the families met."

He couldn't recall the boy's name or other information concerning the incident. I felt that he knew more but didn't want to discuss it anymore. He said he didn't want to provide a written report.

*Drove to the library to review old news articles for 1979-1982 to attempt to locate any new times concerning the subject or alleged rape cases. Nothing located in the newspapers.

*Contacted detective Dan at the Mineola Police Department. He provided several names of teachers for me to contact.

*Dorothy:

She recalls Rita vaguely. Remembered that Rita was expelled for having liquor in her locker. The liquor was in a thermos bottle. She located Rita's class photo on page 34 in 1980 yearbook (sophomore class). She did remember hearing about Rita making allegations against a male but couldn't remember any details of the incident after fourteen years.

*Lynda:

She remembered Rita as a troubled girl but had no knowledge of the alleged rape.

*Lisa:

She remembered that Rita ran with a rough crowd. She might have been into drugs or alcohol. Lisa was in her class but didn't associate with her or her group.

*Teresa:

She knew Rita well. She said, "that Rita had a bad reputation for sleeping around. She was in a rough crowd and always in trouble. She ran with two other girls and they were in the 'thug' gang."

*Jenny:

She thought Rita was a flaky person with various mood changes. She recalls Rita being expelled for alcohol on campus. She recalled something concerning an alleged rape but no details.

During the time in Mineola, TX I contacted other individuals who knew her as a classmate or student. Many knew or heard about her reputation. Some recalled hearing about the alleged rape incident but none could provide specific details. None would provide written statements since it had been 13-15 years ago. Also, most could not provide factual information only hearsay or some vague knowledge about her past.

*Drove to residence of Johnny ______, Rita's father, in Dallas.

Johnny was very ill and it was difficult to interview him due to noise in the home. I taped the interview, as he wouldn't write anything.

Johnny said, "he believes his daughter even though she does lie, but not about the two alleged rape cases (referring to Mineola and Oklahoma incidents)."

He said, "Troy and his wife in Mineola helped his daughter in dropping the charges-he thought it was due to her moving home and the fact that he was very sick."

He said, "that he couldn't remember much about things that occurred 14-15 years ago.

He recalled the alleged rape in Mineola as being at night, the boy was raunchy and lived at the edge of town and drove a pickup with a gun in it.

He said Rita left school when told she wasn't going to pass.

He said, "Rita did drink but no drugs. She was sent home from school for having alcohol."

He feels that Rita has had some trouble and a pretty rough life. He felt that maybe he should have done more to help her.

He said, "that she was sent to a doctor in Tyler to check for drug used when living in Mineola." This is why he says she didn't use drugs. He couldn't recall the doctor's name.

He said that she spent time in Terrell State Hospital about 3-4 years ago for alcohol treatment.

OF INTEREST:

He said, "that Rita didn't want to testify in the Oklahoma incident but the detective put pressure on him and Rita for her to testify.

He wanted her left alone but the detective wouldn't hear of it. The detective came across as threatening to the father.

He said his son was in the Air Force when Rita had all of her problems and couldn't be of help.

He did say, "Rita is a pretty emotional person who will not back down."

Dad gave the impression to me that he cared about Rita and felt guilty about the past family problems.

*Contacted retired principal Larry:

He recalled suspending Rita for three days for having alcohol in a Thermos while in biology class.

He said, "Rita missed a lot of school and I felt it was due to a broken home."

He thought she used alcohol as a means to escape her problems. She didn't fit in well at school and preferred older people for friends.

He said, "I felt she had a mental problem in school and needed help."

He met the father and discussed the situation but never met the mother.

Larry provided us with the following written affidavit on November 27, 1995:

1.   I was contacted by Thomas Vannoy of Southern Security Associates of Belton, TX, in October 1995 concerning former student Rita.

2.   I served as high school principal for Rita in 1981-1982.

3.   Rita was suspended from school for three days for bringing alcohol to school in a thermos.

4.   Parents were notified before suspension and informed of the charges. Johnny (her father) attended the hearing along with myself and Rita. Her mother chose not to attend.

5.   After the "due process" hearing from all parties involved, Rita and her father agreed with the three-day suspension.

6.   For the remainder of the school year, Rita seemed to be depressed and for the most part remained isolated from the majority of students.

7.   During Rita's four years in high school, her attendance was erratic with absenteeism and tardiness.

8.   I offered my services to Rita when she returned to school and told her I would be there for her if she needed someone to talk with. She would never open up and share her problems with me. She kept everything inside.

9.   After Rita's suspension, she was not a discipline problem for the remainder of the school year.

*Contacted Manuel:

He remembered that Rita ran with the thugs. That she was a sweet kid but a "dingbat" and real naïve.

*Contacted second husband's brother, Charles _______:

He said he didn't know about her past history but knows about Rita while she was married to his brother.

He said, "Rita is a schizophrenic. She is the only person I have ever known in my whole life who really has two personalities."

He said, "She is a liar and will lie about simple stuff. One time she wanted to give us a dress for our little girl. Rita said it came from Neiman Marcus but the tag said JCPenney."

He recalled that Rita wasn't a good mother. She would go out and leave the small child at home and when Kevin came home from work, she wouldn't be there.

He recalled the time she called Kevin from OKC and said she was pregnant. They drove there to locate her and get Kevin's car back. They found her working at Pizza Inn and she wasn't pregnant, another lie by Rita.

He feels that, "she has a mental problem and that on occasions as he and his wife were talking to Rita that she would change personalities and become a different person-even changing her voice."

I was able to obtain information that indicated the male involved in the alleged rape incident could be Charles _______.

He remembered Rita and allegations made by her against him. He was a college student working at the First Baptist Church as Music Director.

He didn't wish to talk about the incident until he thought about it and discussed it with his wife.

*Charles called me to discuss Rita. He expressed his fears of having his name in the newspapers.

Charles gave me the name of the minister of music, Tommy _______, who was at the First Baptist church during the Rita incident. He said, "that Rita had made allegations against another male as being homosexual." He thinks Tommy could help on the case if we can locate him. He could live out of state.

Charles said, "Rita talked about being pregnant and taking a lot of pills to get rid of the baby."

He said, "Rita alleged that he had made a pass at her." (He didn't go into detail and was very evasive)

No report was made to the police, as it was resolved between him, the minister and Rita's parents.

He said, "wanted to do the right thing (with my case) but didn't want to testify or see his name in the media."

He requested that I, "attempt to contact others for information and as a last resort he might provide a statement."

I feel he could be beneficial to your case if we can get him to give us a written affidavit. Copy of tape sent for your information only.

*Drove to Sulphur Springs, TX to interview Kevin.

Kevin was the second husband of Rita. They were married in August 1983 and divorced in September 1984.

Kevin didn't want to write a statement but did provide a taped interview.

He said that he was 33 years of age and Rita was only 20 when they were married.

They were married after Rita was legally divorced from first husband Jeff.

They were married when the baby from the first marriage was six months old.

He said, "that she was always becoming hurt and going to the hospital when nothing was wrong with her."

He said, "She was the type of person that when she wanted sex, she would try to get into your pants no matter where."

He said, "that only once did she ask him to have anal sex and he refused."

He said, "that Rita was a liar and lied to him about being pregnant."

He said, "that Rita didn't talk about her past problems but was upset over being adopted."

He said, "That she was after males, she would dress sexy and smile at men."

He feels that Rita is a liar and believes a lot of what she tells other people. That he wouldn't believe anything that she had to say.

I have included his taped interview. I will have it typed into a statement and see if he will sign it (he does sign it in May of 1996).

*Contacted Peggy in Mineola, to solicit information on Rev. Michael K. Haynes who was the minister of the First Baptist Church during the time Rita made allegations against one or more persons.

*Rev. Michael operated the Bell County Ministries for the jail and also worked within the State Penal System. Rev. Michael couldn't recall much about Rita. He asked me to call back in a few days after he thought about it.

Rev. Michael provided us with an affidavit, bless him:

****

My name is Michael K. Haynes. I was the head pastor of the First Baptist Church of Mineola, TX from 1979 to 1982. Sometime between the fall of 1981 and the spring of 1982, I called a meeting, which included me, one of the staff members of the church and the family of Rita. I do not recall the exact time of this meeting due to the number of years since it occurred.

Rita, a teenager, had accused my youth director of rape. However, I doubted the veracity of Rita's claims because I knew something of her personal problems, and I did know the young man who was my minister of youth. Nevertheless, I felt it necessary to get everyone together and attempt to discover the truth because I knew that the situation was potentially serious and might get out of control.

We determined that Rita was not telling the truth and dismissed the accusations as false. Her mother and father moved to the Dallas area sometime following that meeting and I heard nothing else about any of the people involved until I was called by investigator Thomas Vannoy of Southern Security Associates in Belton, TX. He told me of a young man named Matthew Thompson, who was serving a 15-year sentence in Oklahoma because of the testimony Rita. He asked me if I remembered the incident, and I told him I had only a slight recollection. However, upon reflection, I do recall the meeting and the false accusations made against the youth minister of First Baptist Mineola. Apparently, Mr. Vannoy feels that this statement might shed some light on the fact that Rita had a prior history of making such claims against others.

If indeed, Matthew Thompson is innocent of the crime he has been accused of, I feel it is necessary for someone to speak up in his behalf. However, I do not know whether this is the case or not. I simply know what happened in my study during the meeting between the parents, myself and the youth director of the church.

*

We asked Mr. Vannoy to do some investigation of former detective David Leewright to see if we could come up with any good stuff about him. All he got was a former colleague who advised him sharply, "he was no longer employed by this department, and they didn't know where he was living or how to contact him."

Vannoy continued to try to contact the first husband. He obtained his address and sent an inquiry to him. No response.

He contacted a psychologist in Temple, TX who advised him of the difficulty of obtaining information from Terrell State Hospital. He suggested having my attorney obtain a court order from a Judge seeking release of her records. She had records. Based on what Vannoy told him, he diagnosed her as a substance abuser with a personality disorder.

Vannoy contacted the local police departments, but unfortunately nothing was found about Rita.

In November, Vannoy was able to obtain the name and telephone number for the Youth Director for the First Baptist Church in Mineola during the Rita incident. Vannoy spoke with this man over the phone. Either this man was not the one accused by Rita or he was keeping his mouth shut about anything to do with Rita. I'm not sure he is the one that was involved. This goes to show how difficult it is to get people to open up about things, if even to help an innocent man get out of prison.

Vannoy's report continues…

I contacted Tommy and asked if he "was the Youth Director in Mineola in 1981-1982." He advised me that he "was the right Tommy who had lived in Mineola."

He said that he "didn't remember having a problem with Rita. She was a high school girl. Her mother worked at the church office. She was an odd child but I never had any problems with her that I can remember."

I then asked him several questions in an effort to gain additional facts concerning Rita:

Q. Did Rita ever make any allegations against you?

A. No!

Q. Do you recall her making allegations against anybody at the church?

A. No, I really don't. She always had problems at school.

I replied, "Okay."

He said, "You know, I'm trying to think, isn't she an adopted child?"

I replied, "Yes, she and her brother were adopted by their parents."

He said, "It's been so long I kind of lost track."

I replied, "It was about 1981-1982."

Q. Do you remember her making allegations to the church minister or someone else in the church against you?

A. No!

Q. What do you recall about her?

A. I just remember that I would hear her mother talk about the kind of problems Rita was having at school. She was kind of slow, you know, and all of that, but I just don't remember a lot. She was not really active in anything. I had the youth choir, you know? I don't remember her being in the choir.

Q. Do you recall her making allegations against any member of the church or younger males in the community?

A. No!

Q. Do you remember anything about her involving alcohol?

A. I really don't.

Q. Do you recall anything about her alleging she was pregnant?

A. I really don't remember any of that. Now, it could have taken place, but I don't remember her having…it seems to me though that there was one time when she did say something about being pregnant. I might have heard it from her mother but I never heard it from her.

Q. You don't remember who told you?

A. No! I'm sure it would have been her mother or someone in her family.

Q. Do you recall anything about the family?

A. Not really. (Then he made the following comment)

I don't really remember anything about her, except they had trouble with her in the office. She would talk about things and it seems it was always somebody else's fault and it never worked out to be her fault, according to her mother.

I think they tried very hard to do everything for her but evidently, she's one of those kids you can't do anything with.

He said he "knew she was a problem child."

He said he would think about it some more and contact me later. I believe that he could have some personal knowledge concerning Rita that could assist our cause.

I contacted him once again and he said, "she was a child who had problems but he never really knew what they were." He was sorry that he couldn't help with the case.

*Contacted Gracie in medical records at Parkland Hospital in Dallas concerning Rita.

Under the 1st married name, the following entries were made:

August 3, 1982 – emergency room

January 2, 1983 – emergency room

February 13, 1983 – emergency room

February 17-20, 1983 – inpatient (gave birth)

February 22, 1983 – emergency room

March 4, 1983 – emergency room

July 6, 1983 – emergency room

The clerk said that the computer had been purged. It would require a release from the patient to obtain information concerning treatment.

Under my pressure and persistence, trying to leave no stone unturned, Betty would provide another affidavit to us in 1996, however reluctantly. It is just as well to include it here:

State of Texas, County of Dallas

Betty Wright, deposes and states:

1.   Wild thinking of things (by Rita).

2.   Did not see her drink. Don't allow it in my home.

3.   Married (to her son) in Duncanville in our home. Divorced maybe Dallas.

4.   Personality changed a lot. Always thinking she's hurt or someone going to hurt her.

5.   Said he (her son) was drunk, when we would be together all day. He would be just fine. She would go off alone and pout and say he was drunk. He would just be eating dinner and talking with his brother. No one drinking.

6.   No date recalled for Parkland Hospital incident in Dallas.

7.   She drove Jeff's car to my house once in the middle of the day. She said she stopped to get gas and a truck ran over her at the station. She was crying out of control and going on about it. I checked her over. No marks on her at all. I told her she was Okay, but she said no. I called her father at home. He wanted to talk to her. She was fine in seconds. Crazy like this all the time. Just one thing after another.

8.   No police report that I heard of. I think the neighbor might have called them or took her to Parkland. Her mother called me. I went to find my son. There he was asleep at home. He said she had got up and got all dressed up. He said they had a fuss but he went back to bed. He didn't know what she went out for.

9.   No copy of this or lawyers involved. My son was only with her a few weeks. It is hard to remember, it was so long ago. But when someone needs help, you just know it. Don't understand why the parents don't see that.

10.   Don't know the reason for no reports. Maybe they did not make one. She was not hurt and this was told to my son by the Doctor and whoever else at the hospital.

11. This was just how she would do. You tell me if that's normal.
Sitting up in the bed at 2:30 in the morning when husband is asleep and
going to work at 5:30 am. Bows in her hair. You don't sit up and work
on your hair at 2:30 in the morning.

12. Yes, I remember Rick and Rita taking the baby, Kim, away from
us. We wanted to keep her. Rick cussed me out. Later Rick called and
apologized to me and my son. Jeff even helped with Kim and little
Ricky when Rita was in Terrell Hospital.

13. After their divorce, she called me and said she had cancer, but
asked me not to tell her parents. Crazy.

24 July, 1996. S. Matern-notary

In December, Thomas Vannoy provided his closing summary:

I, Thomas Vannoy, Investigator with Southern Security Associates,
investigated the background on Rita for Mr. Thompson.

I contacted approximately 40 people in person or by telephone
during the investigation. Some were in high school with her as students
or teachers. Others knew her through other experiences in the
community or other locations prior to the incident involving Matthew
Thompson. The following interesting comments were repeated by
various individuals who knew Rita:

*Rita had a drinking problem in high school.

*Rita made allegations against one or more males alleging some
type of sexual offense. The offenses were never sustained.

*She complained about illness and went to the hospital when
nothing was wrong.

*Was considered a liar.

*Associated with a tough crowd known as the thug gang.

*A person with mood changes.

*Committed to a State Mental Hospital.

*Untruthful about being pregnant.

*Had a bad reputation in school.

*Unfit mother for her two children.

*Had an excessive sexual desire.

I personally believe that Rita had serious problems before the incident in Oklahoma in 1991. Had the court and jury been aware of her past history beginning in high school that maybe the trial could have had a different verdict. Hopefully the system will review all the information obtained since the first trial and provide Matthew Lambert Thompson another opportunity to prove his innocence.

*

For now, this was the new and newer evidence we would present to the district court in Ada, in early 1996. It was getting pretty personal there. The Judge was a woman who lived on Constant Street in Ada. I could see no other logical determination than her giving me a new trial.

I was really showing off with all of this new evidence. I could show my friends the facts proving my innocence See, I haven't just been blowing smoke all of these days! You know, they probably didn't even care if I were guilty or not. But I did. Gosh help me until the day I die, I will prove my innocence.

I felt comfortable with my cellie Albert. He was an athlete too, into sports, and we gelled pretty clean. He was a cannabis lover, but deep into Lifeline. I was smoking pot and daydreaming about my business idea. I seemed high-centered, feeling I should be on the streets instead of in here.

Monday, November 27, 1995

I talked to Thomas Vannoy and Garvin today. Thomas said he has one affidavit back and was writing on the other four. Garvin thinks this evidence will not be considered because of our due diligence. I need it there for cosmetic purposes anyway.

Josh visited Sunday. Krissy and I were sitting for a picture with him and all of a sudden, he leaned back and kissed both of us. I thought it was special. I hope the pictures come out good.

*

Every year around Christmas, the staff would pass out simple sacks of candy, fruit, etc. to all of the inmates. They would do this early in the morning, usually a couple of days before Christmas. We all ho hum and joke about the meager presents, but deep down it is appreciated, as an act of kindness. This year they did it about 5 am on the morning of the 22nd, a Friday morning.

On another morning soon around this time, I awoke to the sound of the guard's key turning in our door's lock at about 2:45 am. In a few time-slowed microseconds, my gut felt, but hoped against, the words that would come from the officer's lips. Please say my cellie's name, he doesn't smoke pot.

"Thompson, Matthew Thompson, #162066."

Stepping into the cell, waiting for recognition by one of us, the officer was polite.

"I need to transport you to central control for a urine analysis."

Nothing saved me. I was UA'd and tested positive for cannabis. I was graced with bail but would face thirty days in disciplinary segregation within the next couple of weeks and would be shipped to another yard. No room at Harp for pot smokers.

The drama club had come back together in the fall and we were putting on a three-play special the weekend of Christmas. All of my energy was wrapped up in my two roles. I was a priest at a mid-century American prison on the night of an execution in one play, and a gold miner in a comedic play. My last bit of fun at Joseph Harp.

Sunday, December 31, 1995

Bah Humbug! Well, this place stinks. I am so sick of being here. I am tired of watching good-looking women on television or watching fishing shows and shows showing people having a good time. I'm sick of seeing the same idiots. Something about prison brings about different relationships with people. The mental and emotional stress makes you need and appreciate good friends you make in here. But on the other side, the feelings of disgust multiply towards the people you don't like.

This holiday season was the worst yet for me. I feel depressed and that turns into anger about this whole thing. Plus, I got the dirty UA, and Mom and Dad went crazy over that. I'll go to DU (disciplinary unit) here soon. Pretty much sick of being here.

*

By this time, Joseph Harp was under rule of the Gestapo and it was expected of you to rat on your supplier, if you wanted to stay at the prison after receiving a dirty UA. Yeah, in prison, have unsuspecting men rat on their suppliers, get stabbed and killed. The Gestapo's conceit was dangerous here at Joseph Harp where forty percent of the inmates were sex offenders and murderers can find an excuse for their earthly bloodlusts! Quite a progressive prison movement in the eyes of a dead man's poor mother.

On Wednesday, January 10th I was informed to pack my stuff. I was going to DU. A few goodbyes and I was locked in a single cell on the disciplinary unit. My friend Trent was next door. That was cool.

My teacher was allowed to come to see me in DU. I had an Intermediate Accounting II class that I was enrolled in. He brought me my books, assignments and such. I would be able to keep up, as the first few weeks were slow. I was faithful that I would go to a place with the college program, probably Stringtown, or Lexington. That was a priority in this place.

A few days into my (DU) sentence, I had my day to talk with the deputy warden and committee about the drug-free philosophy and my chance for bettering the grace of Joseph Harp and its managers. Heck, my unit manager showed up on my behalf. He believed in me and had heard me talk over the phone with my attorney at critical times in 1994 and 1995. He also was the unit manager that let me slip to C-unit without a program failure, with the fabricated "attorney's instructions" story in 1993.

They didn't buy my carefully concocted story of how I found the weed right in front of the officer's eyes as I was leaving the shakedown room of the visiting room. Somebody just left it there, you know? Yeah, well to heck with you and your misguided back-stabber information system. It won't work. These were my true thoughts as I waited my last days out at Joseph Harp.

Chapter 14   Lexington Correctional Center

Luckily, I only had to stay in DU for two weeks. I was given time served, so another knucklehead could take my place. Thank you, I won't argue about the other two weeks. I was happy to be able to watch the Cowboys and Steelers in the Super Bowl. We had listened to the playoffs on the radio. I was just going up the road to Lexington Correctional Center (LCC), the medium yard. I had heard that Lexington was more like a real prison, with more violence and trouble. Sounds fun.

Of course, I had been at LARC in January and February of 1993. L.A.R.C. is the name for the collective complex. There is a minimum-security prison visible from the highway, a medium yard built like Joseph Harp, and the Assessment & Reception units, which are maximum security. I am told the college program is strong. That is all that matters. I'm good for a change. What's up with earthquakes on my birthday? Kobe, Japan on January 17th.

On Wednesday, January 24, 1996, I hit the LCC yard. After only a couple of hours of being admitted, I was given a cell on Unit 4. I got settled on the unit and spent the day exploring the college program, the track, and the yard. The education department was cool with a computer room and two talkback-TV rooms. I could type a new narrative here. At Harp we were limited in access to PC's. We used more like a "word processor" there.

From the start I could feel the different energy of this yard. It was night to the day of Harp's atmosphere. Whatever you want to call it: evil energy, negative energy, frustrated energy.

Like walking into a restaurant, club, or room full of people. We all can describe the atmosphere, ambiance, essence we feel in the place. Same thing. Why is this yard so different? I thought about it. Same people, same sentences, same crimes. What makes it different? I think it is the A&R units.

The transition from a county jail to A&R to prison happens to every inmate, even death row cases. A&R is the first "prison" a person goes to. I can't tell you the horror that many men experience, whether physically or most likely in their soul, when locked down in the A&R cell waiting for shipment. These energies and thoughts are renewed every day as the process goes on at LARC. Pain, sadness, and despair, man.

Thursday, January 25, 1996

I got to LCC yesterday. Called Garvin and he sounded like he had done some real thinking about my brief. Sounded like he made some changes. He sounded somewhat "proud" I guess. Talked to Josh for a long time last night and he really needs to understand why I can't come home. He asks so many questions.

Ready for the Super Bowl. Dallas and Pittsburgh once again!

February 2, 1996

This is the coldest weekend since the temperature has been recorded. Two below last night and five below tomorrow night. The heat doesn't work worth a darn! It's probably 35-40 degrees in my cell! It stinks.

Thursday, February 8, 1996

My experience in DU at Harp was just that, an experience. The first few days were really very relaxing. Trent was in the cell next to mine. I read a few good books. The *Aquitaine Progression* was very cool. I would like to write a screenplay about that book.

I got some good quality thinking time and even came up with some more ideas. I quit smoking for those fifteen days and for one day here. I am going to try to quit again. I think about Krissy a lot. About her pretty eyes and face and mouth and hair. And her legs and…I guess just about all of her!

I think about Josh a lot. About future quality time and teaching time with him. He has a lot of challenges in his life, with my situation and past. He needs some understanding and guidance through his life.

I read a book here last week, *Boy Wonder*, a fictional story about a man and his rise to the top in Hollywood producing movies. Quite a ride.

My new cellmate Jerry is quite a character.

*

Jerry and his friend Rick, two cells down, would become a great relief to me as friends to laugh with and hang out with. Both were small in stature but big in bravado. Jerry had light brown, straight hair and Rick had a lot of blonde hair, and looked sort of like a "not so spectacular" Vince Neal of the rock band Motley Crue.

Tuesday, February 27, 1996

We finally filed the motion last week. (February 20th) I feel very comfortable and confident about the legal soundness of our brief. My opinion is that it will interest the Judge. We'll see.

The statement from Rev. Michael was signed November 16, 1995. We filed February 20th, more than ninety days. It probably will not be admitted as new evidence.

Friday, March 8, 1996

Talked to Dad and he told me we had been awarded an evidentiary hearing by Tom Landrith! March 18th or so. He also told me of a police officer in Massachusetts and his observations of Rita.

I felt sort of caught off guard about the news. I am so grateful. My soul feels such a drain of emotions that I feel spent. Kind of scary too, thinking of being "outside". My brain is really in overdrive. I'll gather myself for the hearing. I have to think about what to do, where my money will go, for what and how much.

I sprained my foot the day before Dad told me about the hearing. Also, that show on Fox or ABC about the guy named Matthew accused of rape and he believed in his mind that he had done it even though he didn't. It aired March 7th.

Tuesday, March 19, 1996

The hearing was not yesterday. The State has until tomorrow to respond to the brief. I hope a new date will be set then. It is hard to wait. This is a long week.

Thursday, March 28, 1996

Talked to Garvin just now and he said that our application was denied and we don't even get a hearing. I just don't understand.

Monday, April 1, 1996

I went through a lot of depression the last four days. The weather is nice today. That seems to help me.

*

Oops! Just kidding about the evidentiary hearing Matthew Thompson! Didn't mean to get your hopes up. The Judge in Ada heard and ruled on our motion for a new trial on March 22, 1996. Included were the affidavits from Massachusetts, the statement from the boyfriend Mike, the statement from the minister in Mineola, an affidavit from the first husband's mother, Betty, and an affidavit from another attorney (a friend of Garvin's) stating his opinion that he believed that I deserved another trial based on the new evidence and my attorney's failure to investigate Rita's past.

The Judge said that the new evidence was not "outcome determinative", that even if it were presented at trial, I still would have been found guilty. There was no explanation of the reasoning involved. In my eyes, the ruling looked like a kindergarten student had prepared it. It was a two-to-three-page pre-printed form of yes and no answers to the very essential questions about the case. Like the Judge was just filling out a survey questionnaire or something. Maybe the prosecutor had to offer help and guidance, like he did with the jury instructions at the trial.

We appealed the Judge's decision to the Court of Criminal Appeals but they affirmed her decision. We were devastated and couldn't believe they wouldn't give us a new trial.

The molestation charges were still ongoing in Massachusetts. We were informed by Rick's new attorney that he had found more evidence of Rita's behavior. She had been arrested for arson and had been caught in another lie about being beaten or raped. In 1995, she called the police one day to say that Rick had beaten and/or raped her. The attorney sent us a copy of the incident report by the officer that responded to the call:

*

On 3/5/95, at approximately 9:00 pm, I was dispatched to 208 High Street. Dispatcher Burke stated that he received a call from a Marie Martin of 149 School St. Burke further stated that Martin received a call from a "Rita" of 208 High St. in North Andover. Marie Martin stated that she is the foster mother of Rita's children and that the children live with Martin. Martin stated that Rita told her the following: That she found a note at her house, allegedly left there by Rita's ex-husband Rick. Rita told Martin that the letter threatened both of their lives. I then proceeded to High Street to investigate.

Upon my arrival, I was met by Rita. I explained to her why I was there. She stated that in fact she did get a letter and related the following story to this officer: She stated that she just got released from Framingham State Prison for attempting to commit a crime. She stated that she was charged with trying to burn some property down. She stated she now lives at 208 High St. with her boyfriend, Eddie, who works at Haffner's Gas Station. She stated she also has another roommate, Gary. She stated that her ex-husband's name is Rick. She stated Rick was arrested and charged with rape and molestation of one of their own children. She stated that she hates her ex-husband. She stated he used to put guns to her head and beat her. She stated that she just recently, as of two days ago, moved to 208 High St. She stated when she arrived home at 6:00 pm on this evening, she found a note pinned to the door of her house. She then showed me the note. It stated: "Marie, I love my son. I will burn you cunt, for Rita. Pick up your last check." The check was signed but this officer could not make out the signature. Rita told this officer it was Rick's signature.

Rita also stated that her children now reside with a foster parent by the name of Marie Martin. She stated she called Marie to let her know that her husband threatened to burn her.

This officer listened to Rita and this officer observed her to be nervous. During the course of the conversation with Rita, this officer heard her state at separate times that, the note was pinned to the door, and then said that it was taped to the door, and then that she found it at the foot of the door. I then asked her if her husband knew she was staying there and she stated no. I then asked her how could he leave her a note if he did not know where she lives. I then observed her to appear to be confused. She stated he must have found out. She stated he burns places down where she used to live. She then showed this detective a check made out to her by her husband. The handwriting of her husband on the check did not match the writing on the note.

I observed the note to be written on a light bluish envelope. I also observed in the room numerous cards with light blue envelopes. These cards were from Hallmark. I observed one card without an envelope. I then observed the envelope with the threatening note on it to match up to the hallmark card without an envelope. As this officer started to question her about this, Rita became more nervous. I started not to believe the story of the threatening note. However, at this point, I did not tell Rita my suspicions. I was able to confirm that there was in fact a restraining order against her husband. I told Rita I would get in touch with her husband and talk to him about this matter. She stated she wanted him arrested. As I was about to leave, the phone rang. I then heard Rita start talking into the phone. She stated the following: "I know this is Rick. You can't make threats to me over the phone. Yes, I got the note." At this point I went over to her and took the phone from her. I then identified myself as a police officer and asked who I was speaking to. The male subject stated he was Mike Burta. I then asked him why he was calling. He stated that he is losing a roommate and was going through the newspapers looking for a roommate. He stated he was reading the Tribune and the 2/20 edition has an ad in it with a number stating someone was looking for a roommate. He stated he had no idea why the girl started to talk about something different. He stated he was just trying to find a place to live. At this point he told me he currently lives at 14 Walder Rd. #12. He gave me his home phone number being xxx-xxxx. I told him I would come by to confirm this.

I then hung up and asked Rita why she tried to pretend that the caller was Rick. She stated it **was** Rick threatening her and that he was lying to me. I then told Rita I was having a hard time believing her and that I doubted her story. I asked her if she in fact wrote the note. She would not answer this officer after this. I told her that I believed the last caller to be legitimate and that if I found out she was making a false report, I then could charge her criminally.

I then proceeded to 14 Walder Rd. and met with the caller Mike Burta. He showed me the ad in the paper and he was legit. I explained to him why I had to check on him and he stated the girl really started to confuse him. I then proceeded back to the station. Once inside I contacted Marie Martin and explained to her what had transpired. I then explained to her that I thought Rita was making up the whole story. Marie explained that a lot of people believe she did this. At this point we received a call from Rita's psychologist. She stated that Rita just left a message on her answering machine stating she was going to kill herself. At this point myself and Officer Patnaude went back to the residence and spoke again with Rita.

She stated she did threaten to kill herself. At this point we called for an ambulance to come to have the subject evaluated. The psychologist called back and stated that if Rita refused to go to the hospital, then she would "pink-slip" her. Rita finally agreed to go to the hospital. Officer Patnaude followed her up. This officer does not believe the note was left by the ex-husband. This officer however requests extra checks of 208 High St. for the well-being of Rita Gasteau.

Signed, Detective Mike Gilligan.

*

Nice name, Detective Gilligan. Sir! This was the last straw. It is one thing that a man proclaims his innocence and has a legitimate case for it, but this was getting ridiculous. Again, I was amazed at my good fortune in discovering evidence detailing her pattern of lies, and this officer caught her red-handed, but this evidence was post-1991, so Garvin didn't plan to use it.

I had been at LCC for several weeks. My cellmate and I were already friends and I had made new friends, of course telling them of my innocence. I just couldn't resist, it was who I was and where I was in my life. When I found out we had been given an evidentiary hearing, I was so happy. In one minute, my thoughts were of me walking proudly out of prison. This was it, what it felt like to be redeemed. Then I learned that there was no hearing and my mind shifted to another occupancy.

Lexington was in fact a different yard than Harp. I was fortunate for my cellmate Jerry and his buddy Rick. They were both cool guys that I would maintain good friendships with. We had a lot of fun and did some crazy stuff. I would take Rick and Jerry with me in my boat if the big flood came. You know? We were solid. They told me all the gory stories about the violence on this yard.

My experience of violence at Harp was minor. However, James and I saw a guy get his teeth kicked in with steel-toed boots, right next to us. It horrified me. We were just catching some rays, eyes closed, laying on the boxing ring at the track. There was a young man, laying on his side, asleep, a few feet away. We heard a crunch, and then we saw a couple of more kicks, as the wearer of the boots shouted something about ratting, and then made his way quickly back to the yard. The kid rolled off the ring, but was on his feet, bent over. After 30 seconds maybe, he looked up at us and said, "What happened?" We told him. His teeth, and blood were all over the ring. We said, "You should go to medical." We showed compassion and concern, then made our own way quickly back to the yard. He did go to medical. But yeah, LCC was even more of a battleground than Harp was. Harp was the safest prison in the system. This place had a reputation for violence. Must be the energies.

Rick, Jerry and Rick's cellmate had a good hustle putting up shelves in guy's cells. Their cell was two down from us, and Jerry was always there, leaving me alone to read or think, but we talked and got along when he was in the cell too. From the start, I smoked pot as it was so abundant, cheap and the UA process was easier to beat.

There were a few guys from Ada here and one of them had been looking for me, putting the word out for me to look him up. Gore was his name. Yeah, Glen Gore. I remembered he and his brother, but had never met Glen. Glen and I talked and discussed Ada and all of that. He hooked me up with some weed and was cool. He had heard from the visiting ministers that I was a good softball player, and I was recruited for third base. We had some fun playing softball that year (we won the yard championship) and would continue to interact over the next few years, with softball, the gym and the visiting ministers from Ada.

My thoughts were on a business I had thought up, school, the next appeal and new books of learning. I found *Einstein, The Life and Times,* by Ron Clark, and was off into Al's world, completely enthralled. Cool. I did some deep, deep thinking in that cell, not wanting to ever finish the book. Back to the journal entries that year.

Tuesday, April 9, 1996
The Unabomber got arrested last week. He reminds me of Jeff, the runner at Harp.

Thursday, April 18, 1996
Talked to Craig (one of my attorneys that worked for Garvin) for the first time today. He wishes to come meet me. That makes me feel good. He thinks we'll get a hearing in the next three months from the Court of Criminal Appeals, appealing the post-conviction denial.

Tuesday, April 23, 1996
Craig came up today. We talked about the case. He said after the Judge refused our rehearing motion, they called some "state officials", trying to help me. I felt good about Craig's care for my situation.

Wednesday, May 15, 1996
Josh cut his leg last weekend, six stitches. I talked to a LisAnne at KFOR and asked to talk with Anthony Foster. Craig called him.

*

The second husband Kevin decided to sign the prepared affidavit on May 17, 1996, after a phone call from a friend (me!). It read:

*

My name is ______________

I don't know how to start this interview, but in the short time I was married to Rita a lot of strange things started to happen in my life that are really hard to forget.

I never thought much about it until I received the phone call from a private investigator that brought a lot of it back.

Rita was the kind of person who would keep you so confused that you didn't know if you were coming or going half the time. Everything she would accuse me of, I found out later she was doing.

It is my opinion she's not a good mother. Her daughter would scream and beat her head against the wall every time she was around Rita. She was scared to death of her.

Rita would always seem like she was becoming hurt and would need to go to the hospital for some reason or another. I found out later through her mother that was nothing new. And there was nothing wrong with her.

Rita would claim that people were following her and by the way she dressed I wouldn't doubt it.

I know that she got fired from a couple of jobs for stealing.

The people that were supposed to be following her were because she led them on. She had people come to the house that was kind of strange to me. She had people call and give like a code word and if that code was given, she would talk to them.

I didn't actually find her here…but I had just started a new job down here in Sulphur Springs and I did find our car over in Commerce. I knocked on the door, and as I went to leave, I heard this guy say, "Rita, that's your husband, you need to get home."

I went back to work and she beat me home. She said, "that she had gotten sick and stayed over at a friend's house."

I never could understand how this could happen because she is the kind of person that couldn't find her way down the street.

208

After we had moved down here, we were living in a trailer park and she met some people at the Pizza Inn or Sonic or somewhere. One day she came home and said, "that she just had to get away, and that she had joined the Air Force Reserve." This I knew was totally impossible because I was in the Army National Guard and still am. A wife and husband can't both be in the reserves without someone to take care of the child.

I came home, but she had packed up her stuff and the car was gone. All of her things, her radio, stereo and everything gone. There was a note that said, "Go pick up Kim." Kim is her daughter, who is my stepdaughter. Kim was about 16-17 months old at the time. She was at the day care so I went to get her and I didn't know what to do with her. Because you know it's kind of hard working and trying to take care of a baby. So, I took her to my parents who lived in Mt. Vernon. My mother kept her for about a week.

Rita would call and every time she would call collect. Somehow, she ended up in Oklahoma City.

Well, I finally convinced her to come and get Kim. As I think back now, it was probably a big mistake. I should have called her ex-husband to come and get the baby or even Rita's mother. Every time she would call me, I could hear Kim screaming in the background, "Daddy, Daddy", which I assume she was talking to me because I saw her first step, her first word was Daddy and she was always so happy around me. She was always screaming when Rita was around.

Rita would just go lock her in the bedroom and put the little gate across the door and the child would bang her head against the wall. But when the child was around me or my mother, she was just so happy. I still worry about her.

I finally decided that I was going to Oklahoma to try and get all this stuff straightened out. I found out that Rita had filed for divorce and this was after she said, "she wasn't going to file for a divorce, because she was pregnant by me." I found out that this was false and she wasn't pregnant. She would call and say she "was as big as a basketball."

So, my brother went up with me to find out. We went to OKC to track her down at the Pizza Inn where she worked. She brought the car to me and had a couple of big guys with her and said she "had signed the wrong papers." She also said she "was in the Air Force permanently and couldn't get out."

I just feel she is the kind of person who will stress you out. She would just call all the time. She would call me at work. I wish I had the phone bills that amounted to about $400-500. I don't know who she called but she called all over the state of Texas, and swear up and down she never made the calls.

I could come home from work and she would just be screaming and yelling at me, accusing me of seeing other women, writing them notes and stuff.

I must admit I wasn't used to someone getting up in my face like that and I did slap her a few times to try and calm her down. There wasn't any talking to her, and that may be one of the reasons she finally, you know, filed for a divorce.

I gave her the money and she filed for a divorce. I couldn't take her screaming, yelling, accusations, and I just didn't feel like it was right to have to hit someone to have them calm down.

When we would go up to see her parents in Dallas, her dad would go, like, "Rita, it is your fault. Why do you act like that?" There is so much about her I will never understand.

I think she could be a wonderful person. I don't know what her problems are and why she's so bad about accusing people all the time.

When I met her, she was very flirtatious. I was 13 years older that she was. She was 20 years old and I was 33.

I was single for nearly all my life and this was somebody who was hard to resist. I fought her for a long time and like any other human being, I just gave in.

She would ask me if it was Okay to do things after church, and you know, I just wasn't into that kind of stuff. I just wasn't used to someone asking me if I "would have anal intercourse with her." I said no.

She didn't mind where you were if she wanted to have sex with you. If you were driving down the road in a car she would try to get into your pants. I don't know why she got this way. When I first met her, she was really sweet and just looked like, you know, an angel. She was going to church, had a little baby and looked so sweet.

Then she got a job at a dress shop and came home one day. I will never forget it. She had on a flowered dress that was really short. She had her hair cut off real short and frosted. She said, "What do you think?" My gut feeling was, and I said, "You look like a whore."

Rita couldn't keep a job. She would always wind up at Pizza Inn or restaurants. She could always find a job at restaurants waiting tables.

When she finally came down and got the rest of her stuff, it was September 1984. She gave me the other set of keys to the car and registration that I had mailed to her. That was the last I heard from her. I thought that was just wonderful.

Apparently, it seems like she still has some problems and I am really lucky I got out of it when I did. That's about all I got to say about it.

Thomas Vannoy then went on to ask Kevin some questions:

Q. When you went to Commerce and found her; was she at another man's house?

A. I assumed that. The car was parked out front and it is hard to mistake the car we had. It is one of a kind. When I went up the stairs and knocked on the door, this guy came to the door, and the voice said, "there is no one here, I live by myself." When I knocked on the other door, I hear someone say, "Rita, it is your husband and you need to go home." Or something like that, as it has been over ten years ago. I didn't see her or anything, but you know, I couldn't swear she was in there, but I just have to assume she was.

Q. You didn't know the man?

A. No. I didn't know him but she was going over there a lot, saying, "she had a job." But it was probably someone she met over here, most likely a college student or something. I'm sure he is long gone by now, but I left a note on the car and told her that she needs to get home. You know it is kind of funny that she beat me home. I had to go back to work but she beat me home and was at the trailer house when I got there. I wouldn't doubt that Kim wasn't locked up in the room all the time she was gone. She just didn't care much about that baby.

Q. Where did you meet here?

A. I met her when we were going to church at the Gospel Lighthouse in Dallas. I was trying to find my way back to Christ and I did. There were a lot of Christian people in my class, young adults and one of them knew her. I kind of felt sorry for her. She had just gotten divorced…well she couldn't get divorced until she had the baby, until it was legal.

I met her and went over to her house to meet her parents. Her Mom and Dad were really nice. I went back to see them and then I was off for two weeks on vacation. When I came back, we went to church with her parents.

We went to classes on marriage and I said, "I want a marriage that is going to work." So, we went to classes on this marriage and she was sitting there, going yea-yea, I'll be willing to make it work.

I decided this was great and then she called me at work all the time, and I almost lost my job because she was calling all the time. She would say her ex-husband was harassing her all the time and bothering her. I said Okay, we'll move. So, I just packed up one day and moved down here and got a job out where I am working now.

So that is one good thing that came out of this. I don't know why but it just seems like her problems got worse after we moved down here. The lying was more and more and she had to go to the hospital more. She would think she was pregnant and lie about it. I don't think she ever told me a word of truth in her life. I could not live with those lies. I just couldn't take it anymore. I was so stressed out. I couldn't eat, sleep and was sick all of the time. I could hardly go to work.

Rita was the kind of person, I mean, I don't think anyone could torture you more than she could. I don't even think she realized she was doing it. I don't know what she thinks.

Q. You met her in 1984

A. Met her in 1983. I think we got married in August 1983 and divorced in September 1984. We moved here in April 1984 and then I went to work for U.S. Brass in Commerce in May 1984.

It is like we were here and it took two months for the divorce to be finalized in September. So, about June is when she left to go up there to Oklahoma. She came down from Oklahoma one time to meet me over at

212

her aunt's house. She even called some guy from over there as if it was nothing. She would call people up with me standing right there and it didn't even faze her.

Q. Was she still married to Jeff?

A. No. They were divorced. They were married like three months. She got married and started screaming at him and he couldn't take it anymore. Their divorce couldn't be final until the baby was born. Kim was born in February 1983 and I married Rita in August 1983. Kim was a six-month-old.

Q. Did she take good care of the baby as far as you know?

A. Not in my opinion.

Q. Did she leave the baby by itself?

A. Well, what would you think when you got home and there's a note saying, "I got to get away"? Then you get a phone call from Oklahoma City. Then you have this year-old child. I was 33 years old. How am I going to take care of this child? My biggest mistake was marrying someone 13 years younger than I am.

I can't condemn her too much, for I was just as gullible as these other guys. Maybe she felt sorry for me and wanted to get out of it and leave me alone. I don't know!

She was the one that went out and filed for divorce. I just didn't have the heart to do it for I loved that baby so much. I hated to leave the baby. I would have gone through hell for that little baby. I can't have children and here is that little baby six months old calling me Daddy. She took her first steps in front of me and you can't resist something that loves you like that. I went through all these hard times, as long as I could, just for that little girl. But when she filed for divorce, that was it, you know? That was it.

Q. After she filed for divorce did you see her?

A. I saw her that one time when she came back and got her stuff. When the divorce was final, she brought me a copy of the papers, or I think she brought me a copy. But she came with her dad and some guy. I think it was the same man, pretty good sized, I think it was someone up there from Oklahoma. I took her stuff to her and was nice to her.

Q. When you were married you suspected she was running around on you but you never actually caught her. Did she ever talk about possible emotional or mental problems prior to meeting you?

A. No. I thought she was a pretty normal person at the time. I did find out later that one thing did bother her a lot. She couldn't cope with the fact she was adopted and she couldn't find her real parents.

Q. She was adopted and I understand her brother was adopted too?

A. Yes.

Q. Did they get along?

A. I don't know. I met him one time. The parents were really good people but it seemed like the parents were too old to be adopting at the time. I'm not saying anything, her mother was a nice person, but you know, her mother never really had that mother's instinct. There was really no emotion. Her mother didn't hug her like her dad did. Her mother was kind of cold acting to me.

Q. You met the parents a few times but have you seen them since the divorce?

A. I loved the parents. I didn't want any more heartache on their part. I worry today about Kim. I just pray for her and hope it turns out Okay. It is out of my hands. I had to get on with my life. I have a good wife and two wonderful children from my wife's previous marriage. I would have to say, "Rita did me a favor." I would have stayed where I was for twenty years or more and would have never gotten away from there. I have to thank her for getting me away from there. I'm sorry that she has gotten so many people in trouble along the way.

Q. What about the stalking offense in Sulphur Springs?

A. I filed a report. Rita called me and said there was a guy sitting outside waiting on her to get off work. I went up there at the Pizza Inn and waited until she got off work. I then went inside and I guess it shook her up when the police went to the Pizza Inn.

She didn't think I had called and she said, "That's him." I told her to go home and I would follow. She slowed down and let the guy pass me. It looked like she wanted him to know where she lived and didn't care that this guy might come by and beat me up.

I couldn't protect her from people she went after. This is a girl who brought home from the Sonic $20-30 in tips. She could dress the part. Everyone else dressed in pants, she would wear shorts, stockings and real glossy lipstick. She could make herself look beautiful and attractive and all she had to do was smile and the guys would fork over the money.

Q. On the stalking offense, did the police ever stop the man?

A. They talked to him and said he wasn't really a good person.

Q. That was in 1983 or 1984?

A. It was 1984. We moved here in April 1984.

Q. When you were married, did she ever want to simulate being raped?

A. No! We had a good marriage until we moved here and then really there was no more relationship. She was gone, working at night, and I worked days. There was never anything like that with us.

Q. Did she ever want you to slap her around?

A. No! The only time I slapped her was when she got up in my face and started screaming in my ears. I just couldn't take it and had to calm her down. Our sexual life was pretty basic, pretty normal. There was nothing bizarre about it, except some suggestions she would make sometimes, but I would say no.

Q. What type suggestions would she make?

A. Oh, about oral sex and stuff like that and I would say no I'm sorry.

Q. You said that she wanted you to have anal sex with her?

A. One time while we were up in Dallas and I said no we can't

Q. Do you know anything about her being in a mental hospital prior to meeting you?

A. No! She did tell me one time that when she was in high school, she had a friend whose room was just full of drugs. She also told me she knew handwriting experts. This was a girl who could blow more smoke than anybody I knew. I kind of think she would believe the stuff she made up. When she started telling something it just got better. The stories kept changing and I knew they were not true.

Q. You are convinced that she had a habit of lying to you? Maybe a vivid imagination?

A. I think so. I think she had a real good imagination. Just like people stalking her, and I could never understand why she would say she was pregnant and she wasn't.

She would just keep the story going even in Oklahoma she would keep the story going, "Oh! I'm as big as a basketball." But when I confronted her in Oklahoma, she just lost it and said, "What are you doing here?" I said, "I have come to get my car."

Q. When you went to Oklahoma to get your car, was she pregnant?

A. Nope!

Q. Did she tell you over the phone that she was pregnant?

A. Yes! I knew it was not true, as I can't have children.

Q. Did you ever meet any of her friends from Oklahoma?

A. I didn't want to meet any of her friends. I didn't want a confrontation. The divorce was final and I told him, "If you want her that bad, you can have her. It is your headache now. I have to get out of this nightmare now."

Q. Can you think of anything else that might be beneficial?

A. I can't think of anything.

This is Kevin again and this is all I have to say about the experience I had being married to Rita. I really don't know anything else I could say that would add or take away.

My statement is based on truth and I believe everything I said. It is a memory that is burned into my mind and will never go away no matter how hard I try to forget it.

Rita is the kind of person…I don't know what her problems are and I hope she gets better. I believe with all of my heart that she is a habitual liar and actually believes what she says. I have no idea why she is this way. This is all I have to say.

*

Monday, May 20, 1996

Talked to Anthony Foster at Channel 4 today. He recognized my name from the letters. He said to give him a week to investigate. I was pleased with his attitude and treatment of me as a human being.

Saturday, May 25, 1996

Thomas Webb III was set free yesterday after almost fourteen years.

*

I knew Thomas Webb III at Harp. A black man with softened features, well-educated and kind, he was on E-unit and we had some interaction with softball and a Christmas play. One day we were talking and I told him of my innocence. He looked me in the eye and calmly stated that he wasn't guilty of the crime he was in on. He was really into his spirit and had met a wife at the Christmas play who had come in to sing.

I was enthused. I looked at him with concern and tried to inspire him to fight until the end to clear his name as I was, giving him my thoughts of what to do. He appreciated my concern but felt his energy was better directed somewhere else. It wasn't long after this, though, when I was at LCC, that he and his wife hired attorney Box and he was released soon thereafter. I was surely right behind him.

Thursday, May 30, 1996

Today the appeals court refused our motion. Same reasons as trial court. I am really mad and looking for another avenue. Got to talk to a TV station.

Wednesday, June 5, 1996

Monday, I received the copy of the decision and was just disgusted. I immediately set out to write my own rehearing brief, and mailed it today to Garvin.

Larry Stadler had his time cut from 17 to 10 years and from first-degree rape to second degree.

Police came at us four deep on Monday night. My cellmate is a heat wave! Pam got one juror to sign so far and hopefully more will.

Chapter 15   Juror's Affidavits

Again, we were perplexed as to why the ruling was that this new evidence would not have had an impact upon the verdict, that I would still have been found guilty beyond a reasonable doubt. Garvin came up with the idea of showing my jurors the affidavits from Texas and the boyfriend's affidavit, and asking them what effect they would have had on the whole body of evidence. This was probably not going to be allowed in a strictly legal way, but my goodness, if the jurors say they would have acquitted me, then that is a powerful statement. Is the Judge just smarter than all of these people who saw all of the evidence as well? These people had no political agendas or loyalties. We got seven of nine that we were able to contact to agree with us. What else do we need to do?

With the juror's affidavits, the second husband Kevin's signed affidavit and a more complete one from Betty, we would reload and go with it to the federal district court.

I met an inmate named Larry Stadler one day on the ballfield. A friend from Harp, Sam, introduced him to me, as Sam knew about my case. Larry was in his twenties but was balding and getting a gut on him. His body was sort of pear-shaped, and his skin and hair red with the Irish in him. Larry had a similar situation as mine, in that he claimed he was innocent of his crime. We began to hang out a bit and talk. His case got a lot of publicity because of the time cut and he was really bummed out about that, but he had already done one year, so he would have only three more to knock out the ten, if he stayed out of trouble, which he did.

Larry told me his story. He, his wife and another girl had gone to a bar near Tulsa one night. At the bar, the girl was drunk and was lost to them. They suspected things when she walked out of the manager's office with her hair in a mess, giggling, stumbling and straightening her clothes.

He said she was so drunk that when they got back to the apartment complex, he just carried her to their bed because her apartment was upstairs. He said on the way home, they had to hold her head up as she was passed out. His wife left for a few minutes to check on her mother or something, and then called him on the phone. After speaking with his wife on the phone about what to do with her, he went to wake her up. He said he gently began to shake her and call her name to wake her up. He said she woke up screaming rape and the rest is history. That was his story and my observations saw truth in it. I dreamed passionately of helping investigate the woman's history when I was released. I could actually **help** him. He had a beautiful wife that came up every weekend, a supportive mother, and he didn't use drugs. He would be okay until his release date.

Friday, June 7, 1996

Today was another one of those days where the end was in sight. Like I would be out tomorrow. I talked to Pam tonight after she had talked to most of the jurors. The older man, heavyset, the foreman I believe, was very stubborn and just couldn't accept that maybe I was innocent. The young, pretty girl was the one that really pushed for conviction and the State's selling price of 30 years (she and the foreman were the 2 who wouldn't sign the juror's affidavits).

Gore told me about a talk he had with a female friend of his from Ada. He said she told him that I had raped an "old woman"! Can you believe the rumors that start? This girl used to work for the police as an informant and hung out with those fine detectives on the force. I'm sure they filled her head with these fantasies for fun. Crazy. I've never done anything against these people. Or maybe it was Gore living up to the warnings to me from other people about his lying. He did watch my reactions with a funny look in his eye, now that I think about it.

Pam and I spoke during interviewing of the jurors. She woke up my naïve self, about exactly what a rape kit is. She thinks fingernail and skin scrapings **would** be there. The doctor and whoever else did the kit must know something.

If there was **her** skin under her fingernails (I believe she scratched herself across the chest) and they withheld that evidence or the rape kit altogether, then that would be cause for a new trial.

Wednesday, June 26, 1996

I finished my narrative today, *Lamia.* I need to perfect it now. Thirty pages, single-spaced.

Talked to Garvin today. He said he hoped to finish the brief by Friday.

Talked to the brother Charles Haley (I called him on the prison phones!). Time will tell if he decides to sign the affidavit.

Sunday, July 7, 1996

The last four days have been 105 degrees, 108, 110, 106 or so. HOT! Setting records. I can't remember any hotter days. Vannoy has been working on getting more affidavits. We won the yard softball championship.

Tuesday, July 16, 1996

About a month ago or so, another friend of mine named Rick (another Rick; a black fellow who lived in the cell next to me) and I came to the realization about Anthony Foster. Rick went to school with him and grew up around his family. Today Rick told me that Anthony Foster lives across the street from his brother! What a small world, huh?

Tuesday, July 30, 1996

I mailed the packets to Gerry Spence and the KATT. I am so excited.

*

I mailed to attorney Gerry Spence a copy of my narrative and a videotape that summarized the case and the new evidence. He is the attorney with the buckskin coat that is always on television. He had a show on CNBC. I thought he might be able to help get my story out. Garvin was a friend of his and was my current attorney, but I felt he would understand my seeking Gerry's help in getting my story out. He did send me a reply saying that he wished me well even though he couldn't help at this time, which is more than I can say about all of the other people and organizations that I sent information to. I sent Rick and Brad at the KATT a copy of my narrative only.

Thursday, August 8, 1996

Last night I had a dream about having to face the death penalty. I was on a dream-like death row, more like the basement of a gymnasium or something. We were able to walk around and stuff though. All of a sudden, they told us that one of us would die tonight, and we wouldn't know who until right when they were ready to do it. Short dream. I woke up soon after they told us one would die! Scary.

Tonight, Hatch dies at OSP. It has been all over the TV. He killed Brooks Douglas's parents.

Spence was on *Late, Late Show* last night. I missed it.

Monday, August 12, 1996

Garvin fired me. He will represent me until the next hearing. A bad day.

*

My attorney was pretty mad that I sent the information to Gerry Spence. Perhaps he felt betrayed, I don't know. I just always felt that the way I needed to go was through the media to reach American's souls; that somehow things would work out if people were made aware of this injustice. Everyone other than me felt that the appeals system would grant the relief we sought, but I was the one seeing it fail at each step and was continuing to sleep on a metal bunk each night.

He agreed to continue with the next appeal, to the federal district court, and to represent me if I got a hearing. I felt stressed and embarrassed a little because the packet did not achieve its intended effect, but I was comfortable that I had done what I needed to do. I knew that this would probably be my last attorney for my appeal. I would do it myself.

Sunday, August 18, 1996

I had a dream last night about being back around 1920 in Ada. I had the period clothes on and could see and feel them. I could feel the time period essence in the air. I was close to the Ada Middle School, walking around. Neat dream.

Friday, August 23, 1996

Well, I wrote the letter to Dad about Garvin and his response to my video, and the letter asking him to return to my case. Dad should get it tomorrow.

I have been researching for the 10th circuit if I have to do it myself. I'm going to try to get someone to take it pro bono, though.

Last night about 7:00, they took blood for the DNA database. What an invasion of privacy and a possibility of being set up. My cellie is so afraid of being set up. He should know.

Josh started first grade. Dad said when he got home Wednesday that Josh was doing his homework.

I had another guy ask me if I used to be at Conner's (Dick Conner Correctional Center, in Hominy, OK). I look exactly like a guy at Conner's, a man named Frank.

Sunday, August 25, 1996

Josh and Mom came up today. I told Josh again as best I could about my situation. It is hard to tell a six-year-old about a rape case. I said that it is weird with grownups sometimes, that they can't admit their mistakes.

Tuesday, August 27, 1996

Boy, last weekend was really a bad one. I have really had a bad month. Probably the worst month yet. Garvin, the rodeo tryout, the sweat lodge. I think I had somewhat of a nervous breakdown the last week or so, but more like a mental overload, a misfiring of emotions and thoughts, a drain and depression. I seem to be in better spirits today.

I will try to go back to Joseph Harp to work and the atmosphere seems better there. I wonder if the Indian (leader of the sweat) put bad medicine on me that day. If he did, I believe I shall prevail.

Thursday, August 29, 1996

That Tiger Woods' guy's first day of pro career. I feel he may break all of the records and change golf forever (he is black).

I had been trying to contact the Montel Williams show, and Larry Stadler was contacted by them this week but doesn't want to appear on it. I will!

I'll always remember the mosquitoes all over the TV and room. Also, bad bagworms this year because of the "reverse" precipitation over the last six months. They cut down the shade tree outside of our cell because of bagworms.

Dad will talk to Garvin on Thursday about things. I am ready for him to file and get on with it.

September 17, 1996

Dad talked to Garvin today. No change in his stance. He'll take care of any oral arguments or hearing if needed. Then I'll be on my own which is fine now that he has shown his true colors.

I come up for pre-parole tomorrow. What a joke.

Wednesday, September 18, 1996

Dad went before the parole board today. Nothing spectacular. They gave him two minutes to speak.

*

We filed the brief in the United States District Court for the Western District of Oklahoma on September 18th, the same day I came up for pre-parole. I sent each of the parole board members a copy of my narrative and a cover letter explaining myself. They probably thought I was a jailhouse nut. Maybe it was a bad idea, but it is what I did.

Garvin did another good job with the brief. Included were the affidavits from the jurors and from the second husband, but no mention of the arson or Officer Gilligan's report. I am of course hopeful, but I am preparing by myself a brief for the 10th Circuit Court of Appeals in Denver, CO if I am turned down by this judge.

In October of 1996, The Western District Court requested a transfer of our brief to the Eastern District in Muskogee because of the magnitude of appeals in the Western District. We agreed.

Thursday, September 26, 1996

Had a dream last night. Jack Nicklaus, Josh and I were at a Ken's Pizza, fixin to eat pizza. Jefferson Starship's "Lay it on the line" came on the jukebox and Jack began to sing. He sang well. I joined him and we stood up and sang the whole song. Josh looked at us like we were crazy. We finished to a standing ovation. I woke up to the song on the radio. Been thinking about starting a cookie business.

Wednesday, October 2, 1996

The Albert Einstein show last night was quite a jolt.

Today and last night the police were looking for an aluminum piece of trim from the door's windows, thinking of course that it could be sharpened and used as quite a sword.

A few days ago, there was a minor stabbing. An Indian stabbed a Mexican. The Mexican did some sort of damage to their sweat lodge. I realized that this could escalate into a homicide. The Mexican disrespected and more or less mocked the Indian's very soul; their spiritual intensive type of life; their very God. If one of those Indians is a killer, he might kill that Mexican. And that trim makes quite a fatal weapon.

October 17, 1996

We were locked down for two days so the DOC soldiers could take our always dangerous wooden shelves. But we got a pint of ice cream and have fried chicken tonight for dinner, so we want shakedowns as much as possible.

I had some strange dreams last night. In one dream I had to carry someone to the emergency room because traffic was stopped up.

Reminded me of my dream where I went through empty halls and elevators of a hospital.

One dream I was at a swimming pool and Pamela Anderson was there and we were friends. We were talking and it felt really comfortable.

Saw Josh Sunday and he said he wanted his Daddy home for Christmas, and a Ninja Megasword.

October 18, 1996

Last Tuesday I talked to Sgt. Ford about his call for count time (time when inmates are counted). He really winds up and bellows, "It's count time!" very loudly and drawn out. I asked him, "Have you ever lived by a railroad track and at a certain time a few times a day the train whistle blows and eventually drives you mad so you have to move? Know what I'm saying?" Today was his first day back and he voiced a short, to the point call for count time. I hope it continues. I'll buy him a Snickers today for incentive. Just rude.

Friday, November 1, 1996

Talked to Rick's attorney today. Rick was acquitted of three counts of child abuse and three counts of assault. Good news for him.

Monday, Veterans Day, November 11, 1996

Thinking of habeas corpus in Eastern District. Funny, but I look forward to their denial so I can have control of my appeal in the 10th circuit. Wrote Gerry Spence again, and Garvin a couple of weeks ago.

Had a bad day Sunday, Sunday morning especially. Happens after days and days of prison, the bottling up of emotions, the resistance of the psyche to slip into reality. A mini-nervous breakdown, that I experienced as anger first, then depression. I recognize the importance of the track, the gym, the library and ball-field. And drugs, coffee and cigarettes too. The ball-field was my escape but it was closed today. What a sorry place to be. It is a nightmare unless you really wanted to come here. Some do.

Friday, November 22, 1996

Dave (Rick's cellmate) got shipped to Texas and my cellmate Jerry moved in with Rick. I talked to Craig today and Cindy Garza (Channel 5) called him! I then talked to her. I am working to put together some information for her such as Rita's statement and her trial testimony.

Monday, November 25, 1996, 2:30 pm

I went by and saw that I have legal mail today. I can't explain the tension I have from now until 3:00 pm when I can pick it up. Kind of like waiting for the results of an important exam that you were unsure about. You really don't want to even look at it, but want to run and hide. I think that it may be from Craig about Garza, but I am reserving myself and preparing as if it is a denial by the Eastern District. Of course, a reversal needs no preparing for. But I'll be Okay in a day or so and will get my habeas for the 10th circuit going.

Thursday, December 12, 1996

I have talked to Garza on the phone. Talked to her last night for about twenty minutes. I will call back tonight to talk her into coming and seeing me. My case is before a magistrate, Judge Payne in Eastern District.

I made wooden Christmas ornaments for Mom, Dad and Josh.

Dad sent me three books on physics. I am probably half finished with my habeas corpus.

Geoff is my current cellie. I hope his wife hooks me up with a girl named Ann.

Finished humanities class today. It changed my life. Will take Administrative Policy next semester.

Saturday, December 14, 1996

Talked with Rex the other day. Rex is an older man who was convicted of setting his wife on fire, killing her. Rex has the beginnings of Alzheimer's disease. He's forgetting what day it is and names and such. We talked for a while. I told him about my grandfather and of my interest in neurology and asked if I could ask him a few questions about it. We talked of several ideas, mine being to exercise those functions, i.e., to do repetitions of recalling names, the days of the week, etc. to strengthen these functions. Rex is also taking melatonin and says he feels like a million bucks. Rex is a respected man here, a former petroleum geologist. He said to me, "I can tell from the way you express yourself and talk that you will be a great doctor or whatever you endeavor. You will be very successful." No doctor here, but I sure was humbled by that. But he has Alzheimer's, right?

Christmas, December 25, 1996

Well, another Christmas (#5) in prison. Another look from beyond of the beauty of X-mas. Talked to Josh at Mom's earlier. He sounded like he had the whole legion of superheroes: Batman, Power Rangers and Stretch Ninja. I was watching one of the parades. Buzz Lightyear had a float and it made me think of how different growing up on the verge of the new millennium is, versus the 1970's. The computer age! The hardest time in here is leading up to Christmas. Once it arrives, it's better. Then the NFL playoffs, bowl games, etc. lead you into the New Year.

The last six months have been a very rich and dynamic development for my mind and soul. The discovery of Leonardo's zest for life (learned in my humanities class) and the great men of history changed my passion for life. The book on Einstein has been a deeply spiritual experience and sparked my love and life as a theoretical physicist, quantum theorist and searcher of the "machinery of life". Fascinating.

Geoff moved in a couple of weeks ago and is very smart. He is a licensed embalmer and can hold discussions with me about medicine and physics.

Garza, or should I say the channel 5 producer, slammed the door on my plight last Thursday. What a good laugh I got from that one. He said the reason for not continuing with my story was, "What if he is guilty?" There is risk in everything.

Thursday, December 26, 1996

I was thinking of about a month ago when I was going to move to Unit 6, my buddy's reaction. He actually got mad, like I was abandoning him. Angry. I have given him so much encouragement and positive direction. Maybe he didn't have anyone like that growing up. I bring so much energy to those guy's minds. I know I've changed their perspective of life.

I was talking with Geoff about the death of Larry Stadler last night. I had been trying to identify the "fog of dread" that I felt had moved all over the prison or at least on this unit. I felt it in my soul and was trying to place it, identify it. Geoff quoted the Bible about the fog of the demon hanging around for 2-3 days reaching to others. Good that Geoff could admit he knew what I was trying to identify. I thought of the Indian man at the sweat.

*

Larry's suicide was selfishness at its peak. The ultimate definition of selfishness (because of his mother and family). I can hear Larry saying, "I'll show them."

My friend Larry Stadler hung himself in his cell on Christmas Day 1996. His wife left him in September and broke his heart. It was just a downward slide for him until he took his life.

His wife came to see him every weekend. She was really pretty, probably too pretty for Larry. She was his life and rock. She came to see him as usual one Sunday, but the next Tuesday he got a letter from her stating her intention to leave him. She really took it too far in my opinion. She said that she was leaving him and moving back to Minnesota, that she had never loved him and that the last five years (how long they had been together) had been miserable for her.

Larry came to my cell to tell me about it that day in September. I tried to just be supportive, understanding and let him know that heartache happens. He was really confused, as could be expected. He wanted to believe that her girlfriend, and her girlfriend's husband had something to do with it, asking her to leave him and move to Minnesota. It may have been that simple, with his wife just being a fickle young girl who needed to get away. However, I felt the intensity of the letter explained her intentions and feelings clearly, so what do you say?

Larry weighed 240 pounds in September. He was at 180 in December. He quit eating, or just quit going to the chow hall. I wasn't alarmed at this because his cellie worked in the kitchen and they ate plenty, off of his hustle. I had noticed his weight loss, but figured that this was just a healthy reaction to his plight. Get in shape. He continued to come by and talk and I did my best to help.

A day or two before Christmas, I was talking with him in his cell and he was whining about how his mom didn't do this, or that, on time. He also was still in denial about his wife leaving him. I thought that he needed to face the fact that his wife was gone and that he was in here. He just wouldn't believe that she was really gone.

On Christmas Day about 3:00 pm, he called his mother and was upset about the conversation. Count time was at 4:20 pm. His cellie was working in the kitchen. Larry took his belt and attached it to the top bunk and then threaded an extension cord through a hole in the belt and made a noose with the rest of the cord. He did all of this with his door closed and his "jigger" curtain up (something that covers the 4" x 12" window for privacy while doing private business). The guard discovered him about 4:30 pm and after attempts by an inmate to revive him, he soon was carted out of the unit.

I was just freaked out after count finally cleared and I heard what the holdup had been and who had died. I thought about my harshness with him a couple of days ago, but took comfort in that I was just trying to help. Perhaps I would be a little more sensitive if the same type of despair happened to another friend, but I handled this one the best I could. With about two years to discharge and a chance to redeem himself in his love's eyes, now he was just dead.

1996. This was a year of ups and downs, lessons and puzzlements. The first year at LCC had been different. It started so well with the news of a possible hearing, which to me at the time meant I would be going home. The denial of the hearing and the appeal to the district court in Ada brought James' pessimistic words that much closer to my reality. It had been a year and a half since I "would be out any day". My contact with the interested television people was just another tease, although I felt Ms. Garza was a true soul.

I had written The Innocence Project in New York earlier in the year. It was a program set up by Barry Scheck and another attorney to offer helping in getting innocent men released from prison. They were currently involved in helping Ronald Williamson (and Dennis Fritz), who was convicted in Ada, with his case. Mr. Scheck answered my letter, but stated their inability to help me as my case was one of consent and would not be helped with any DNA testing.

I had gotten back into my old habit of pot smoking with the drug's abundance on this yard and the UA's being easier to beat than at Harp. The jobs here were limited and I was happy to be able to be a student and not have to hold a meaningless job. After an Intermediate Accounting class completed in the spring, I changed my focus and major to Marketing. I was interested in gaining knowledge for my business. I knew accounting and didn't want to do it as a career.

My life was inspired and forever changed by the study of Leonardo da Vinci in my humanities class. He was just so grateful to be able to awake every day and have the opportunity to seek more knowledge and wisdom. The Einstein book also gave me great energy as I focused on his views and theories. I felt lucky to have thought up my business ideas and would spend countless hours daydreaming about them and formulating plans in my head. My self-pity thoughts were balanced by my future opportunities.

My friends Rick and Jerry (my cellmate) were good tonic for my soul. We were able to joke around and got along good. I'm not always able to just hang out and talk with "the guys". They were my brothers. We loved each other like family in this unfortunate situation.

Larry Stadler's death was a trip. He was simply heartbroken and lost his spirit to live. That is such a vital process in here; wake up every day and find a reason to live on. When times would get tough for me, I would remember my cellmate with LIFE plus twenty. I believed in his innocence, although I didn't believe there were many truly innocent.

Perhaps one out of every hundred. Should that one just be sacrificed for the good of the system?

As 1996 closed, I was blending in, just another DOC number with a quantity of days next to that number on my time sheet. I was more and more grateful that the jury did not give me that thirty years Ross asked for.

Chapter 16 Still waiting for release

Thursday, January 2, 1997

Great day so far! I've resumed my workouts for the last three days. I've come out of a 15–20-day rut, from the holidays. What an emotional time for me. For every good period, there is as much or more lonely periods. And easy to be frustrated, because I can't get out!

Called Craig on Tuesday and he said a letter from Drew Edmondson had arrived or something. Not clear what that meant. He said call back today. What is so funny is that I'm not going to call because I have this sense of hope for good news. Why spoil it, at least for today. A good feeling is hard to come by.

Beautiful weather today, must be close to 70 degrees. Finishing up *In Search of Schrodinger's Cat*. Every particle has an equal partner that mirrors its movement. Action at a distance. Einstein put it well as he called this "ghostly" communication. Beautiful concepts to imagine.

*

I was able to find a book in the library at LCC about diagnosing mental disorders (*DSM-III: Diagnostic and Statistical Manual of Mental Disorders*, Third Edition, American Psychiatric Association). I was amazed at some of the specific patterns of behavior that it listed, and Rita seemed to exhibit.

The book stated that many times it is difficult to pinpoint one specific disorder to a person's behavior as they may exhibit behaviors of two or three disorders. I could see Rita within several categories of explained behaviors of the text.

Some of the information under Histrionic Personality Disorder:

The essential feature is a Personality Disorder in which there are overly dramatic, reactive, and intensely expressed behavior and characteristic disturbances in interpersonal relationships.

Individuals with this disorder are lively and dramatic and are always drawing attention to themselves. They are prone to exaggeration and often act out a role, such as the "victim" or the "princess," without being aware of it.

Behavior is overly reactive and intensely expressed. Minor stimuli give rise to emotional excitability, such as irrational, angry outbursts or tantrums. Individuals with this disorder crave novelty, stimulation, and excitement and quickly become bored with normal routines.

Such individuals are typically attractive and seductive. They attempt to control the opposite sex or enter into a dependent relationship. They may make suicidal gestures or attempts. Frequent complaints of poor health, such as weakness or headaches, or subjective feelings of depersonalization may be present. During periods of extreme stress, there may be transient psychotic symptoms of insufficient severity or duration to warrant an additional diagnosis. A common complication is Substance Use Disorder, particularly in women.

There were also behaviors under Borderline Personality Disorder that I recognized:

There is impulsivity or unpredictability in at least two areas that are potentially self-damaging, e.g., spending, sex, gambling, substance use, shoplifting, overeating, physically self-damaging acts.

The person expresses physically self-damaging acts, e.g., suicidal gestures, self-mutilation, recurrent accidents or physical fights.

Sunday, January 19, 1997

Last Tuesday or Wednesday, Ford shook us down and found my can (for smoking). He didn't write me up. Called Dad and was told about Judge Payne's order for the State to show cause why this writ should not issue. I felt that it was too hopeful. Friday was my 30th birthday. Strange, I've felt somewhat down. I am getting tired of this yard and may look into a minimum security. I finished the *Chaos* book, the "flow" of life, as Plato saw it. Michael Jordan in a flow.

Sunday, January 26, 1997, Super Bowl Sunday

Cellie had a visit. I'm waiting on Ms. Hiner to bring the paper. Thinking again. Played my first chess game last night! Played until 2:30 am on Geoff's computer chess game. J.R. and Barry had their little skirmish of violence. Blood all over the sidewalk. Oh, the situations that arise. One person decides to throw a punch or make a threat and the other guy must retaliate to save his honor and courage.

Gravity provides an ever-wonderful mystery, and the strange attractors, the force particles. There is great stress in my current rhythm of life. My cellie's great nervous energy and stress transfer to me. My nerves have progressively worsened since his arrival. God help us with the Eastern District.

Consciousness. Just now I was thinking of when I was very young and we all went to the Robbins' house and we were singing hymns and I couldn't read yet, but their boy my age could, so I mimicked the other singers, pretending I knew the words. Maintaining my pride?

February 21, 1997

What an intense month since school started. I got the job in the kitchen but resigned within a month because the last two guys that worked there died, one from cancer. I recognized how close my desk was to the kitchen electrical service box and just got paranoid. I got my blood work today. I'm normal! Knock on wood. Found the book, *Unseen Hands and Unknown Hearts*. I dreamt of Garvin last night. We were outside in his yard, he had a big home and a spacious airplane (leer jet) and had to leave quickly because of danger or trouble. About all I remember.

March 13, 1997

Last evening there was one of the most beautiful full rainbows I can remember outside of Hawaii. It looked as if one end sat in Ada and the other in Norman! Ha.

I've been busy with the policy class and am learning a lot. I read the book *Pyramid Power*, the golden ratio and all. I'm mailing to Jenny Jones today. Tomorrow is Einstein's birthday.

Saturday, March 15, 1997

I was just thinking of the young kid who I have been encouraging for months to learn, read, etc. I was planting the seed. Now even though we had a falling out, I see him reading in his room and in the library. He is a different person from one year ago. He quit making getting high his only quest for the day and actually has a month of clean time. The seed is growing.

Monday, March 17, 1997 (six years since meeting Rita)
Bad day. Got mad at stupid computer for losing my text. Then found out the State responded finally, but don't know details yet.

*

The State responded to our brief. Basically, they just used some mumbo jumbo to paint me as an idiot and a guilty idiot at that. However, they really didn't have any comeback for the juror's affidavits, which was a relief. They said that their affidavits were "inconsequential", which is showing disrespect for the juror's intelligence. Who should be in a better position to decide if our new evidence is outcome determinative, the Attorney General's hired help or the jurors who heard the case?

Wednesday, April 16, 1997
Long day today. We completed our oral presentation of USG (U.S. Gypsum) for the Policy class. I moved to Unit 6 yesterday. Had a good conversation with my cellie Harjo.

Thursday, April 24, 1997
Much better since moving up here. My spirits are much better day-to-day.

*

I had to leave Unit 4 to save my nerves. The noise was always loud on the unit and with me reading a lot; it had an effect on me. Unit 6 was a different type of dorm, with more room to move around and higher, sound deafening ceilings. My first cellie was a fragile, older Indian man who told me of a spiritual awakening he had that I thought was interesting. He said that as he was having a heart attack many years ago, God spoke to him and told him that he would not die. From there he began his spiritual journey of development, continuing today. After a few weeks with him, I then moved in with my friend Jon Davis.

I continued to read and study both on my own and for my classes. Chess had become an obsession to me and I was studying books and practicing hours a day. The chess was the same as the Einstein theories. Maybe I was always too scared to learn.

Tuesday, April 30, 1997

Had a dream last night about Mam (expired grandmother) & Papa. We were in my mom & dad's room as it was before renovation. Papa had gotten some new golf clubs with intricate designs on them. We were looking at them. I noticed how small the head on them was, hard to hit with. My sister was sitting in Dad's burnt orange rocking chair. Papa said, "Mam, come look at these." Or something like that. Mam very politely and charmingly said she would backtrack later, examining the clubs then.

Then Mam told us to **speak up** in life when something bothers us or we need to say something. She lay on the bed and I took her hand. She grimaced in pain (like she had arthritis) but bore it so I could hold her hand. I could really feel her hand. I was crying pretty much all through the dream and as I woke up. I feel closer to Mam now.

Monday, May 12, 1997

Sent story to Barbara Walters and Larry King a couple of weeks ago. I got a postcard from Larry King thanking me for writing him. I have story to Connie Chung ready to go tomorrow.

Finished our Administrative Policy class. Good class. I got a 169 on my achievement test, John 162, Marshall 156. National average was 155.6. I felt proud. Of all of us.

Having a rough time of it lately. Severe prison burnout and boredom. Josh came up Sunday and read to me. That was a trip. Got an aloe vera plant.

Friday, June 6, 1997

Not too much to write about. Moved in with Jon Davis a month ago. Mom got a new knee Tuesday. Got twenty-five pages done on my Bermuda Triangle solution novel.

Friday, June 27, 1997

Quasim Alim (a fellow inmate; worked in visiting room) told me he had a dream last night that I went back to court.

Tuesday, July 1, 1997

Today my friend Geoff got hit in the jaw (face, cheek) with a 2x4 (piece of lumber) over that crap with Alfonso. Alfonso got shipped to the Walls (Oklahoma State Pen) but the guy who hit him is still here. Bad deal. Broke his jaw, cheekbone, skull, and bones of the orbit. Hit him at Vo-Tech, Geoff just coming around the corner and never seeing it. He said he woke up, not knowing what happened but went to the bathroom, saying "he fell". Crushed his sinus and lucky to not have damaged his brain.

Monday, July 21, 1997

Got my chessboard July 9th. I have gained tenfold in playing strength since that time. Remarkable. Had R.C. beat and made a stupid move. The night before that I beat Geoff playing black, my first win against him. Dr. Seigbert Tarrasch (one of the original Grandmasters) says there is only one correct move, what the position demands. Probably a lot like decisions in life.

I've lost fervor for my novel, need a voice recorder.

Sunday, August 3, 1997

Last Saturday Josh and Dad came up for Benny Boeck Day. I had a joyful time. We ran around the bases (Josh and I) probably ten times.

My mental stability has been wavering. I am just getting completely burned out of this place. I have no job, nothing to provide self-esteem but exercising, thinking, and studying chess. I am seriously considering transferring.

Asked Cindy Garza to come see me. I just don't feel like I can be understood over the phone or through a letter. She hasn't even answered.

Tuesday, August 12, 1997

This summer has been a huge bore, without a class or a job, I was terribly pressed to find things to satisfy my self-esteem. This week I'll send in the money for the Governmental Accounting class. Chess is improving. No word from Judge Payne.

Saturday, September 6, 1997

One of my dreams last night, was that Judge Payne was not the man reviewing my case but that someone named William was. I think I saw his name on the opinion written, but I don't remember what the opinion said.

Also dreamed of Dad and I, stopping at a convenience store to buy Coors beer, which was on sale. He bought Heineken instead.

Tuesday, September 23, 1997

Yesterday and today we (the whole yard) were shook down because of a stabbing last week. We were shook down by one of the biggest maggots. His hero must be the head cop in *Shawshank Redemption*. They took a lot of stuff. Took the tin box that I got at Harp. I had a quarter and the lady on the unit wanted so bad to write me up for it. I still laugh at the look on her face when she saw it. She's one of those people that really gets off by telling on people or writing them up. These shakedowns really make us hate the police even more, them throwing our stuff around and shoving it in a corner. Oh well, I don't let it stew in me.

Sunday, November 17, 1997

What the problem is with most of the sorry cops is that they have no respect or appreciation for the sensitivity in the human interactions associated with shaking down a person's cell or body down and giving orders. Any sensitive, sophisticated person would realize that some respect, understanding and friendliness is necessary to facilitate a tolerable situation that wins for both sides, for harmony. It's the same in the world with the haves and have-nots. Selfishness and lack of concern for mankind makes the problems with society.

December 1, 1997

I wonder how many men are in prison for the following reason or set of circumstances: someone is raped in a certain area of town. A man with a criminal conviction for rape lives in that area. He may be unfortunate in that no one can verify his whereabouts during the time in question. He may not have an alibi and the paranoia of the police leads to another conviction.

By the way, imagine Rita playing her mind on Leewright. He believed her illusions, I think. His paranoia flowed right along with her lies. Did he or any other, screw her?

December 19, 1997

I had especially good spirits today. Rita's birthday…Meaning? Beautiful day. Clear and 65 degrees.

Sunday, December 28, 1997

Cindy Morgan read *Lamia* (my narrative) tonight. She and I discussed it and other things. She certainly thought it was interesting. She said, "This could be a novel." She had good vision of the police's case and related mostly with that, I felt. I was characteristically overly defensive when we talked. She read it very fast. I was impressed with her brainpower.

*

Cindy was a female guard I became friendly with who was interested in my case. She treated me with respect and trust. Maybe she could spot a decent person in all of the trash that was in here. I talked with her a lot.

Mothers' Day
May '97

1997 ended with the same anticipation of release that had plagued me from the beginning. Perhaps my time would have been easier if I were guilty and knew that I must complete my sentence to get out. This anticipation of release was like a cruel trick played on my hope spirit. But what a gracious trick, I realized.

The college classes that had been so important to me were running out. I was coming to the point where I only needed upper-level courses to graduate that weren't offered through the college program.

My cellmate Jon Davis had been shipped in May and Bobby Powell (James Powell my friend at Harp!) had lived with me since. Jonathon Davis was the smartest person I met in prison, and he and I worked together with the Policy class. Tall and straight of bearing, Jon was born and raised in Maryland, but had wound up with an Oklahoman LIFE sentence fifteen years ago. Fluent in computers, I would have him in a second as a business partner. He always reminded me of the comedian Steve Martin when he smiled, the way his eyes pull up on the outside corners.

Bobby Powell was young and working hard to improve himself as I was. He was a good person, witty and cool. We got along well and were able to have a lot of laughs and talk about women, the times of our lives, and do our *Dumb and Dumber* impressions.

Chapter 17 Pro se brief

January 10, 1998

How about that insane guard on our unit squeezing that guy's testicles and shining the flashlight at his rear end?

Had the dream the other night about famed attorney Gerry Spence roping a horse and carriage that I was riding in. What could that mean?

*

One of the guards was just sadistic and mentally ill. He had choked a guy to death at the Walls (McAlester, OK, Oklahoma State Penitentiary) a few years back and was continuing with insane behavior. This inmate was in a wheelchair, his lower calf deformed from a wreck or something. Out of the blue, right in front of everyone, this guard decides to shake him down. It's like 6:30 am and the guy is returning from breakfast. This guy didn't even do drugs, he was just minding his own business.

The situation was really weird. The guard grasped the guy's testicles until he yelled out, and then shined his flashlight and got close up to look at the guy's bottom. The guard always worked the graveyard shift because the staff knew of his peculiarities. His MO was to enter inmate's cells at night, shining his flashlight in their eyes to wake them up and try to provoke them into a write-up or more. Simply mentally ill.

Thursday, January 22, 1998

Had a dream last night about the eyes. A blonde girl with perfect brown eyes, looking at me and smiling a glorious smile.

Last Saturday was my 31st. Josh wrote the letter on the computer the week before asking his question (What do I do every day?). I answered him last night. Makes me realize how dull my life is.

Tuesday, February 17, 1998

Same thing day after day. Oh, the insanity of some of the DOC employees. I have been trying lately to just stay focused on the present. That is my new philosophy. The future looks good if I'm out and exonerated of this crime, but other scenarios are only depressing. Waiting for possible word from psychologist at Framingham (mental hospital in MA) that I wrote. Not much chance of correspondence, I fear. Hopefully the videotape will get to Dad this week.

Had a dream last night about being in a Lincoln and driving through Ada, remarking at how much it had changed. Went to a small house in the country to party with Terry Teel, Jay Johnson, Kathy (high school classmates) and others I can't specifically remember. Had a small golf hole or something there and Greg Norman was out hitting some balls. We were inside changing to go swimming.

*

I made a videotaped summary of my case and Dad sent a copy of it and a copy of my narrative to five places (Primetime Live, Dateline NBC, Sally Jesse Raphael, Maury Povich and a man in Texas who helped get an inmate off of death row), hoping to spark their interest in my case. No responses at all.

On March 15th, 1998, my friend came over to smoke a cap with me. Right after he left, the guard appeared at my cell.

"Mr. Thompson, #162066, they want you in central control for a UA."

"Okay." I said with a false confidence, like "no worries".

My world came crashing down in a hurry. I drank a lot of water before I went, but failed the test for marijuana. I was looking at thirty days in the disciplinary unit. A jail within a jail. At the time, my hope was to discharge this sentence completely in the early summer of 1999. Now I was looking at November of 1999. The worse part of it would be telling my parents and kid that I must do more time in prison. Why do I risk everything just to smoke pot?

On March 20th, 1998, I was sent to DU to do my thirty days, and finally called my dad from there with my evening phone call. I decided to appeal this write-up to see if I could beat it. I didn't appeal the one at Harp. By the time I went to DU, I had prepared my appeal.

On April 3rd, after fourteen days, Ms. Morgan (she was working DU) informed me that I had beaten the write-up! I was as happy as a bird. Because of lack of bed space, it would be another nineteen days until I was completely off of DU. During this time, I would be allowed freedom during the day, but had to come back to spend the night in DU. After a few days on Unit 4 living with my friend Pigg, I was moved back to Unit 6.

Wednesday, April 22, 1998

Just got out after doing 33 days for a dismissed write-up. Just happy to be out.

Sunday, April 26, 1998

Krissy and Josh came up today. I told Krissy about her trapezius muscle and her metabolism. Somehow, they had thought I was going to be out in December. When she told Josh this, he animatedly slammed his fist on the table, an act I recognized as disappointment and frustration. Pain hurts our feelings. I talked about some pretty heavy moral issues with Krissy. Josh was named the Johnson O'Malley student of the year for the second grade!

Monday, April 11, 1998

It is starting to get hot again. I am getting back into shape, feels good. HOPE…for good news from the Judge. I watch the mail…and dream of getting a letter from someone who is to help facilitate my release. I see the unit manager…and hope he is going to say that I have a call in his office from someone asking to speak with me about my case. And I still hear the rattle of the keys in the same way.

The prisons are changing. Seems that the new director's vision is to really make prison unpleasant. Understandable.

I ordered some books on entrepreneurship today through inter-library loan. Hope to be able to learn something. It's chow time. Later.

Monday, May 18, 1998

Josh's 8th. Mom and he came up yesterday to visit but were told my visits were restricted, and they had to leave. Mom cried and both took it hard. It was a mistake by these people in not dismissing my sanctions from the write-up. I feel guilty for getting the write-up in the first place.

Josh got a hacky-sack for his birthday from me. I am not sure he knows what to do with it so I'll write him. I hope he and Krissy can play. Great exercise. I am comfortable with my cellie, Donnie. I guess I'll remain on Unit 6. Started OSI job today. Got UA'd tonight and passed it. Thank goodness.

Saturday, May 23, 1998

At work Friday I held up my four fingers to the guy who owed me the soups for so long, and he showed his left fist to me and counted his knuckles with his right hand, one, two, three, four. I told Bobby, "He's asking for it." He owed the soups to me for months. About 7:15 that evening, I followed him up to the unit. After summoning my courage along the way, I went to his room. He wasn't there but as I was walking down the stairs, he appeared from a room and walked towards me. I was almost at the bottom of the stairs, he above me. I asked him if he had my soups. He said no. I asked why. He moved down, even with me and said they screwed him at work, only giving him so much. I said I needed them tonight. I said he needed to borrow from someone and pay me now. Finally, I said, "I'll be back." He brought the soups by right after count. That was honorable. We just communicated. And are friends!

I talked to Josh and Bobby (my nephew) last night. I sure would like for him to come up with Josh and to bring the hacky-sack.

Some days in here I am on the verge of insanity. I have to actively participate in keeping myself together and rolling through the hard times with serenity. I of course think of the guys with life sentences and such, whose plight must be deadening compared to mine. It's funny though. If you get 10 years you have a hope. If you get 20 years you have a different hope. A life sentence dashes many hopes but a new one will arrive. Even death row, right up until the final breath, there is hope given you. Inspirations and enthusiasms drive us. You either use it or lose it, Life.

Saturday, May 30, 1998

With all of my aspirations, I still am and will be upon my release just an innocent man wrongly convicted. Really just a fool tricked into six years of prison.

Mother is so dire and filled with dread. The things she says to me, spook me. She just can't understand why I am not out. I think I have dealt with that question myself, "Why can't someone with overwhelming evidence get an immediate hearing?" I remember an excerpt from a legal ruling that I read that stated, "It is better that a hundred guilty men go free than one innocent man be imprisoned." I realized very quickly, with the district court's denial, that the image of American justice is apparently a faded fantasy. Mom is just now coming to that realization.

Wednesday, June 10, 1998

Last night's sunset (when about twenty tornadoes rolled through OKC) was memorable. High altitude cloud cover reflected yellow and golden, while lower supercells in the distance were red, burgundy, blue and orange. Looking back towards Ada were three light reflections that reminded me of the northern lights. The sunset reminded me of a renaissance religious painting. Del Greco or such.

Thursday, July 9, 1998

It's been 100 degrees since Monday. Saturday four people DIED, heat related. Four more since. Last night my cellie, Shawn, got stabbed by Pigg. Didn't really hurt him though. I hope he can find some other way to live his life.

Shawn and Pigg had a little disagreement over some drugs I think, and Pigg made a "not very effective" shank with a disposable razor blade and some tape. He confronted him and cut him, but Shawn just had a shallow cut across his trunk and side.

Saturday, August 8, 1998

I've had four or five cellies since Shawn. I hope to keep the one I've got.

We're working on going to find and interview Rita. I hope we can get a confession from her.

Ordering all I can from inter-library loan about business, taxes, insurance, etc. Reading James Michener's *Hawaii*.

Thursday, August 13, 1998

Pam's birthday. I just called Dad and he told me that the Eastern District had denied my petition last May. Garvin changed addresses and the court just now found him. The court basically deferred to the decision of the post-conviction decision. I am very hurt right now and I know I'll need a few days to recover, although I am already rewinding and looking to the future. It is just unbelievable.

Last week we found out that perhaps Rita had accused three more people. I will try to call Pam later to see where our next move is. This literally has taken my breath away for the moment.

*

Judge Payne, United States District Court - Eastern District of Oklahoma, ruled that the juror's affidavits were not admissible. I was heartbroken and find their continued conservatism puzzling. He ruled that evidence of Rita's past false accusation of rape, and all of the other evidence of her behavior prior to 1991, was merely impeachment evidence and would not have made a difference in the verdict. Same as post-conviction appeal, basically. Heck, didn't know about it, was watching for it, for near three months.

Pam did some searching for Rita in Massachusetts. She was able to talk with a man (a police lieutenant) there who had information that Rita had perhaps accused THREE more innocent men since the last we had heard from her (in 1995). However, this information is hard to obtain because of the victim's rights statutes that keep this information confidential. We think that Rita is living as a transient around New Bedford, Massachusetts.

Wednesday, September 2, 1998

I won the yard chess tournament that was held last weekend! I played two rounds Saturday, one Sunday and the final against

"Louisiana" Monday and finishing last night. Won a case of pop. I have sure put countless hours into studying chess over the past twenty months. The warden came to our cell last night; he seemed to me a smart aleck and condescending.

Tuesday, September 29, 1998

Saturday Josh and Mom came up for the ball-field event. He told Mom it was the greatest day of his life. A special day. Mom was upset watching the guard pat-search me as I walked them out.

Another disappointment in that I've not heard from the investigative reporter that I wrote, Jack Cartwright from Texas Monthly Magazine.

Wednesday, October 7, 1998

My appeal was denied again (a request for a re-hearing) by the Eastern District. I'll probably end up doing the next round myself, but will meet with Craig next week.

Saturday, December 5, 1998

I'm currently working on 10th circuit appeal. I have until December 31, to file it. I still need some affidavits, especially the Campus Corner affidavit. Hope to get them soon.

Friday, Christmas Day 1998

Well, nothing exciting but not too down either. Lots of thoughts this morning of worldwide kids and their excitement and joy. Thoughts of all of my family and my son, hoping only for joy and fun for them. I had Dad get him a copy of *Island of the Blue Dolphins* to get him interested in reading. Another Christmas dinner here. Grateful just for that. Watched *Burden of Proof* and Gerry Spence with his new book about the problem with judges and lawyers. Just what my "being" has experienced in the past seven years. Six and a half months to go! God help me.

*

The highlight of the year was the time spent in DU for the misconduct that was eventually dismissed. Also, while living on Unit 6 in 1998, my friends John Daniels, and Tommy Ward, both from Ada, were on this unit. Tommy and John were old friends. I knew John from school (he was in my sister's grade), and he had lived in the neighborhood for a while. Tommy, I had met one time before, in 1983.

In the summer of 1983, John and I worked for the same mowing company in Ada. One Saturday, John and I had planned to go swimming. When I went to pick him up at his grandmother's house, at 5th and Cherry, Tommy Ward was there. That was the first time I had ever met him. He was nice. Quiet. I remember his straight-down, blond bangs, similar to mine. Long, over his eyes. I drove the three of us to Pennington Creek in Tishomingo. We swam and had a good time. The next year in April, Denise Haraway was kidnapped. Later in the year, Tommy would be arrested for her murder, along with Karl Fontenot. Soon after, author Robert Mayer would come to Ada to research and write the book, *The Dreams of Ada*.

At LCC, in the evening for supper, they released you after count time, one unit at a time, to the chow hall. Tommy, John and I would often sit together. Tommy's hands shook from nervousness, all the time. Well, one day, being ornery, I fronted him out a bit, just among us, and asked him if he had kidnapped and killed Denise Haraway. He answered me, in all ways I could understand, NO.

My appeal was continuing to show me the reality of the justice system. I guess I can understand. It is there to keep the ninety-nine percent in prison, as much as anything.

I felt fortunate to be able to continue my appeal, at all, to the 10th Circuit, after all of the mistakes. I had close contact with the court clerk there in Denver, telling me what I needed to do to "preserve my appeal". After finding out about the ruling in August, and with continued help from Craig, and Garvin's office, I would end up successfully filing the brief on the last day of 1998.

In October I moved to Unit 3. My friend Don Vaughan was looking for a cellie, and knew of only a couple of guys on the yard that he could get along with. I told him that I would move in with him. I was good for a change by this time.

Don was a 60-year-old man that had two life sentences and had been in for 40 years. 40 years! Man. He was as strong as an ox and lifted weights every day. He also did, like 1,000 push-ups throughout the day. He had the physique of a 30-year-old. Never asked him who he killed. Killed someone in prison also.

Wanting to assure my release from prison, I quit smoking marijuana for all of November, December and half of January before slipping and starting back.

I knew this black, old-school convict, Boone, who I also knew, from years ago, at Joseph Harp. He would talk with me about where he was now in his education, contrasting with such a lack of guidance growing up. He honestly, did not know his ABC's, until a few years ago.

He said, "You know, I'm still recovering from all of that and fighting to overcome it. Hell, I can spell most three- and four-letter words now. Pretty good for an ignorant fuck who couldn't say his ABC's!"

He is exaggerating some, but his eyes are like black steel, and a look of determination covers his face. I get a shiver in my head, his intensity being so powerful. He smiles and looks up in his mind for a few seconds before continuing, with a story he'd told me before.

"My mom would have a different boyfriend every few weeks, it seemed. Some were cool, but some were just losers, and so I would try to kick their ass, to get my mom back. So, I was 9, 10, 11, fighting grown men. Took out a lot of aggression on them, I guess. Damn sure was NOT scared, of any one of them. Scared of everything else I think, though. Man, what a screwed-up time that was."

I always had a good rapport with him. He was one of the most courageous men I have ever met. Can you imagine the courage it takes to admit you don't even know your ABC's, and then go about learning them? Man, what an inspiration!

I filed my pro se brief in the 10th circuit on December 31, 1998, hoping that my version would create some understanding. It felt good to finally give my own presentation of the case. No one knew my case better than I.

I was beginning to understand what James had told me years ago on our walks at Joseph Harp. The courts won't question the verdict, but just look at the procedural soundness of the trial.

I did the best I could to point out her inconsistencies and provide an explanation for the confession, as I failed to do that at trial. Some of the highlights of the brief:

****

INTRODUCTION

How strange and INEXPLICABLE that a woman could falsely accuse men of felonious beatings and rape, time and time again, as if it were an uncontrollable habit or addiction. This incredulity is what resulted in my OWN doubting of my sanity in the days leading to my arrest and on the day of my arrest, resulted in my conviction, and continues to hamper me in my appeals.

*

Here I have the chance to talk about "the confession":

CONFESSION

With evidence that someone other than Matthew Thompson caused her injuries (Mike Bryan), evidence that she has falsely accused men of beatings and rape before, and that she is a person who lies more than she tells the truth (second husband Kevin's affidavit), WHAT EVIDENCE DID THE COURT RELY ON TO DETERMINE THAT A REASONABLE PERSON WOULD STILL HAVE FOUND MATTHEW THOMPSON GUILTY OF THIS RAPE? COULD A REASONABLE TRIER OF FACT STILL FIND BEYOND A REASONABLE DOUBT EVERY ESSENTIAL ELEMENT NEEDED TO PROVE THE CRIME OF RAPE? The logic must be that Matthew Thompson made some incriminating statements that an innocent person would surely not make, that he confessed.

For two days I DENIED her statements and accusations. I was certainly confused and incredulous, but figured it was just her own confusion and imagination. Finally, AFTER TWO DAYS OF DECEPTION, LYING, AND CONFUSING TACTICS, at the end of the conversation at East Central University, I implemented the STRATEGY of admitting some fault and telling her what she wanted to hear, hoping she would feel better and then LEAVE ME ALONE! Although I was wary of her and her "girlfriend" because of the death threats she sent to me, and ironically asked if she went to the police, my innocence forbade me to imagine that she would be secretly recording our talk for the police and for the last two days had been attempting to help build a more believable case so the police could arrest me for a rape I did not commit! I felt compassion for the woman, even though I did not understand her position, and certainly her allegation of my role in it.

The next day the police asked if I would like to give a voluntary statement. I agreed and told the whole truth of what happened. Period. I believed they would investigate my side of the case.

On the day of my arrest and the moments of my giving the "confession", I must say that I was devastated by the accusations by her and the police, and the reality of the arrest on those charges had me sincerely and actually doubting my own memory, and gravely, in a much deeper contemplation, my own sanity. I vividly remembered the truth that I stated the day before on videotape, instead of what THEY were saying was the truth. The valium was a further consideration that made a mental malfunction on my part that much more imaginable. I just wasn't capable, with my own upbringing and sense of morality, to fully factor in the reality of her just lying about such a serious matter, against me, a person who had brought her only pleasure in the few hours that we were together. I trusted her and the detectives. Like a CANDID CAMERA set-up; people will doubt their own mind, even when the truth is right in front of them. This was no different, only on a much deeper issue, and a much deeper doubting of my sanity.

For what it is worth, for I can't at this time prove it, I gave the confession with a promise by Detective Cosper that "a statement to please the DA would result in the charges being dropped and that I would get some help in a drug treatment center." I was to deny the truth of the previous day's video, verbally acknowledge that my confusion about the facts was caused by drugs, and give a possible scenario of the events. That is just what I did. I was searching for the truth that everyone knew to be true but me.

It needs to be understood that AT THE TIME I GAVE THIS STATEMENT, ALL I KNEW OF HER STORY WAS HER ACCUSATIONS OF THE KNIFE AND THAT I ABDUCTED HER, MENTIONED BY HER IN OUR MEETINGS, WHICH I ALWAYS DENIED. Had I known of her ridiculous story (the descriptions of the person and car), had I known the true nature of the charges against me, I would surely have snapped to the conclusion of her untruthfulness and would never have given a false statement making ME look like the insane one. Over the next few days my attorney told me of her story and I realized I had foolishly helped the State build a case against an innocent man. I never had the chance to explain these facts to the jury as my attorney advised me not to take the stand. Lastly, SHOULDN'T A CONFESSION SUPPORT THE STATE'S VERSION OF THE FACTS? IT DOES NOT.

*

The critical importance of immediate investigation. Opportunity fades:

PROMPT INVESTIGATION

A.   My initial attorney did ZERO investigation for over five months after my arrest!

Wrongly accused, I trusted my attorney, much like a child trusts his parent, or a patient trusts his surgeon, to listen to me, search for the truth, and promptly and thoroughly investigate my side of the story, her version of the facts and the prosecutrix' background. Incredibly, and with no exaggeration, my attorney did ZERO INVESTIGATION OF MY CASE UNTIL OVER FIVE MONTHS PASSED AFTER MY ARREST WHEN HE FINALLY HIRED AN INVESTIGATOR.

1)	If he could have promptly found a patron or employee at Hardee's that saw Rita Gasteau and I sitting together in Hardee's, her story would have been destroyed and mine revealed as the truth.

2)	Had we obtained Hardee's cash register tapes with an employee (Rita) discount of food and drink, then a regular-sale ham and cheese sandwich and water shortly thereafter, then two six-packs of Bud Light from the twenty-four-hour Texaco within minutes of the Hardee's tapes, this circumstantial evidence could have been used to back up the truth.

3)	Had the employee of the Texaco remembered me coming in that morning and seeing Rita Gasteau sitting happily and consensually in the car, we could have backed up the truth.

You are aware of the vital importance of a prompt investigation of an alleged crime. CAN A FIVE-MONTH LAPSE BEFORE EVEN BEGINNING AN INVESTIGATION MEET THE REQUIREMENTS OF CONDUCTING A "PROMPT INVESTIGATION" AS STATED IN A.B.A. STANDARD 4-4.1? Prompt by definition is immediate; immediate being close to the present time. DID HE "EXPLORE ALL AVENUES" AS REQUIRED BY THE SAME STANDARD? I am not exaggerating when I say he explored ZERO avenues. With an evidentiary hearing, my attorney and the investigator could be asked to testify about their investigation in this case.

CONCLUSION

With an attorney who did no investigation for five months, who did not point out basic inconsistencies and not possibly true statements to the jury, who failed to find available evidence of the prosecutrix falsely accusing men of beatings and rape in the past, who could not procure the deposition of a witness who would take credit for causing the prosecutrix' injuries (the boyfriend) that the State always knew the whereabouts of, Matthew Thompson in essence had no representation at all.

With oral arguments, I could clarify the evidence and procure any needed testimony you may request. My innocence would be clear with a personal appearance. I ask you for a new trial in which I can present a

fair and thorough case. I would of course still risk the possibility of
another conviction. I don't want a free ride, just a fair chance. Thank
you for your time and patience.

****

Chapter 18   Fritz and Williamson freed

January 22, 1999

It is a great day when I get an inter-library loan book in. I'm stoked to absorb *Legal Master Guide for Business*. Good author. I came in early today, feeling on edge. Just sick of everything and my nerves are restless because of it.

Saw Josh, Mark, Dad and Mom on the day before my birthday. Josh has a chess set that he got for X-mas. We set it up and played a game. He knew how to set the pieces up already. Interesting day. Filed my brief on December 31st.

Sunday, February 7, 1999

Five months to go. My last few months since September or October, I've been here on Unit 3 in my own private cell. Don is at the clay shop from dawn to dusk-thirty. Every day, I meet the sun at my window, see it as I am going to work at OSI and then watch the sunset out the side window on my quad. I say, "Hey God! Thanks for that beautiful painting, evolving and recreating itself every second."

Wednesday, February 17, 1999

Tonight, I was UA'd once again. Clean! A potential nightmare was in reality just an inconvenience. I wonder if quitting my job had anything to do with the testing. Such an invasion of privacy. Suppose I was depressed as a result of my job/incarceration and instead of buying a box of Nutty Bars to feed my depression, I smoke some pot. My choice of one herb over another plant, chocolate (cocoa), would result in more time in prison.

Saturday, February 20, 1999

I spoke with Ron and James about the wonder and glory (just about life), as well as some of my own wonders. Such as…if I think of my friend, does somehow, she receive (or CAN receive it) stimulation of her nervous system from my strong essence of her in my mind and aura?

In effect, I'm e-mailing her, Krissy.com, with her essence, her mathematical vibration that is her fingerprint, of her Being. Also, like when you are focusing, praying for someone. Like an old phone, one piece of equipment to hear/receive, one to talk/send.

Thursday, March 18, 1999

I read in the paper this morning that Williamson and Fritz (the Debbie Carter murder case in Ada) have been cleared by DNA. Another blunder by Pontotoc County officials. Tommy Ward will not have DNA evidence to test.

Thursday, April 15, 1999

Today Ronald Williamson and Dennis Fritz were released from prison for the rape and murder of Debbie Carter. Also, Glen Gore was implicated as the prime suspect after DNA evidence matched his. Glen escaped from the trustee building yesterday and there is a manhunt on for him. Glen was the one who told me that the girl thought I had been convicted of raping an 80-year-old woman.

*

My friend Mario and I were playing chess in my cell when we heard the news of Williamson and Fritz's release on the television. I was confident against any player on the yard, but Mario had my number. I only beat him once or twice. He was a black guy who claimed to be Italian/Moorish. He said he was a Moorish warrior. He was a cocky yet peaceful fellow who enlightened me in the Muslim beliefs and ways of thinking. Anyway, he had told me weeks earlier about his "chess friend" at Conner's. He spoke about their games and that the guy studied books to learn the game like I did, and was always working on his case like I did. As the camera moved to Dennis Fritz, Mario said, "That's him! That's him! The guy I was telling you about. We would play chess. Fritz! Yeah, Fritz!". Mario knew Dennis Fritz from Dick Conner Correctional Center.

Today I have legal mail. I find out about mail at about 11:00 am and can't pick it up until 3:00 pm. I just can hardly bear the wait because I know it's some kind of bad news. It has been over four months since I filed my brief. It could be dismissed because I failed to show a federal right or question denied me by the district court. This saying more or less that they weren't even going to consider much of it. Their law clerks probably dismissed it before it reached the Judges, or suggested that it be dismissed by the court. I'm going to be madder than heck. Another pummeling. My body is in turmoil. My stomach tied up in knots. I get fidgety and can't relax. Can't read. Keep taking deep breaths to try to release some endorphins or such to counterattack my stress hormones in their wild escape. I'm getting ready for the body slam!

*

April 28, 1999 was a great day for me! I received legal mail in which the Tenth Circuit in Denver granted me a hearing! They also appointed me a federal public defender (I didn't ask for one). Between the time I saw that I had legal mail (about 11:00 a.m.) until I picked it up at 3:00 p.m., I about went crazy. I was just certain that such an early answer was a denial of my appeal. I had prepared myself for the "body-slam to the spirit" that a denial would have been. So, I was ready for that as I set out to read the letter.

I took the letter to a small rose garden, sat down and slowly opened it and began to read. When I read that I had been granted a hearing, I had to double-check to see that they had not made a typo. I'll always remember thinking, as I digested the letter: "Hey, this is **GOOD**!" I must have read this letter twenty times that day and the next. More than a few times my eyes welled with joy that someone finally had given us a small crumb of the bread of life that we sought. Thank you for just this small crumb of hope for our hungry souls.   I have spoken with my appointed attorney and he will file a supplemental brief on my behalf and then the State will respond to that. I should expect oral arguments or a hearing within six months or so.

Wednesday, April 28, 1999, 8:30 pm

I keep the letter with me, here in the cell, its face up on the bed to be read a few more times today. I showed it to a few. Good thoughts from everybody.

I read the word "granted", and look at it time and time again, soaking up the pure joy that one word conveys. Yet I keep testing its truth, like a mirage.

I didn't ask for counsel, but okay. First thing I said at the rose garden was "Well, this is GOOD!" I was so excited. I could not understand when "appellant" gets a favorable ruling! I had to look to make sure he wasn't calling us each other.

I was so nervous from 11:00 am to when I got the letter. I could not find the handle on my attitude. I had no patience. All I could think about was how to control my nervous system to deal with the powerful stress hormones that were juicing out through my body. I was preparing to have my heart and nervous system "twanged" and bowed by the Judge. It's like coming to their open door, begging and pleading your case, sure that he is convinced. He looks at you with shark eyes, laughs at you and slams the door. Then he threatens to sic the pit bull on you if you don't leave his property. Like a public whipping or being strapped up like Rambo in the leach pit and having them pound their fists into your body. It is a beating just like that, but to the spirit instead of the body. Your spirit is greatly diminished for a while like when Obi-Wan Kenobi lowers the tractor beam in *Star Wars*. Remember that sound?

Tuesday, May 4, 1999

Last night were the killer tornadoes in and around OKC. Mario is from California and he was making fun of me when I began to get worked up as the tornadoes closed in on the central part of the State. He could see my apprehension, and was laying it on. However, I knew the fix we would be in if the tornado decided to hit LCC. Sure enough, we were locked down. I prayed that I wouldn't die today in my cell.

May 20, 1999

Don went up for parole yesterday. A typical encounter. Those people don't even know how to act when they are around a "killer", a murderer. Don was misunderstood and they put his next parole date off "indefinitely". Those parole hearings are very emotional for an inmate. I remember mine, and I remember how long it took for Bo Baker to return to normal after his.

I played a couple of games of twenty-one (basketball). Got fourteen in the first, with a late start. Won the second. Two blacks and two Indians were good, and a couple more decent white guys. One of the Indians won the first. Good athlete.

My days are very dull and I must admit I'm not handling things in the best way. Just such a lack of fun. Robbie Knievel to jump tonight on Fox.

Sunday, June 13, 1999

Last night I passed their UA. I'm just reflecting some tonight. Beautiful weather. Rain and sun have made the trees shiny and green. Mild temperatures. Last summer was drought and 100 degrees about this time.

Twenty-nine days left. Just took a slow walk around the yard, looking for Antonio Gambino on the mail list. Went to see Rex (not the older man Rex) today, talked about his kid learning piggy-back and wearing him out. Josh and Mom came up yesterday for the last time. Josh and I played poker.

Sunday, June 27, 1999

Last night I passed another UA with a little help. On Thursday I signed the Sex Offender Registration Form.

*

I would have to register as a sex offender for the next ten years with the police department of the town where I reside and also would need to report any change in my address or vehicle. I was embarrassed, angry, sad, and full of pity as I filled out all of their forms, stating my itinerary and place of residence upon release. Now the fun really starts. Which would be more difficult, being in prison or being in Oklahoma as a registered sex offender? Well, I'll take my lumps and be happy to be out of prison.

It was Saturday, June 26 1999. About nine in the evening, there was a knock on my cell door. I perked up, and so did the butterflies. I turned my head to look. It was the guard. Oh no.

"Mr. Thompson. They want you at Central Control."

"Yes sir."

What? They just UA'd me two weeks ago! Why again? What do I have to do to get out of this place? I have just 16 days to discharge. God help me.

I stayed in a friend's cell for an hour, hiding out and drinking all of the water that I could. When I was peeing about every ten minutes, I walked slowly toward central control. Thoughts of despair, shame and embarrassment flooded me, but I pushed them back. I expected to beat this thing even though I had been smoking. Went to central control.

Finally, it was my turn. The door was popped for me to transfer to the shakedown room to give the UA. The best possible guard would be in there with me. Cool! I had a chance! I reached down deep for some courage, summoning it.

We entered the room and he shut the door, handing me my cup. I walked slowly to the toilet, feeling surprisingly calm as I began to play my hand.

"Sir, I've got sixteen days to discharge a sentence for a crime that I am not even guilty of. My wife and kid, we would love you forever if you would turn your head and let me get to the faucet, and water."

It came out so smooth. Surprised me. I felt the wife and kid would sound better than "still friends", and kid.

After a two or three second pause, he said:

"Are you dirty? For what?"

"Weed."

I knew with that question, and not a NO, that he would help me. He had some compassion in his eyes and voice, and I guess a little adventuresome spirit too.

"Probably. Look man, I swear to you, I'll send a money order for $100 to you as soon as I hit the streets. I don't make trouble, but just smoke a little weed. I've been in six and a half years for something that I obviously didn't do."

He thought about it for a few seconds. I was so happy. I still knew, he would help.

"I don't want your money. Can you get me a SHANK?"

"Heck yeah. Why, so you can get promoted or something?"

"Naw, it just makes me look good, for right now."

"I promise."

"Okay, go ahead."

I went to the faucet and ran a few centimeters of water into the cup. He took it and we stood at the door, waiting for them to pop the door for us to exit the cell. I talked some more about my case and also just some small talk. He was interested in what I would do when I got out.

As the door was popped, I said, "Thanks, man!" and went to wait outside until he gave the thumbs up. It was funny to me as he tested the sample in front of the other guards; it was the clearest urine ever. His thumbs-up was a wonderful sight and I strolled back to the unit, counting my blessings.

A shank was a homemade knife. It could be made out of anything, just as long as it did what it needed to do. My old friend, Bo Baker, helped me get one. I didn't ask too many questions. This guard worked the chow hall in the evening. One evening we just kind of stepped around the corner onto the back yard, and I passed him the shank. It was the real deal too. He was impressed, I think.

My old buddy Sgt. Ford on Unit 4 had been promoted to a lieutenant in the last year. Ford had been a shank and drug bloodhound and had set records for discoveries on Unit 4. He even found a butcher knife in the garden one day.

In June, my appointed attorney went over the "record on appeal" and discovered that the videotape that I gave to the police the day before my arrest, which I have always said is the truth, had not been part of the record on appeal since after the direct appeal (the first round of the appeal). On post-conviction in the trial court and then in the federal district court, this videotape had been left out. My attorney set out to find the videotape and have it included in the record on appeal or whatever other legal action he saw as beneficial considering it was withheld from the earlier appeals.

My attorney contacted prosecutor Chris Ross about the video. Ross said that they did not know where it was. A few days later, after continued persistence by my attorney, Ross said that they had now found the videotape. My attorney filed for an extension of time for filing his supplemental brief so that he could go about getting a copy of the videotape and then prepare his legal argument for this issue.

Chapter 19   Free from prison

Wednesday, July 7, 1999

This afternoon I discovered that I leave Friday instead of Monday! I felt like a kid the day before leaving for Six Flags. Wound up! Having a great shock of joy thrust upon me. I'm gathering my resources for the next step of my life after this planning stage, the implementation of my hard work into achieving my dreams for a comfortable life.

I called my sister to call my brother to call my dad, without mother hearing, to tell he and Josh at the exact same time about my Friday release. Dad may want to try and surprise my mother, who I talked to today about car information. She thinks Monday is the day. I'm not sure Dad and Josh can pull off a surprise, but I wanted to let him have an opportunity.

*

I would be leaving prison in two days with God's grace. I was soon to become a number and name of a different sort, a free man. I felt blessed that I would go through the remainder of my life with such a perspective on life and freedom. However, I was a little worried about life on the streets as a convicted sex offender.

Within three days I had to report to the authorities in Pontotoc County, to register as a sex offender, and set up payments on all the FINES, from my conviction.

Friday, July 9, 1999

Well, today I discharged my sentence. Six years, seven months and one day. Josh and Dad were there when I was ready at about 11:00 am. Josh said, "Dad, you're a surprise." A surprise to Mom. Dad got a speeding ticket on the way up.

*

It was just reality at its best. When we got to Ada, and were coming in on West 14th street, I noticed mostly that the trees were six and a half years taller and fuller. Interesting. I ate a hamburger at Folger's, visiting with the angels as I savored each bite. The Folger brothers are like the

Grandmasters of Hamburgers. One of the Folger's (Jimmy) came over to me. He looked me straight in the eye as he shook my hand.

"Matthew, welcome back. We're glad to have you." He was sincere. Welcoming.

"You made it." He hugged me after that. That meant a lot to me, more than he could ever imagine. They believed in me, and were letting me know they were on my side.

Josh and I went to Wintersmith pool, swam for about 45 minutes, met his friend Beau and then walked home. We talked with, and about, the trees. I showed him a "singing" cottonwood tree. I hung out with my nieces and nephews and Josh. Then went to Teri's for an hour. Josh and I then walked to Braum's, to get a chocolate milkshake. What a joyous, refreshing and stress-free day.

I stayed at my mom and dad's house for a few weeks, before I was to move to Norman and be a full-time student at the University of Oklahoma. One day I was up in Norman to find a job. I saw a carpenter at a house. He hired me and I worked for he and his crew for three weeks before school began. What an experience.

My next job was as a waiter and room-service delivery at the Norman Holiday Inn. That was a good job, slow, yet paying pretty decent. I had to quit that job because I was denied an alcoholic beverage server's license. No convicted felons.

Friday, September 17, 1999, in Norman, OK

I am a student at the University of Oklahoma, taking twelve hours. Life is good! Next week, Thursday, September 23, 1999, my attorney has fifteen minutes of oral arguments in front of three Judges of the Tenth Circuit!

Friday, September 24, 1999

Yesterday were oral arguments. I talked with my attorney and he said everything went well. He said that the Judges asked many questions and even allowed him to go over his fifteen-minute time limit so that their questions could be answered. Now we just wait for their ruling.

Saturday January 15, 2000, in Norman, OK

Hurray, Monday is my 33rd b-day, but today the 10th circuit denied my petition. I was so excited when I got the mail, just knowing that it could only be good news this time. I was wrong. I made it through the first few sentences of my attorney's letter, to where he said, "Sorry for the bad news." That was as far as I got.

Thursday, April 13, 2000

I received in the mail the brief that my attorney filed with the Supreme Court of the United States. I had not talked with him since January, and had written off my appeal as over and through.

June 2000

With some help from a friend, I got a lot of the documents from my adoption in 1967, and found and met my biological parents. I had always dreamed of who I was, and where my DNA came from. My natural surname is FINN! Like Huckleberry Finn, you know?

*

My birth mother, Gayle Neal, was a nursing student in Tulsa. I was born at the Salvation Army Hospital, in Tulsa, OK. She gave information about her family and siblings, and the name of the alleged father and his family. In addition, there are copies of the legal documents prepared in Ada by my grandfather, mom's father, attorney Harvey J. Lambert. Both parents were from around Henryetta, OK, but Bill mostly grew up in Checotah, OK, just down the road.

In September 2000, the Supreme Court denied my appeal. My appeal is over, and vanishes like the wisp of smoke…that Rita's story is. That first chance lost, at the Oklahoma Court of Criminal Appeals, was simply unrecoverable. However, I realize that from the start, this case has been doomed anyway.

I graduated with a BBA from University of Oklahoma, in December 2000. In the summer of 2001, I wrote this book. Ninety-nine percent of it.

One day I had to go pay on my fine, in the courthouse. As I was coming up the stairs to the third floor, I was noticing a lot of people. I soon realized it was a hearing for Glen Gore. I was right there, standing to the side, and detective Jeff Crosby was standing there too, as Glen was led out, and down the stairs. Glen and I made eye contact.

"Hey Matt." Being friendly.

"Glen." And a nod.

Uncomfortable situation. What was I to do? One other thing, while bringing up detective Jeff Crosby again, I want to say that I never had a single issue with him, and he always treated me with respect.

I continued to seek interest in my story. I bought a HUGE "literary agents & publishers" book, and wrote "half a hundred" of each, as writers do. Nothing.

In January 2003, early one morning, I CALLED IN to The Howard Stern Show, morning radio show, and was ON THE AIR! I was struck with fear, and don't know how I was able to speak. I talked with Howard, the crew, and soon in on the conversation, was a lawyer friend of Howard's, sort of supporting me! During this time, I had contact with an agent on Long Island, and he heard me on the show! I thought my ship had come in. Nothing.

In 2007, I thought John Grisham's *The Innocent Man* book would help me. It always seemed like things were going my way, but nothing would develop. New sex offender laws, just continued to pass. In 2008, I was within one year of being OFF the sex offender list, after ten years (1999-2009). Then I received a letter stating I was to be on the sex offender list, now, for LIFE! But with help by OKC attorney David Slane, I was finally removed in 2013. What a nightmare, living in a community as a registered sex offender.

Ever since the beginning, craziness has always been there. I was just intrigued with the coincidental dates and numbers that came up. Remember the 911 attack, and the numbers of the flights, dates and other weird stuff? The coincidences.

Of course, the biggest coincidence is the birthday of the man fitting the description, and driving the car, is November 4th. November 4th is the date I was wrongly convicted at trial. Here are some more numbers, dates and circumstances in my case:

11-4-92 – the date of the guilty verdict at trial, a Wednesday.

11-4-72 – Birth date of the man fitting Rita's description, as well as driving the yellow car she described, Johnny Conners.

907 S. Constant – the home I grew up in.

907 E. 12th #6 – the Big House attic apartment where Krissy and I lived, in 1990.

907 E. 12th #7 – the small apartment home, behind the Big House, where Rita and I had consensual sex in 1991.

March 17, 1991 – the day I met Rita, St. Patrick's Day. Both of us have green in our eyes; she was from MA with a Boston accent. Lot o'green, lot o'Irish.

12-8-91 – later in the year, after my arrest, Krissy and I married.

12-8-92 – after the 11-4-92 conviction, she (Judge Kilgore) set my sentencing date, allowing me to remain out on my bond, until I reported to the Pontotoc County jail (the Sheriff) on this day, a Tuesday, to await transfer to prison.

12-8-82 – Ten years earlier, Debbie Carter was raped and murdered in Ada (John Grisham's book *The Innocent Man*). Dennis Fritz and Ron Williamson were wrongly convicted of these crimes, and later exonerated for. DNA match, Glen Gore, then plead guilty, to avoid the death penalty.

7-9-1999 – date of my release from prison. There are a lot o'nines involved, as with the street addresses.

Chapter 20   What to do if falsely accused

Detectives are not your friends

Don't talk to the police or detectives at all. Nothing you say to them will help your case. They are trained in psychological interrogation that can make you possibly confess to a crime you are completely innocent of. They will use any means necessary to get you to say the wrong thing. It is uncomfortable, scary and stressful to be locked in a cell and charged with a crime you didn't commit. But the detectives can't help you get out, or help your case, or help you. Period. Don't talk to them. Tell them, "I am innocent of this crime, so that is all I need to say right now, until an experienced attorney is on MY SIDE."

Investigation, investigation, investigation

First of all, if you have been wrongly arrested, then you are in serious trouble. Talk about being in a tight spot. But if you're truly innocent, then you deserve a good defense and a good chance. Start gathering evidence!

Time is of the essence, not a minute to spare! You're first efforts in this deal have got to be hiring a private investigator to get all they can about your side of the story, the girl's side, her past character and history, interviewing any witnesses or people that may have had contact with you on the night in question, etc. While the time is still right, a strong investigation ASAP is your one strong chance! As soon as time fades away, so may any evidence that can prove your innocence.

Cases are won or lost based upon investigation. A lawyer is good for maintaining communication with the prosecution, pleading for your release or lower bond, and advisement on your rights and the law. They will work well between your investigator and the State and may even know of a good private investigator for you to use.

However, without you **insisting** on the investigator, the method of investigation and how the money will be spent, an attorney might be inclined to pocket the cost it would take for a good investigation. He may see it as his own fee. Your attorney is probably not a licensed private investigator.

A court appointed attorney would be at no cost to you and would work with the State and any investigator you may insist upon. He is obligated to help your case, and a few phone calls or appearance or two by them won't hamper you here at the start, as long as the investigating gets done. In fact, if you have money for either an attorney or an investigator, a free attorney and a hired investigator right now would be your best bet.

Whatever it takes to get a proper investigation done on your case…that is what you must do. If you want to hire your own lawyer, pay him $500 to represent you until the preliminary hearing and spend $1,000 or $1,500 on an investigator. You'll never regret it.

Private investigator

In my case, I believe that with proper investigation from the start, I would never have been brought to trial. If I would have paid a good investigator the $1,500 it took me to bond out, the chances are that the case would have been dropped. With hard-nosed investigation for just a few days immediately after my arrest, the investigator would have found stuff then that we eventually found 3-4 years later. A qualified investigator will work awfully hard for a week for $1,000 to $1,500.

The investigator we hired while I was in prison and filing for a new trial was an excellent investigator. He was well organized, covered all angles and was very effective. I want to use him as a good example of what you need to do and expect out of your private investigator. Very detailed, documented, discovery of possible evidence. If you are really innocent, then there is information out there to help you. There has to be!

Once they are finished, you've got in writing (or digitally), times, places, people, statements, or evidence that may help you. So, you can "race it around" too! You should consider re-investigating again if your case is set for trial. New evidence could come up, people could change their statements. Think about the simple fact in my case, of boyfriend

Mike Bryan being in the same room with his parents, made him keep his mouth shut that day. You never know what you might find.

Preparation is key

With a good initial investigation, some research into the laws of your state, and a knowledgeable attorney, you can prepare a good case for trial. Unfortunately, rape shield statutes in many states make it very difficult for a defendant to prepare a case. Most states will not allow evidence of the woman's past behavior as part of the defense. It is really the truth, that the State can file a rape charge with only the accusation from the alleged victim. There need not be any physical evidence, nor a medical report, or any corroboration of any kind. Her false words are enough. Oh, how powerful they are.

Although there are good trial attorneys out there, most aren't really experienced in rape cases beyond what they learned in law school. HELP your lawyer, find and watch instructional videos, tutorials, WITH him. From this research; write down, and prepare a basic OUTLINE for your defense. Complete this preparation, work from your outline, and continue with it. As stated before, keep investigating leading up to trial! People may feel a need to open up, and tell the truth, as your case nears trial. If you can find anything favorable, evidence about her past behavior maybe, it may help you. You may not be able to present it at trial, but it might be a key piece of the puzzle, might persuade the DA to drop your case, or reduce a charge or something. Evidence that you have in your possession, as proof of your innocence. You never know what might happen. Good luck. Thanks for reading my book.

May fortune shine on you, and on us all.

Author's Note:

Go To:

RATTLE OF THE KEYS

on

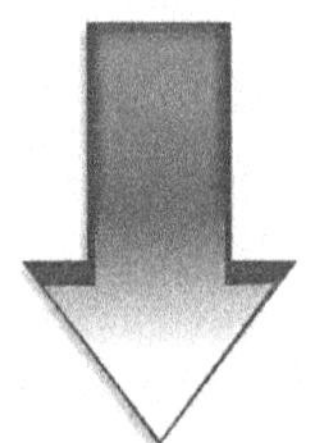

New information, ALL the PHOTOS, and more; in COLOR, new
videos, and new topics to come, on my YouTube site.
Get there, and Subscribe so you won't miss it.